ANTARCTIC COMMAND

Also by the Author—

ANTARCTIC CONQUEST

ANTARCTIC COMMAND

by

FINN RONNE, Captain, USNR

 THE BOBBS-MERRILL COMPANY, INC.
A SUBSIDIARY OF HOWARD W. SAMS & CO., INC.
Publishers • INDIANAPOLIS • NEW YORK

All photographs used in this book are official U.S. Navy photos, unless otherwise noted.

First Printing

Library of Congress Catalog Card Number: 61-7893

AUTHOR'S NOTE:

The story I have recorded here is one of men living in a hostile environment and under great nervous stress. As such, their behavior occasionally assumed a degree of eccentricity and intensity which would not be representative of their normal demeanor. That statement is as true of the author as of the people I describe.

The Antarctic night during which human beings must live in hibernation without the natural benefits of sunlight and the stimulus of variety produces abnormal incidents. This singular environment tests the basic fibers of a man's personality in situations which he might never meet again during his life.

In the interest of accuracy I have recorded incidents that occurred during the expedition which might possibly be interpreted as unfavorable to some individuals. I am most sincere in assuring my readers that this is done in the spirit of scientifically interpreting our isolated sociological environment and most definitely not as a result of any personal feeling.

I trust that this book will be read with a maximum of tolerance for individual behavior. This story will show how extremely important it is that we realize the full extent of the personality formula before selecting personnel for such expeditions into remote areas.

I know that the men who shared this great and important adventure with me at the Ellsworth Station in the Antarctic have long since forgiven and forgotten the many petty grievances which arose during the extraordinary conditions of our isolation. I praise them all for their sacrifice and dedicate this volume to them and to the men of the Antarctic, past, present and future.

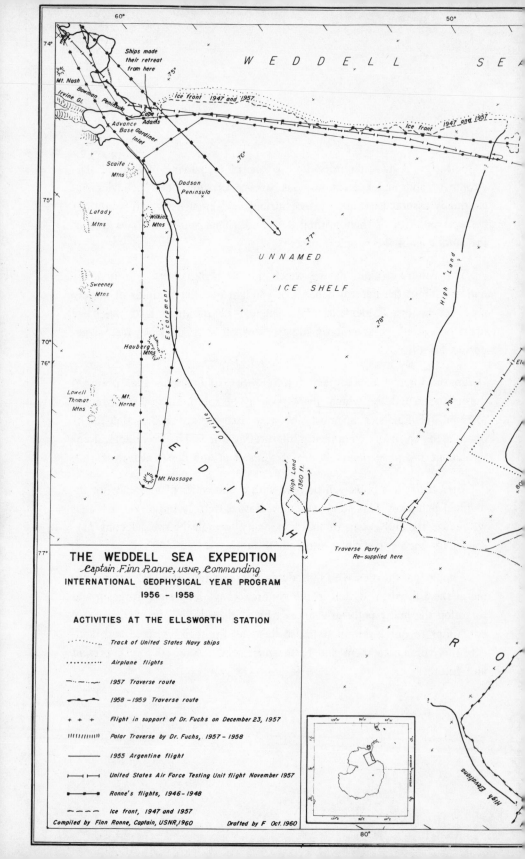

THE WEDDELL SEA EXPEDITION
Captain Finn Ronne, USNR, Commanding
INTERNATIONAL GEOPHYSICAL YEAR PROGRAM
1956 - 1958

ACTIVITIES AT THE ELLSWORTH STATION

.... Track of United States Navy ships

⋯⋯⋯⋯ Airplane flights

—·—·— 1957 Traverse route

●—●—● 1958 – 1959 Traverse route

+ + + Flight in support of Dr. Fuchs on December 23, 1957

‖‖‖‖‖‖‖ Polar Traverse by Dr. Fuchs, 1957 – 1958

———— 1955 Argentine flight

⊢—⊢—⊣ United States Air Force Testing Unit flight November 1957

●—●—● Ronne's flights, 1946 – 1948

— — — Ice front, 1947 and 1957

Compiled by Finn Ronne, Captain, USNR, 1960   Drafted by F Oct. 1960

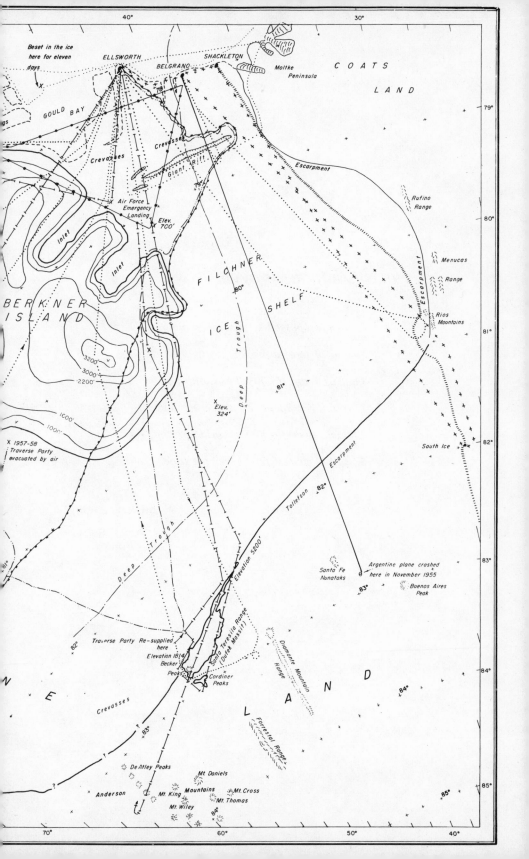

THE POLAR NIGHT IS OVER!

O, I have passed a miserable night

So full of fearful dreams, of ugly sights

That as I am a Christian faithful man

I would not spend another such night

Though 'twere to buy a world of happy days

So full of dismal terror was the time.

W. SHAKESPEARE,
Richard III, Act I, Sc. 4

CONTENTS

Preface   13

CHAPTER

1   On Our Way   28

2   On The Ice   40

3   Friction   49

4   Race Against Time   60

5   Snapping To   74

6   Flying Weather   87

7   Antarctic Fever   98

8   Winter Routine   107

9   On Ice   117

10   Getting Tough   145

11   The Cave Dwellers   158

12   Shoveling Out   171

13   Flight Of Discovery   185

14   The Crisis   201

15   The Air Force Unit   218

16   Leaving The Hell-Hole   231

Epilogue   246

Appendix   253

Glossary Of Antarctic And Scientific Terms   269

Acknowledgments   272

ANTARCTIC COMMAND

PREFACE

July 1, 1957, WAS THE BEGINNING OF THE GREATEST SCIENTIFIC ENDEAVOR in the history of civilization—the International Geophysical Year, in which seventy nations co-operated in a concerted effort to achieve a better understanding of the world around us. This effort lasted for eighteen months, until December 31, 1958.

It was the third time such a program had functioned. The First Polar Year, as it was then called, took place in 1882 when a few European nations operated a modest geophysical program on the border of the Arctic Ocean. Antarctica was not included because it was then an unknown area in which no man had ever set foot. The Second Polar Year took place fifty years later, in 1932, when more nations with more stations took part, but still there was no station in the Antarctic.

While the Third Polar Year normally would not have been launched before 1982, this particular period, 1957-1958, was chosen because it marked the peak of the cycle of solar activity. Disturbances—sunspots and solar flares—that had been absent during recent years began to reappear and at the middle of the year reached a maximum of intensity in their eleven-year cycle.

Plans for the International Geophysical Year (IGY) began during a scientific conference in Brussels, Belgium, in 1950. By 1955 it had been determined that many of the sciences relating to the environmental conditions surrounding us on the surface of the earth, in the depths of the earth and in the atmosphere above should be carried out also on the Antarctic continent. We already knew from the work of many expeditions, which by now had lifted part of the veil that enshrouded the continent, that the South Polar regions were unique in many ways. The interior of Antarctica consists of a snow-covered plateau almost two miles high that offers clear, rarified air—ideal for scientific upper-air observations. Besides, a number of phenomena in the ionosphere that affect weather and radio waves over the world originate in the polar regions.

Not that the Antarctic was the center of all IGY activities—scientists of the co-operating nations made recordings and studied geophysical sciences in nearly every corner of the entire world—but Antarctic stations were essential for the complete program of many of the sciences. There are certain observations that can be made only in polar regions—seismology, for example, to calculate the amount of snow and ice on the earth's surface, and certain geomagnetic readings. More cosmic rays reach the surface of the earth in the polar regions than elsewhere because the lines of force of the magnetic fields are perpendicular to the surface of the earth at the north and south magnetic poles. The peculiarities of the ionosphere would also be studied. Since the North Polar area lies in the middle of the Arctic Ocean, floating "ice islands" were selected as station sites for observations. These islands, first discovered by Sir Hubert Wilkins in 1937, now for the first time formed a link in the network of observation points. The Antarctic continent was logical as points for observations at the opposite end of the earth.

Many studies were to be conducted at the six scientific stations being established by the United States. One of these six stations would be shared with New Zealand, and our No. 7 station, McMurdo Sound in the Ross Sea, was to be a U. S. Navy air-facility base for logistic purposes only. Nor were we alone in our huge activity. The British, Russians, French, Norwegians, Argentines, Chileans and others all established their own stations for observations. We were to work with all of them in the grim, icy and desolated vastness of Antarctica, where nationality loses its importance in direct ratio to the drop in temperature and increase in force of winds.

The American program was to be carried out at the South Pole Station, where Paul Siple, an old friend of two earlier wintering expeditions, was in charge of the scientific program; at Wilkes Station, where my good friend and former sledging companion Carl Eklund would be science leader; at Byrd Station; at Little America; at Cape Hallet, shared with New Zealand; and, finally, at Ellsworth Station on the edge of the Weddell Sea in Edith Ronne Land at the opposite sector, more than a thousand miles away from the nearest American IGY station. My particular concern was the Ellsworth Station, named for polar explorer Lincoln Ellsworth at my suggestion. Names of other explorers were used to signify the Amundsen-Scott South Pole Station, etc. Here we would study the earth's magnetic fields, the phenomenon of the aurora—brilliant displays of light that range the spectrum in the polar areas. At Ellsworth, as at the other stations, we had another specific task. We were to conduct an intensive investigation into the physical properties of the ionosphere. During the polar night when the sun's rays do not strike the surface of the continent at all, there is no solar radiation. For many years scientists have believed this "deadness" may effect radio signals in short-wave communication since electrically charged particles in the upper atmosphere are the tiny mirrors that reflect radio waves to every spot on earth. It was our job to record results by sending radio waves of various frequencies into the ionosphere. We hoped to be able to forecast radio blackouts and other interferences with radio communication after we had learned the secrets of the Antarctic and applied them to readings taken elsewhere on the earth.

At Ellsworth Station only we would study the newly discovered "whistling atmospherics" or "whistlers." Waves that originate in lightning flashes in the northern hemisphere are believed to travel along the magnetic meridians far outside the region of the maximum atmosphere, then return to earth along a gentle curve that places them at a point in the southern hemisphere, exactly opposite their place of origin. During the course of travel, the energy can be recorded as an audible whistling sound.

Like most of the other stations, we would study seismological problems, sounding the Filchner Ice Shelf on the edge of the Weddell Sea to measure the thickness of the floating ice and the depth to the bottom of the sea. Here we would try to learn more about the earth's crust, the thickness of sediments on the ocean floor and the composition of the various layers. We also hoped to gain a better understanding of Antarctic glaciology and the past and present climate of the entire world. By sending a surface party into the interior we hoped also to learn more of the geological history, get a better idea of the extent to which the continent is mineralized and what economic values may be buried in the land under the ice sheet.

Since the Antarctic has been considered to be the weather-maker of the world, scientists would make all-year–round observations to study the weather in the stages of creation. They would transmit readings to other points of the world so we could learn better to predict, if not control, the ever fluctuating weather around the earth. A full program of surface and upper air observations study was planned, to be co-ordinated with the fifty weather stations set up by the twelve nations on the continent and adjacent islands. With the report submitted regularly by these stations, meteorologists and forecasters at the Weather Central at Little America would be able, for the first time, to draw weather charts of the entire south polar regions.

The standard meteorological program of Ellsworth Station was to include the following operations: three-hourly synoptic observations; twelve-hourly rawinsonde runs aimed to achieve a height of 100,000 feet and provide measurements of temperature, humidity, pressure, wind direction and speed; pilot balloon observations, when required for aircraft operation, to determine the upper air velocities; continuous recording of air temperature, barometric pressure, wind direction, sunshine duration, mehispehere heat flux, surface albedo, solar radiation. We would also try to measure the precipitation and depths of snowfall and snow accumulation on a daily basis and collect snow for precipitation chemical analysis.

To do this whole job we needed scientists, aviation specialists and a military unit that would assist in the housekeeping maintenance of the camp while the work was going on. A selection committee of the IGY chose nine civilian scientists and technicians. The Navy chose ten aviation specialists under a senior aviator and seventeen enlisted men of a construction battalion unit, in charge of an officer of the medical corps. He was also to serve as our doctor. I was chosen to command the entire station because of my well-known interest in exploration of the Antarctic and my lengthy command experience there. I quickly learned that those in charge gave only lip-service respect for that experience. Their way of managing an Antarctic mission is not the explorer's way, even though our forces always superbly conduct operations of resupply and logistic support.

All of my experience in the past had been as a member of professional field-exploration forces and as leader of an expedition of my own. My feeling for the Antarctic was genuine and deep; even the area to which we would go to establish the Ellsworth Station was old home-town territory to me. Its very name, Edith Ronne Land, honors my wife. Over a period of twenty years, my father Martin Ronne sailed from Norway with Roald Amundsen on his expeditions to both the North and South Polar regions, including the expedition when Amundsen first reached the South Pole in 1911. After the death of Amundsen in 1928, my father was coaxed out of retirement to go to the Antarctic again, this time with the American Commander Richard Byrd. He was the only one of the forty-three–man wintering party who had ever been there before.

On my father's death in Norway in 1932, Byrd invited me to visit him in Boston. As a result of this meeting I became a member of his 1933-35 expedition, and it was the beginning of an association which lasted until Byrd's death in 1957. Already an American citizen, I had come to America in the spring of 1923 to reside and was then on the engineering staff of Westinghouse Electric Corporation at Pittsburgh.

When Byrd asked me to go south with him in 1933, I served as the expedition's ski expert and dog driver, and on sledge journeys operated the radio.

On the first day of March, short weeks after arrival, four of us headed south on the Ross Barrier with three dog teams to select a location for the Advance Base where our leader planned to spend the winter. The temperature fell to −65°, and we became entangled in the same crevasses that Amundsen and his four companions crossed on their way to the pole. From the joys and hardships of traveling behind a loaded dog team, as well as from the cold depths of my sleeping bag while blizzards whirled around our thin cotton tents, I gained respect for the eternal white, disarmingly peaceful and always unpredictable Antarctic continent. Thirty-one days and 500 miles later, Little America's crudely built makeshift barracks took on the air of luxurious castles.

We had encountered many dangers on our field journeys. In the camouflaged pattern of the snow, perils are lurking everywhere. The surface may look smooth, but suddenly your dog team slides into a dark chasm. Then you discover that you are in a network of crevasses. It may take you many days to get clear of them. After a while you learn to know that the hollow sound your ice pick makes on the unblemished surface signifies dangerous hidden crevasses underneath, but such detection requires considerable experience.

You may also be caught in a blizzard that springs out of nowhere in a minute or two. The low temperatures can give trouble, even during spring and early summer. They numb you and chill you to the bone. White blotches appear on the skin that is exposed. These blisters easily will become frostbitten and they can be nasty.

Still, I loved it all, even though there were months of winter darkness and sometimes dreary idleness in the polar camp. Many a man's nerves are on edge in these times; I have seen strong men show their strength and weaklings become dangerous in the boredom of the long night.

Then, when men are cooped up together for months, you have a rare opportunity to study and learn about your fellow man. There are no secrets in a polar camp. Even a man's thoughts become an open book; you can tell what a man will say long before he speaks.

Nowhere does the summer sun shine so clearly and brightly as in the Antarctic. Nowhere do the stars glitter so luminously as during the winter when the Southern Cross is straight overhead. Nor will anything in life so captivate you as the Aurora Australis in the awe-inspiring colors it produces across the sky.

The sights of the Antarctic will stay with me forever. For sheer, utter desolation, it is the most magnificent thing in the world. The isolation—it makes you feel that you are standing on another planet. The glaciers, even with their dangerous crevasses; the huge icebergs many city blocks in size; a seal putting its stubby nose through the lead in the pack ice to look you over with suspicious eyes; the rugged, massive and frigid mountains, devoid of vegetation, serene and majestic: truly, in the Antarctic you feel you are lucky to be alive.

That was how I felt on my first expedition to the most southern continent of the world, and that is how I have felt on each of my three other wintering expeditions since that time.

On that first trip, standing on top of Mount Nilsen in the Rockefeller Mountain group, 120 miles east of Little America, I scanned the endless white landscape where sky and snow joined together to the east.

At that moment, I began to lay plans for a small sledging expedition of my own—a whaling ship would put a party of five ashore on Palmer Peninsula. Then we would be picked up at the Ross Sea side of the continent at the end of the same summer season. We would live off the country, eating seals we could find along the coast. And we would travel across completely unknown land; except for Lincoln Ellsworth's trans-Antarctic flight, no man had passed the interior.

Through a series of coincidences, my modest plan resulted in the creation of the United States Antarctic Service Expedition of 1939-41, supported by the Department of Interior and the Navy. I found myself assigned second in command to one of the two bases that were established. Mine was the base on Stonington Island in Marguerite Bay, on the east coast of Palmer Peninsula.

During this expedition, I led the Main Southern Sledge Party that sledged 1,264 miles in eighty-four days and followed the extension of George VI Sound to where it terminates in an open sea. This discovery proved that Alexander I Land actually was an island, which meant that Russia's Von Bellingshausen never sighted any part of the Antarctic mainland in 1820, thus eliminating this supposition as a basis for any of Russia's future territorial claims. On the western side of this island my sole sledging companion on the final phase of the journey, Carl Eklund, and I found an open body of water which the United States Board on Geographic Names called Ronne Bay in honor of my father.

Before I returned home in 1941 the World War II was about to descend on the United States, so I applied for a commission in the United States Navy via radio from a trail camp when I was still 500 miles out in the field. Once back in the United States, I was immediately commissioned a senior lieutenant and remained for six years on active duty, advancing to the rank of commander.

Toward the end of World War II my eyes and hopes again focused on the Antarctic. Two-thirds of the continent's area was still unknown and, in the field of science, only the surface had been scratched.

Much of my energy, perseverance, patience and money went into the creation of the Ronne Antarctic Research Expedition 1946-48.

With the loan of a Navy ship through Congressional legislation, Air Force airplanes and supported by private organizations and individuals, my small, compact expedition of twenty-three people whom I personally interviewed and selected sailed south for the Antarctic on our 1,200-ton diesel-electric–driven wooden ship, *Port of Beaumont.* Investigations were made in eleven branches of science, and many new mountain ranges and glaciers were discovered and covered in 14,000 trimetrogon photographs with numerous ground-control points. The first flight into the unknown followed the extension of the Palmer Peninsula mountain chain to where it gradually diminished and disappeared into smooth, featureless snow terrain that stretched on southward. An escarpment, dotted with mountains and small nunataks sharply defined the western limit of the level but crevassed ice shelf to the east. Another flight that took us 900 miles from home base followed the seaward boundary of a previously

18

unseen ice shelf southeasterly where I first located Gould Bay and high land to the south of it. Then a landing was made on our southwesterly flights to the south of Bellinghausen Sea—in unknown area. Later we made the first landing on Charcot Island before heading for home base.

The results of the expedition were even greater than I had hoped for. By paring expenses to the bone and taking qualified, unsalaried applicants, my expedition cost a mere $50,000 cash — less than the present price of several good dog teams.

My dream of exploring stretches of the unknown continent had become a reality, and the men with me had met the challenge. To these able men whose interests and hearts were in the attainment of our objectives I owe my deepest gratitude for the success of the expedition's scientific and geographical program.

In the spring of 1954 I was able to persuade several members of Congress that we should continue our work in the Antarctic. With modest funds I hoped a number of airplane flights, strategically plotted, might cover, in aerial trimetrogon photography with adequate ground-control stations, much of the still unseen areas. Thereby it would facilitate the production of a more accurate map of the continent. Not only was this essential to aid any further scientific studies, but I felt it would be done eventually and I was hoping the United States would be the first to produce such a map without further delay. The Senate Armed Services Committee through the efforts of the energetic and progressive Senator Francis Case of South Dakota urged the White House to dispatch an expedition, and sent the President the detailed operational plan I had prepared.

The President sent the Senate Resolution with my plans on to the Department of Defense, and the Navy was designated to take the necessary action. I soon found myself sitting on the sideline without my carefully drawn plans even being considered. The result was that the icebreaker *Atka* was sent off on a few weeks reconnaissance to the well-known Bay of Whales in the Ross Sea, where so many expeditions had gone before. None of the things I had hoped for came out of that cruise.

The International Geophysical Year has since come and gone but still the maps have not been produced. Nearly 100,000 aerial photographs which were taken on the Navy's "Operation Highjump" and by my own expedition have been lying untouched since 1948 in Washington, because of the lack of designated funds to work on them.

At the time of my proposal the International Geophysical Year Program began gaining momentum. The National Academy of Science, under whose auspices the United States world-wide scientific endeavor was organized, brought in new people and new plans. Finally, the entire program, including the Antarctic phase, was put under the U.S. National Committee for the IGY, headed by Dr. Joseph Kaplan of the University of California. Dr. L. M. Gould, the widely respected president of Carleton College and second in command of Byrd's expedition in 1928, was appointed chairman of the Antarctic Committee. Congressional support for many million dollars was obtained and the huge machinery soon got under way.

The military would also play a leading role in the IGY program by providing logistic support with icebreakers, cargo ships, airplanes and men. Without them the participation of the United States would have been limited in scope. In addition to the seven stations the Navy was to build in Antarctica, they would also provide continuous logistic support for them.

In charge of Navy's responsibilities was Captain George J. Dufek (soon Admiral), who had experience in logistic support operations in both polar regions. I first met George when he was a lieutenant and a navigating officer on the Navy's barquentine *USS Bear* in support of the U.S. Antarctic Service Expedition 1939.

Later Dufek became Chief of Staff to Captain Richard H. Cruzen (soon Admiral), who commanded our 1946 summer operations in the Arctic. At the conclusion of constructing the first airstrip at Thule, Greenland, Dufek went with Cruzen to the Antarctic on the Navy's "Operation Highjump." He commanded the eastern group of ships which explored sections of the coastal area between the Ross Sea and the Palmer Peninsula. In 1948 he again went to the Arctic with a logistic force in support of our weather stations there. Then in 1955, without any wintering experience and unaware of the problems that arise in a wintering camp, he tackled the most difficult task of correlating our Navy's activities under the International Geophysical Year Program. As such he performed a highly creditable job.

The tremendous proportions that the IGY-Navy program took on— with thousands of men and a dozen ships—was in sharp contrast to previous expeditions that had headed for the Antarctic. Amundsen or Scott or Shackleton, three crack explorers of the past, would be thunderstruck by the immense changes which have taken place in the white citadel they ruled supreme short decades ago.

Inasmuch as my last expedition had explored the Weddell Sea area, I was offered the assignment as military commander of the station to be placed in that area if I wished to return to active duty. Also I was told verbally that the Navy needed my experiences. Accordingly, with my innate interest in the program, I accepted gladly.

On the morning of July 6, 1956, I reported to Task Force Forty-three for duty in Washington, D. C. in my spick-and-span four-striped uniform, ready to get down to work.

My part in the IGY's Antarctic operations got underway under particularly depressing if not foreboding circumstances. A captain in a high

20

position with the Task Force informed me on the first day that the job as military commander at Ellsworth Station was limited in responsibility, and it was definitely not a job I should accept.

"You will be wasting your time," he told me, as he proceeded to show me just why he thought so.

A junior officer, probably a Navy doctor, would be placed in charge of the military housekeeping personnel at each of our six IGY Antarctic stations, and since the Ellsworth Station would also have an aviation unit attached to it, an aviator, another junior officer, would be in charge of that unit. The civilian scientists would have their own senior man to supervise the scientific work at each of the stations.

"If you do not go," said my captain friend, "these three groups will all be independent of one another. All will have to get along as best they can to run the station. They will get some instructions, but harmony among them depends on the individual, and how well he gets along with the other fellows."

"Of course, if you do go," he said, "with your rank and experience, you will be in complete charge of all the military, including the aviation unit." He then pulled out a draft copy of my orders and handed it to me:

"1. Having been ordered as Military Commander of the United States Weddell Sea Base, your duties shall be as indicated below:

"2. As Military Commander you shall be responsible for the performance of duty, morale, and well being of all military personnel under your command. . . .

"3. The Military personnel under your command will be composed of detachments of Mobile Construction Battalion, BRAVO, and Air Development Squadron SIX (VX-6). . . .

"4. Administrative control of military personnel will remain a function of the commanding officers of the respective detachments. . . .

"5. In your dealings with the scientific personnel you will be governed by the provisions of part 'B' to Annex 'N' of CTF-43 Operation Plan No. 1-56. . . ."

After reading my orders with me, my friend concluded: "Unless you are also put in charge of the IGY scientists, you will have only a minor job, one not worth the trouble of a man of your experience really even considering."

It did not seem to be a very rosy picture to have split commands at any of our Antarctic stations. But with the addition of an aviation unit, the situation at Ellsworth Station would be even worse.

If I did not go, I could imagine two young officers out-maneuvering a lonely scientist, who would also like to have a say in running the station where he was going to live for a solid year. There are problems, obviously, when a civilian cannot give an order to any man in uniform, not even to an apprentice seaman. At least if I went I would unify the two military units at the Ellsworth Station, but still I would share a split-command with an IGY civilian.

And, if this was the beginning, what was to come next?

I hopefully disregarded my friend's advice and began to study the Weddell Sea operational plan. I wanted to learn what I would be expected to accomplish. After all, I told myself, I had three Antarctic winterings to my credit. There must be something I could contribute. Besides Ellsworth and Byrd, I was the only American in recent history who had organized and led an Antarctic wintering expedition. I had practical knowledge and well-developed concepts on station layouts, building arrangements, space assignments for the various branches, special food and equipment and many other details. I also had in mind a number of key men possessing extensive polar experience whom I hoped to have included in the personnel roster.

But I soon realized too that there was nothing for me to do in this planning stage. As far as I could see, everything had already been done.

Personnel? I soon learned that the various Bureaus of the Navy had selected the personnel.

Materiel? The Bureaus had ordered all buildings, clothing, food, transportation equipment, recreational gear and many other things—not according to specific needs based on polar experience, but according to Navy standards.

Only the top planning had been done by the Task Force in co-operation with the IGY's planning office. All materiel needed for the expedition had been ordered as for any military operation—basically the demands are the same, they say, whether the unit is bound for the North Pole or Timbucktu.

Looking through the plans of the station layout, I could find only thirty-five bunking spaces for the forty-one men who had been assigned. Based on my own experience, I considered concentrated food essential as emergency rations for plane flights, but none was provided. The small single-engine planes, I knew, were of little value for supplying traverse parties on the ground, far from base. A bigger plane, a two-engine ship, was the answer. A team of seven huskies would be valuable, I thought, for rescue in case of glacier or crevasse disasters.

I submitted a total of eighteen specific suggestions. Seventeen of them were rejected. The eighteenth was accepted. This was a plea for a small skiff and an outboard motor for each coastal station. Then if a man got caught on a drifting ice floe, there was some way of getting him off. Nothing had been provided previously for such an eventuality. I was most relieved, when at least this suggestion was approved only a month before our departure date. Even then I had little hope that it would be delivered to the ship in time. But it was on board when the ship shoved off.

There was undoubtedly some economic justification for disapproving some of my suggestions: the seven-dog team, for example. The previous year they had an unfortunate experience with dogs. Thirty sledge dogs were requisitioned for use in air-rescue operations at McMurdo Sound. The cost of these dogs reportedly came to a high figure compared to the price that I had paid when I bought the same type animals for my own private expedition a few years earlier.

Apparently, too, there was a great deal of dislike on the part of the "new" explorers for the "old" explorers who had experience in the Antarctic. The seasonal, or summer, explorers were the men making the decisions. Not one of them had ever spent a winter in the Antarctic. Like the birds, they migrate south each season, then retreat back to warmer climates and bask in the northern spring's sun, while fall and winter storms of dreadful proportions streak across the Antarctic continent. The general feeling of this group was "to Hell with the old explorers," as one of them even stated later in a Navy-cleared book that described his experiences.

Admittedly, these men are excellent ship handlers and some of them even had icebreaker experience on cruises in the frozen north and south. They were apathetic, however, to the problems facing men who spend the entire year in Antarctic winter quarters. The problems of wintering are vastly different from those of summering. The real issues between men in the Antarctic invariably arise after the ships depart and the marooned men are left entirely on their own. The issues can be kept to a minimum by detailed, careful planning in the early stages, by careful selection of personnel and by using good, sound judgment based on practical experience.

It must be acknowledged too that those who were now in control of all operations had carried out much of the previous season's planned program, of building the Air-Facility Base at McMurdo Sound, but in many areas completion of the task was due more to good luck than good judgment. A number of fatal accidents, which regrettably marred the record, conceivably could have been avoided.

A tractor fell down in a crevasse and killed a young sailor. Another tractor broke through the sea ice and drowned a second sailor. The operation of heavy tractors on sea-ice is just not sound judgment. The advice of those who had been in the Antarctic and who knew of these dangers had not been sought.

The new "experts" took a strange view of the old-timers, and this view was picked up by all who came in contact with them, including those who would winter over for the first time. My captain-friend put it succinctly: "Those who had been with Byrd were all the same—no damn good." The fact that I also came under this category did not have to be underlined any more clearly. This was to be their show.

In my early days with the Task Force I learned of the intended relationship between the military and civilian IGY personnel at each of the stations. It seemed so wrong to me, because of the split command, that I was determined to do something about it.

If any organization is to function correctly, there must be a chain of command where one officer has all responsibility and the final word in running the enterprise. At Ellsworth Station, I learned, I would have complete command of all military personnel including the aviation unit and their operations as related to the program and complete responsibility for all equipment and the installations. Still a civilian would be in charge of the scientific IGY group, with an equal say in some matters. I expressed my fears that this arrangement would create friction, lower morale and hamper efficiency. From experience I knew how difficult some men are to handle in an isolated polar camp, especially where the military and civilians would have different interests and responsibilities. At the Ellsworth Station, the military would be charged with housekeeping duties and support of the civilians in their work. But some of the annoying chores, such as mess duty, *should* be shared by the two groups to avoid resentment, as it was stated in the civilians IGY directives.

I brought all this up with the executive secretary of the IGY. He saw the possible difficulties of the arrangement and said that, if a military officer could be located who would meet the IGY Committee's requirements, he favored single responsibility to lead the scientific group as well as the military. He conferred with his associates when he found that I was willing to serve in a dual capacity. This resulted in my appointment as scientific leader of the Ellsworth Station. The Department of Defense also gave its consent to the arrangement. As it turned out I was the only one at six scientific stations to act in a dual role as well as the only one with an aviation unit under my command. It was lucky for me that I had studied the problem and made this arrangement before we set out. Now I not only had written orders giving me full command of all military activities at Ellsworth, but complete instructions which placed me in charge of scientific personnel as well. I could not foresee any problems that might arise during our Antarctic sojourn with which I would not have adequate power to deal.

Obviously, with the open antipathy toward those who had been in the Antarctic before, I felt like an outsider during the months in Washington before we departed for the south. One petty roadblock after another was thrown in my way. Even in travel life was made just as difficult as possible for me. On a minor trip to deposit some equipment for use on the expedition and see the ship off, it was decided I should either travel at my own expense or not at all.

Yet these were annoyances, not problems. Once we got to the Weddell Sea and the ships returned north after the brief summer such irritations as these would be eliminated, I felt, although many problems might take their place. What disturbed me much more seriously was the absolute turndown I received on my request, as commander of the Antarctic station, to have a hand in picking the personnel who would spend a year with me in the closest quarters imaginable, with no possibility of relief until the year was up. This was true not only of the military, but also the IGY civilians who also were selected without my having the chance to pass on them.

It is the men who make an expedition. Without their enthusiasm and incentive and willingness to work, any expedition would be a complete failure. The ideal type of an expeditionary man, I learned through three previous winterings in the Antarctic, is one who has his whole heart in the venture. He co-operates unhesitatingly. He takes orders and obeys them immediately. He is expert in his own field and can improvise, for he knows there is no outside help available. He does not expect assignments for which he is unfitted, no matter how much he wants them. Of course, human nature being what it is, such men who react well under stress are few and far between, but they can be found and for such a venture every effort should be made to do so.

With a selected group of men of superior character there should be no fear of the somewhat overdramatized difficulties and monotony of life in the polar regions. As elsewhere, a few good men, even in the humbler jobs, may set an example of energy, courage, foresight and mutual consideration that will stabilize the morale of the group. I confess that on all three of my previous expeditions there were several conspicuous examples of misfits, and it was for this very reason that my opinions on the ideal expeditioner had crystalized.

In the selection of the personnel for the Ellsworth Station, as for all the American bases, very little consideration was given these matters. I met my men—60 per cent of them for the first time—after the ships had left us on the icy cliff where we were destined to spend a year together. They were strangers to me and to one another. I did not know their personalities, or even how they got along among themselves. On shipboard I heard constantly that the men had been carefully screened and that there was not a bad egg among them.

The Navy men were chosen on an assembly-line basis. Requests for volunteers were sent to ships and stations all over the world. As the applications were received they were screened. Gradually the applicants were weeded, and the successful sent through a physical examination, including a personal interview-test, designed to eliminate men who showed anxiety, sulkiness, discontent, shyness, effeminacy and dirtiness of mind. This was, perhaps, a better process for screening personnel than most of the earlier expeditions had, but bitter experience had made me a strong believer in knowing a man over a long period of time to learn his weaknesses and strong points and to get an insight into his views and aims. Only then is it possible to find out what the man is made of and how he will react in an emergency, and to living in an isolated environment over an extended period of time.

Later, in the Antarctic, I asked each man why he had wanted to come on the expedition, and a great number of them indicated they were attracted by the glamour and romance of exploration. Some of them also were disgusted with their present jobs or assignments, where they had found conditions intolerable. These reasons, I knew from experience, are some of the least desirable motivations for a man in the Antarctic.

The IGY civilians were selected by a somewhat more individual process. The picking was in the hands of a committee, some of whom did have previous wintering experience. But this selection committee had a very ticklish time in finding scientists interested in spending eighteen months of their lives in the Antarctic. Usually a mature individual is well established by the time he achieves eminency in his scientific calling. Young people, then, were the most likely candidates to choose from, as the more experienced ones were just not available. This is borne out by the Ellsworth group—the average age of the nine civilians was the same as that of the senior scientist: twenty-eight.

Age, of course, should not necessarily be the determining factor in the selection of personnel for a wintering party. An older man may not be as strong physically as a younger one, but he may have other indispensable assets: motivation, and adaptability or willingness to accept discomfort and endure hardship. Mature judgment is always a stabilizing factor in a polar camp. My father, for example was forty-nine years old on his first expedition with Amundsen and celebrated his sixty-eighth birthday while wintering on the first Byrd Expedition at Little America.

On the other hand, the young, physically stronger, active man usually is able to withstand environmental hardship much better and is able to acclimate himself more readily to the cold. But even more important, a younger man is less likely to develop physical incapacities than would the older one. I have found that men in both categories are needed and essential in any wintering camp. It is my belief that the same balanced assets will be found necessary in personnel who will eventually man our pioneer stations in outer space.

One problem, insolvable and bound to cause dissension, was the difference in pay scale between the civilians and the military. The civilians were to receive between $7,400 and $9,400 per year, plus additional allowances: 25 per cent of their salary for hardship; $816 per year extra for overtime; and their room and board and clothing. Not bad for four of the young men with me who were just out of college. This was quite a contrast to *my* first Antarctic venture in 1933 when I not only went as a volunteer without any salary, but also spent around $600 for some of the things I needed.

The military personnel received no hardship allowance, no overtime payment and no per diem allowance. Even I, as a captain in the Navy in charge of the station, earned less including all my allowances, than the lowest paid civilian under me. And on top of that, the officers were charged $2.25 a day for food every day we were there, while food for the IGY civilians was provided free of charge.

Separately, during the summer months, the civilians and military personnel were assembled at Davisville, Rhode Island, point of embarkation. The civilians were given a quick indoctrination course in procedures to be followed and familiarized with some instrumentation problems they might encounter under Antarctic conditions. They were also taught how to comport themselves in a military atmosphere while aboard ship.

Then, on November 9, 1956, the USS *Wyandot* (AKA-92) was fully loaded and ready to leave. My old friend Captain Edwin A. McDonald, in charge of the Task Group, was on board. It was his job to get us there, get our wintering base built and pick us up after our year's stay. I went up to Davisville to see the ship off and check on some of the equipment. Later I caught up with her at Valparaiso, Chile, and rode the remainder of the way to our destination at the head of the Weddell Sea. There I was to live and work for an entire year with thirty-eight other men none of whom had ever wintered over before. I knew one thing already—my previous Antarctic experience meant nothing to the men "who ran the show back home." How would we fare? Only time would tell. The story of my year in command at the IGY station atop a cliff of ice deep in the heart of the Antarctic continent, is in the pages that follow. I offer it as a report on an important facet of the scientific activities of the International Geophysical Year, but even more as a study in the imperfect science of human relationship, made under the most trying conditions.

CHAPTER 1

ON OUR WAY

W E BROKE OUR LAST LINK WITH CIVILIZATION ON DECEMBER 8, 1956, when we left Punta Arenas, Chile, and headed southeast through the Straits of Magellan. Early in the morning I was awakened by the rhythmic activities of the ship making ready to get underway. The clatter of chain pounding over the wildcat on the windlass told me that anchor was being weighed and raised into the hawsepipe. Slowly we started to inch forward; Punta Arenas disappeared astern, and again our life centered on activities within the ship.

As our two ships, the USS *Wyandot* and icebreaker USS *Staten Island,* which joined us at Valparaiso, swung southeast from barren Tierra del Fuego into notoriously stormy seas, misty cold air greeted us. We headed for the South Sandwich Islands, which in 1774 Sir James Cook mistakenly thought to be part of the Antarctic mainland.

Wind and sea were with us, moving constantly east, shooting through the Drake Passage. At times these seas take on gigantic proportions, as dreaded by the sailors today as they were in the earliest periods of ship navigation. Driven by the hurricane force of the winds, many a ship had been foundered and wrecked on the rocky and wind-raked shores around Cape Horn. The ocean current here gets additional speed by the fresh water flowing into it from the melting snow and ice of the Antarctic, and the seas are a dark steel-blue color which contrasts greatly with the bluish waters of the tropics.

On the third day out we began to see albatrosses, the largest of all sea-birds. These grayish-white birds, some with a wingspread of twelve feet, stood out sharply against the breaking waves and murky horizon. Swooping down upon the ship astern, they examined every piece of scrap we threw overboard and slid smoothly along with indescribable elegance before riding the updraft from the waves. It seemed as if the onrush of the

28

waves would swallow them, but the next moment the birds were in the open and ready to tackle the next wave. Men hung for hours over the railings, watching the graceful performance.

Life on board the ship was routine. The deck officers were assigned to watches—four hours on, eight hours off—while the many passengers continued their leisurely life without care. But at times minor disturbances keyed up dispositions of some of the civilians on board. Not accustomed to life aboard ship and not disciplined in the Navy's traditions at sea, they disobeyed rules and regulations. The etiquette of the officer's wardroom was most often violated and ignored. Some civilians preferred to come for meals in slippers and pajamas, while others favored sports shirts and sneakers. They had been notified of the proper attire actually issued to them for shipboard use: khaki—shirt, trousers and shoes. How some were inclined to create friction showed early signs of what lay ahead. It did not take the executive officer, Commander Williams, very long, however, to assert his authority and to see that they came into the wardroom properly dressed.

When the seas were not too rough we could see the icebreaker from time to time. She usually kept a distance of five miles to our starboard bow. Seeing her lights bobbing up and down on the horizon at night gave us an empty and lonely feeling, although, of course, we were in constant radio contact.

The day we left Punta Arenas, civilian oceanographer William Little-wood began making periodic oceanographic stations. Every hundred miles or so the icebreaker would stop so that Littlewood could record the water temperature and make other marine studies which would provide information on the water circulation and current.

Very near 57° south latitude we crossed the Antarctic convergence, where the warmer waters of the west wind-drift mix with the colder, deep waters surrounding Antarctica. Within a twelve-hour period the temperature of the water dropped from 42° to 34° Fahrenheit.

As soon as we crossed into the colder water, minute shrimps became plentiful near the surface. They provide the food for the penguins, seals, whales and some of the sea birds swarming along the fringes of the continent. In sub-Antarctic waters these shrimp are frequently so abundant that they appear to be as great red tides stretching for miles in all directions. Whale hunting is usually rewarding in these southern waters also.

About a week out, at a time when the seas were running high, we suddenly sighted six small whaling chasers heading into the seas and toward us. They made up part of a Norwegian whaling fleet of twelve chasers and a factory ship for processing the whales. One of the small 120-foot ships hailed the icebreaker. The skipper, a man in his thirties, was a sailor of old-salt caliber. Voluntarily he advised us where we had best start our penetration of the Weddell Sea pack ice and told us whale hunting had been good so far (considering that the number of whales seen in the oceans surrounding Antarctica shrinks every year and the mass slaughtering by too many whaling expeditions eventually will exterminate them altogether). His factory ship, a monster of about 30,000 tons, was just over the horizon to the east, he told us, while the chasers were now headed west, looking for whales. "Go between the Sandwich Island group and then head south on longitude 10 West and you will be able to reach Cape Norvegia, eastern entrance of the Weddell Sea, without much difficulty," were his parting words.

Early the next morning we reached lonely and desolated Thule Island, last in the fringe of islands that guard the northern approaches to the continent in this sector. Huge icebergs were in sight everywhere. I remember my sleep suffered, it was so awe-inspiring to stand on the fo'c'slehead and watch the shining white walls of ice go by. The sights were magnificent with the sun's rays glimmering on the lofty, pure white bergs twenty-four hours a day—sights no one onboard will ever forget. Spread before us were the smooth white fields of sea ice, about eight or ten feet thick, intersected here and there by irregularly broken water leads. As far as I could see were these numerous noble bergs, partly bathed in sunshine and partly tinged with the gray shadow of an overcast sky on the distant horizon. The stage was one of tremendous beauty. It is one of the most majestic and fabulous regions of the earth. I felt glad to be alive and fortunate to view it again.

As our Norwegian skipper had predicted, we sailed on for days before we reached the northern edge of the more concentrated pack ice. Here, Captain Edwin McDonald, our Task Group Commander, and I transferred to the icebreaker *Staten Island*. It was a rough transfer made in a landing craft, as we rode alongside the "breaker" trying to get our gear and ourselves aboard. The seas were running high, and each time the small craft rode the crest of a wave, a man would have to be ready to swing onto the railing of the icebreaker and hold on.

For the first few days the pack ice was very scattered and light but increased in density with each hour as we set a course due south. The icebreaker bucked heavy floes and pushed them aside for the cargo ship to follow. Usually the huge, thin-hulled steel ship kept close to the stern in order to get through the temporary leads before the ice floes closed behind.

On December 20 I was reminded rather early that it was my birthday. At 3:30 A.M. one of the sailors on watch came to my stateroom, woke me up and said it was very important that I come to the CIC (Combat Information Center) because Captain Francis Gambacorta, the skipper of the *Wyandot,* wanted to confer with me by radio. Walking over the icy deck that early in the morning, half asleep, with a nasty wind sweeping in from the east was not exactly fun. I acknowledged his call and he said: "I know you will not mind getting up this early from a sound sleep; I

30

wanted to be the first one to congratulate you on your birthday. Many happy returns of the day! Over."

Still somewhat sleepy I replied, "Thanks a million for your good and welcome wishes. . . ."

Our radio conference continued until breakfast time, primarily a discussion of his famous lamb dishes. We were looking forward to them when we could return to his ship, even though we had already received our share of the dozen or so mutton that he had purchased in Punta Arenas. The climax of the day was a surprise birthday cake after dinner and singing in the captain's wardroom by twelve of the ship's officers before the evening movies.

Within thirty miles of Cape Norvegia the heavy pack ice brought the two ships to a dead stop. Not even with all her diesel power was the icebreaker able to budge an inch. Here, fast in the ice, we celebrated Christmas with religious services and carol singing. The day after Christmas the ice pressure on the ship's sides slackened with the shifting of the winds, and we were again underway. With the helicopters from the icebreaker scouting ahead of us, we followed open leads in the pack and soon entered into an open sea which we were to follow for many hundreds of miles.

At Cape Norvegia an ocean current of about one knot runs in a westerly direction close to the continent's shores. It then shifts to the southwest and flows parallel to the main direction of the Queen Maud Land coastline. This current, sweeping into the southern boundary of the sea, carries the ice floes and huge tabular icebergs with it, keeping the waters generally free of pack ice until it reaches almost 78° South, where it swings northwesterly. We planned to take advantage of this small asset to reach the open body of water, which I had seen in 1947, fronting the Filchner Ice Shelf near Gould Bay at the southern end of the Weddell Sea.

About 250 miles south of Cape Norvegia, a stop was made at Halley Bay Station, the British IGY base already set up on an ice tongue. Later we made helicopter flights over to Dr. Vivian Fuch's Shackleton base a little further to the south on the high barrier. They were then setting up their winter quarters to await the next summer season, when they would commence their tractor journey across to the other side of the continent. Twenty miles further on another brief visit was made by helicopter to the Argentine base, General Belgrano, which was established in 1954-55, the first in this area. General Hernan Pujato, the commander of the Argentine base, described in detail flights he had already made into the interior in 1955. This was of great interest to me as he had viewed mountains later "discovered" by both our Navy flyers in 1956 and the British in 1957.

Our welcome at these bases was overwhelming, and our gifts of fresh fruit and news magazines were more precious to them than diamonds.

On take-off to Shackleton base on December 30, one of our helicopters was damaged when it failed to develop full power. It crashed on the deck of the *Staten Island,* a total wreck, but fortunately no one was hurt. After being stripped of all its usable parts it was dumped overboard when we became stuck in the ice on New Year's Day.

By New Year's Day 1957 we had left the British and Argentine bases far to the east, and penetrated deep into the Weddell Sea. On that day our progress again halted abruptly. Within a few hours the wind shifted and the floating ice field which was ten to fourteen feet thick, built up pressure-ice ridges thirty or more feet above the crushing, heaving and jumbling ice fields around us. We were caught in a vise—not a vise of steel, but a vise of shifting ice that was just as dangerous. The *Wyandot's* engine was stopped. It was a devilish place for a light-plated steel cargo ship. The wind and pressure of the ocean current were from the northeast and the ice pack held both ships tight.

On a number of occasions Commander James Elliott, the skipper of the icebreaker, tried in vain to move his ship into a more favorable position by using the full power of his 10,000-horsepower diesel engines, but the heavily plated steel monster would not budge an inch. To make the situation worse, a blizzard descended. The wind packed enough wallop to dump the hard ice floes and pressure ridges in on the two ships which were already helpless and at the mercy of the elements.

Our two expedition ships were headed for the Bowman Peninsula at the southwest corner of the Weddell Sea in Edith Ronne Land. We intended to build the station about twenty miles seaward from Gardner Inlet in longitude 60° West. But now, for eleven days in January, our two ships were still paralyzed in the ice crushed around us by the shifting winds. In this area of the Weddell Sea, Sir Ernest Shackleton's wooden ship *Endurance* had been crushed by the ice in 1915. I could readily understand why his small ship with a steam engine of only about 300 horsepower did not have a chance to push the ice floes aside and make a passage. Once caught in the ice, the *Endurance* had been entirely helpless, drifting in the pack's icy grip for nine months, until she could no longer withstand the intense pressure and sank.

Already the summer season was advancing, and we were late in reaching our destination. We had hoped to spend Christmas at our base site on Bowman Peninsula, but now more than lateness worried us. The shifting pack ice had cracked the hull-plating of the *Wyandot*. Rivets were torn loose under the constant grinding pressure, and one of her holds flooded. Luckily, this hold was filled with drums of aviation gasoline, that floated in the sea water, undamaged.

During this entrapment, the morale among the men hit a new low. Foreign observers, American visitors and scientists aboard for the summer cruise became discouraged with the slow progress and the many setbacks. The enlisted men, too, wore drooping faces and serious looks, and were tired of living below, in the overcrowded cargo ship, packed in compartments like sardines in a barrel. For nine days the two ships were tied together and barely moved more than a ship's length. Frequent visits were made between them. Slackening of the pack ice, which would occur by the shifting winds, was our only salvation to get out of this Hell-hole, or else we might drift helplessly as had the *Endurance*.

One man's bone is another man's meat. Oceanographer Littlewood had a field day. His bottom trawl grappled along the ocean floor 3,500 feet beneath the icy surface. Other than penguins, sea birds, whales and seals, most people think of the Antarctic region as being relatively lifeless. Yet the Antarctic sea bottom supports as much life as tropical and temperate zone sea bottoms. Although the waters are cold, they contain much dissolved oxygen and nutrients. The late Professor William Herbert Hobbs, historical geographer, once said: "There is more nutritional food value in one acre of the Antarctic seas than the same area in any place in the world, on land and sea." Littlewood's haul onto the *Staten Island* seemed to confirm this statement.

In areas previously void of any type of oceanographic observations, Littlewood found the Weddell Sea bottom packed with all types of unusual crustacean and plankton life. Display trays were filled with many kinds of invertebrate animals including starfish, sea lilies, octopus, sea cucumbers, marine worms, several types of shrimps, scallops, sea urchins, primitive corals and numerous other species that do not have common names. The most interesting specie captured was a broad, flat member of the Crustacea family, which include crabs, lobsters and shrimps. This particular specimen appeared to be sort of the missing link between the trilobites that died out two million years ago and modern crustaceans. The specimen was certainly most unusual if not unique. The largest bottom-type fish brought up was only six inches long.

In addition, Littlewood took samples of the ocean floor itself. With an Orange Peel Sampler he collected sediment and with another instrument called a Phleger corer he obtained bottom core samples and preserved them in a plastic tube for later analysis.

As the ice pressure increased, giving our two ships a heavy list to port, the wreckage of the 'copter moved to and from the ship in the constant movement of the supporting ice floes. Day by day it remained alongside us, like a mascot, poking up through the floes and held by the pressure of them. On the eighth day, as the pressure slackened somewhat, we watched it slowly disappear into 3,500 feet of water.

Delayed and discouraged as the ships complements were, more difficulties seemed to be brewing in another direction. This I felt had been simmering for a long time. Our daily "situation reports," transmitted by radio to the higher echelon, reported one setback after another as slow progress was made towards our destination. It is exceedingly difficult to take appropriate action without being on the spot of the activity. Those located on the other side of the continent receiving these reports would thus judge our situation more or less blind-folded. I was apprehensive that something would soon be heard from that source. And it was! We received radio orders to head for the nearest land, build the station and get the ships out right away. This hasty energetic order was a heart-killing blow to the IGY civilians whose plans had been based on the setting up of the station in the Bowman Peninsula area.

Then suddenly—just as suddenly as the ice had surrounded us—the cloud cover lifted, the wind swung around from the south, the ice pressure against the ships' sides slackened and it grew colder. Instead of resting in a cradle of ice, the ships now floated free in open water between pressure ridges. The change in weather would allow us to continue to our destination, heading westward. That day I shall never forget. It was the most beautiful day we had in the pack. A clear sky, a slow breeze from the south and a most brilliant sun shining over the two ships and the surrounding scenery once again. How good it was to see smiles on the men's faces and feel their spirit rise. Now surely, I heard the officers and men remark, will we make the Bowman Peninsula and get this job done.

At the western cape of Gould Bay we discovered what had caused our entrapment. A huge iceberg, some thirty-four miles long, had broken off from the cape and blocked the western passage. When the wind had shifted, all the pack ice caught in the sheltered side of this giant berg had moved down on our ships.

Carefully we picked our way around the berg and through the dense pack beyond until we reached open water at the western extremity of the berg. Here we saw thousands of emperor penguins standing on the sea ice, hundreds in each cluster. It looked like the whole horizon in that direction was covered with them. A few miles farther west we again saw the ice shelf, which I had followed on my southeastward flight in 1947.

The navigators of our two ships had been taking sun sights continuously and had verified the location of features and the edge of the extensive ice shelf within three to five miles of the determinations I had made while in flight in 1947. They now worked on fine, clear, sunny days, when wonderful mirage effects were observed, just as they occur over the desert. Huge 'bergs and barrier cliffs were apparently resting on nothing with a distant gap between their bases and the horizon. Others I saw were curiously distorted into weird and fantastic shapes and appeared to be many times their proper height. Added to this, the pure glistening white of the snow and ice made a picture which is impossible to describe adequately.

We were now beating our way along the barrier, mostly in open water but sometimes through belts of loose pack ice. The barrier cliff, now on our port side, almost took my breath away. Ten years previously I had flown over it at 10,000 feet; this time I saw it from the deck of a ship. Of all the spectacles on earth, this one is probably the most awe inspiring. It lies there, as sharply cut as by a giant's saw, a flat-topped wall, a white cliff glistening in the sun and reflecting the darkness of the sea, dull and heavy. Most of the men aboard who saw the barrier for the first time merely looked; there wasn't anything to say. It is not even stimulating. It is the end of the earth!

On January 15 Captain McDonald and I made a helicopter flight from the deck of the icebreaker to Cape Adams, the southeast cape of Bowman Peninsula. We were scouting for a landing site in this area. A heavy haze hung over the cape and a light veil of clouds was draped around Mount Austin about twenty miles to the west, so that the black rock outcrops were barely visible. Below us the ice conditions, the geographical features of Bowman Peninsula and the embayments that I had originally picked out for mooring our ships were exactly as they had been photographed and interpreted after my 1947 flight.

A jubilant conversation took place over the intercommunication system in the 'copter. McDonald stated that he would direct the two ships to proceed to the proposed landing site the next forenoon. From the ship's location, open water extended westerly as far as we could see. I proposed to Mac that he should make the return journey northward out of the Weddell Sea along the east coast of Palmer Peninsula. There was a good possibility that open water leads would allow him to reach the outer sea without retracing his path past those huge icebergs. Captain Gambacorta had already begun the boiler cleaning job on the *Wyandot,* which would be completed in the morning. If the weather was good, we would make another reconnaissance flight directly to the unloading site, as the ships also moved forward.

On our return to the ships we flew even with the height of the barrier edge. It measured 250 feet above sea level, higher than any other I have seen in the Antarctic. Below us were many thousand white snowy petrels swarming along the barrier cliff, barely noticeable at first against the blue-tinted cliff with a layer of pure white snow at its upper layer. We landed back on the icebreaker's flight deck and happily related the good news. Our joy did not last long, for during the night, a radio message had been received from the Task Force at McMurdo Sound which discouraged Mac from making any further attempts to carry out the approved IGY plan to locate the station near the Bowman Peninsula. The message was based on consideration for the safety of the men and the two ships, possible problems in resupplying the base the following year and lateness of the season.

A succession of messages flashed back and forth in an effort to gain the concurrence of the high command so that we could follow up the favorable findings of our helicopter flight. But the unalterable decision had been made at headquarters, 2,000 miles away. We were ordered to discard the original plan, to return east and retrace our track toward Gould Bay. With a heavy heart I heard the announcement over the ship's public address system, informing all hands of our future course.

I was disappointed because I was quite sure we had already found a suitable site on Bowman Peninsula. I felt that the base could have been built quickly, and that the ships would have had less difficulty in getting out than in getting in.

Worst of all, of course, was that now we were getting our orders from a command so far away. That command did not, and could not, know local conditions. From their point of view, of course, this decision was best because it narrowed the possibility of the ships getting stuck in the ice. But the simple fact was that Bowman Peninsula was our destination, and by not reaching it, we failed in the first step of the program.

Captain McDonald was as anxious as I to achieve our announced objective, but the orders were quite explicit. I must admit that I was angered by one aspect of the orders to McDonald, which stated, "do not let anyone's desire to make a record influence you." The trouble was the same old one, one that has always afflicted men who journey to unknown lands: jealousy and suspicion that someone else is trying to steal their thunder. Admiral Dufek had just made a record by landing at the South Pole—the first man since Scott to arrive there and the first man to land there in an airplane. Of course, he did not do it alone; the Navy crew of the plane was with him. But, strangely enough, no explorer experienced in Antarctic survival was with him on the flight, although some Antarctic veterans were available to make the flight from McMurdo Sound at the time.

Quite naturally, I was interested in "making a record"—which, in this case, meant getting to the place we were supposed to go. But neither then nor at any other time, was I to allow my personal interest in Antarctic exploration and particularly in the geography of the unknown to keep me from doing the job the Navy and the IGY officials had given me to do.

Headquarters' unequivocal order was a bitter pill to the officers and men on board the two ships, all of whom had exerted so much effort to reach our destination only to be thwarted at the last minute. But in the Navy, and in Antarctic exploration, there are many bitter pills that must be swallowed. I, along with the rest of them, swallowed this one. The ships changed their courses.

About sixteen miles from our destination on Cape Adams, latitude 75° 25′ S, longitude 59° 58′ W, we reversed our course and progressed slowly eastward, keeping the barrier cliff a half mile or so to starboard.

Reconnaissance flights revealed the same huge icebergs in about the same position as observed earlier on our way west. We hugged the steep ice cliffs, hoping to gain an easier entrance to Gould Bay. I spent that whole evening on deck watching the scenery. The shining water was calm, partly free of ice, disrupted only by the wake of the ships. Snow-plow side motions of the bow sped like wedges into the glossy surface. It was getting colder by the minute. New ice began to form but was soon broken by the ships' action, leaving a heavy, gray mass of slush ice in their wake. The sun set over the edge of a huge ice cliff, spattering the clouds like a surging beauty. The icebergs we had just passed on the port side were dark silhouettes against the northern horizon. It was truly magnificent. We seemed to be in a land of fantasy. Our path snaked along the great ice wall; its blue-veined, broken glacier faces fell from tremendous cliffs into a cobalt sea.

The west side of the huge 'berg we were skirting was deeply indented with crevasses. We could see the deep, sharply cut wedges, some of them a hundred or more feet in depth. A few times, years back, I had fallen into some of them, and knew what their cross-sections looked like. Ugly and fearfully dangerous!

On our way west and back, no suitable landing sites had been seen along the high barrier. For 350 miles between Cape Adams on the Bowman Peninsula and Gould Bay, the ice shelf was from 100 to 250 feet high, with no sloping access to it from the sea ice. Many salvos from the icebreaker's four-inch gun had failed to make an indentation in the icy wall. In addition, the sea ice itself was not strong enough to support heavy weights, such as tractors. As we rounded the last cape of the huge iceberg and headed for the east cape of Gould Bay, new radio orders were received from McMurdo Sound headquarters. For the next several days official radio communication between our group and the McMurdo Sound headquarters took precedence over the customary variable weather as a barometer for the lowering morale of personnel aboard our two ships. The new radio dispatch directed us to retreat as far north as Cape Norvegia at the entrance of the Weddell Sea, about 1,200 miles northeast of Gould Bay. We were instructed to establish our station in a small cove, Atka Bay, on a floating ice shelf exposed to the open South Atlantic Ocean in longitude 8° W. To all concerned this was a blow, the severity of which could not be minimized.

The new order was taken up with the IGY civilians on board. To a man they refused to winter if Ellsworth Station were placed so far north as Cape Norvegia. It was near there that a Norwegian-British-Swedish expedition wintered from 1949 to 1952. It was also close to a new Norwegian IGY station. The seismologists felt that nothing new would result from their work there, nor would the glaciologists be able to contribute much work that had not already been done. A location so far north would also be outside the zone for Aurora and air glow observations, thus nullifying the expected observations of that branch of science. Since the other IGY personnel were all opposed to the new location, I got busy on the radio. By the time we had pushed our way through the pack ice to open water beyond the east cape of Gould Bay, my effort produced results.

Through the intervention of Dr. Gould, chairman of the IGY Antarctic Committee, headquarters at McMurdo Sound gave us permission to set up the station east of the forty-first meridian on Filchner Ice Shelf. While not as strategic a location for IGY purposes as Cape Adams on the Bowman Peninsula, this location was considerably more favorable than Cape Norvegia. The trick now was to find quickly a low site on the barrier shelf for suitable unloading on the otherwise continuous 100- to 250-foot–high ice barrier.

The officers on the icebreaker made numerous helicopter flights in search of a low spot to unload the ship. Overcast weather hampered the search, and for a while it looked as if we might have to retreat to Cape Norvegia. Temperatures were getting lower. The summer-season seemed to be coming to an end. Then, on January 26, while on one of the last reconnaissance flights about twenty miles east of Gould Bay, I noticed the ice shelf dipped to a gradual, relatively crevasse-free slope about thirty feet high. This was exactly what we had been looking for, and I asked Lieutenant Newell, the helicopter pilot, to land there. I surveyed the area on skis and located some crevasses that would have to be avoided by the tractors traveling from the ice edge to the smooth plateau a couple of miles inland. It was definitely a secondary choice, but it answered our immediate requirements.

Before the *Wyandot* could tie up at the edge of the ice, the icebreaker's skipper, Commander Elliott, had to go to work. Fronting the unloading site was a jumble of pack ice that was rafted to about twenty feet. It extended for about 300 yards and had to be removed before the cargo ship could tie up. For about twenty hours, Elliott broke away the ice by ramming the icebreaker into the rafted ice. The small broken fragments were carried away by the westerly flowing ocean current. Since we were still a mile or so to the west of the restricted location pronounced in the directive last issued from far-off McMurdo Sound, we radioed for final permission, which arrived the following day.

After forty-three days spent in the pack ice of the Weddell Sea, our quest for a station site was over and on January 29, 1957, unloading of the cargo ship *Wyandot* began.

When Commander Elliott finally tied up his icebreaker to the barrier cliff a quarter of a mile away from the *Wyandot,* he must have given a tremendous sigh of relief. No man deserved more credit than he for having led the way so deeply into the Weddell Sea, in waters where no ship had ever sailed before. At the expense of much needed sleep, Elliott directed the operation of his ship day and night. Once he broke through heavy pack ice for fifty hours without leaving the bridge. After pressing on to within sixteen miles of our original destination, his disappointment had been great when we turned back from Cape Adams. His devotion and enthusiasm for the success of our Ellsworth Station assignment brought him the admiration of all hands.

Equally elated with the end of the trying ordeal at last in sight was Captain Gambacorta of the *Wyandot*. He, too, had spent many wakeful hours of harrowing concern over possible pressure-ice damage to the thin-skinned hull of his cargo ship. Now, both ships were securely moored to the barrier's edge.

CHAPTER 2

ON THE ICE

Aᴸᴸ ʜᴀɴᴅꜱ ɴᴏᴡ ʜᴀᴅ ᴛᴏ ᴡᴏʀᴋ ᴀꜱ ǫᴜɪᴄᴋʟʏ ᴀꜱ ʜᴜᴍᴀɴʟʏ ᴘᴏꜱꜱɪʙʟᴇ. Although it was not their primary job, the officers and men of the two ships volunteered to aid the SeaBees in the enormous task of unloading the *Wyandot* and getting the station in the best possible shape before the ships had to depart. Unloading 6,400 tons of cargo and transporting it two and one half miles to the camp site where the building shells were to be assembled by the SeaBees was an arduous assignment.

For eleven days—eleven short days even though the sun shone all the time—the *Wyandot* unloaded supplies for us onto the Filchner Ice Shelf. Every moment she was in danger from the shifting winds, for a strong blow could pin her against the shelf and bend her plating. Captain Gambacorta moved the *Wyandot* out ahead as soon as she was unloaded; he could not wait much longer if he were to escape the freezing of the pack ice and the forming of new ice in the open leads. At 1:00 on the morning of February 11, the *Wyandot* slowly got underway. Only a few sailors were at the edge to cast her lines loose.

Captain McDonald was anxious to get his Task Group out of the Weddell Sea. He asked me to look over the station and see if I would accept it in its present status. The *Wyandot* had become stuck in the pack five miles east of us, where she had moved to get a head start on the icebreaker in their race to the open sea. McDonald and the ship's crew were all itching to get going. I had skied to the station site almost every day and watched the construction progress. On my last visit I had seen so much work to be done that I did not see how we could be left alone at this stage. The whole station at that time was in chaos, but I promised McDonald to have another look.

Commander James Elliott and I started off from the icebreaker to examine the station. Before we could even get off the ship we had to wait while nearly a hundred SeaBees streamed onto the *Staten Island,* lugging their duffel bags over their shoulders. On the ice scores of others stood around with their gear, waiting to embark for later transfer to the *Wyandot* that would carry them back to the United States. It looked promising. If the SeaBees were ready to leave, the job must be done.

But to see for ourselves, we had to travel two and a half miles inland from the unloading site, for our station was located on the 800-foot–thick ice shelf itself. We had placed it far enough back from the edge of the Weddell Sea for safety, no matter what might happen. Our route to the camp followed the trail that had been packed down by scores of thirty-five-ton tractors that hauled sledge loads of supplies from ship to camp site. The route was very familiar to me. Instead of skiing, this time we would travel by weasel, one of those small caterpillar-tracked vehicles that had been developed during World War II. The weasel was to be the jeep of our expedition. The only other way to travel across the ice and snow was by skiing, or flying; both methods as comfortable and as safe as weasel travel.

The ride to the camp was rough, for the big tractors had broken up the trail in the past few days. It was especially hard going at the beginning, creeping up the steep slope to the top of the barrier, past the warning flags that marked the crevasses—those ever-dangerous cracks in the ice.

At the top we could look back on the *Staten Island* below us; ahead, the white ice barrier stretched endlessly in the clear, dust-free air. Only wind-blown *sastrugi* (snow drifts) broke the surface of the barrier itself. Where the barrier encountered the bay ice, however, sometimes the tremendous pressures had forced ice ridges to rise high in the air.

Before we reached the camp we passed a large mound that looked something like one of the old Indian burial mounds. It was a burial mound, all right, but in it we had cached our tons of explosives for the seismic program. We kept them a long way from the camp, for we were going to be here for a solid year and for nine months of it nobody could help us if we got in trouble. For further safety, we separated the explosives into three dumps and kept them five hundred feet apart. Then, if one cache blew up, the others would be safe enough.

Just before we entered the camp we passed the diamond-shaped pattern that marked the beginning of our radio rhombic antenna system. This system was not completed, I noticed. It would have to be finished soon, for once the icebreaker left the barrier our only communication with the outside world would be by radio.

On the edge of the permanent camp we saw the eighteen Jamesway huts that had been put up hurriedly to house the SeaBees who were building the camp. A few SeaBees moved around the huts. Most of them were gone now, and we would use the huts for storing emergency gear, well away from the main camp. Our greatest enemy, I knew, would be fire. We had to be able to help ourselves no matter what came along. For all intents and purposes we were on our own.

I sat up eagerly as we came within the camp, looking around to see

41

how much had been done since the last time I had been there two days ago. The camp was laid out along a main street, with three cross streets that projected a hundred feet on each side.

A house stood on each side of each street, set twelve feet back from the street line. These were prefabricated houses made of plywood sheeting with four inches of fiberglass insulation between the boards. They were built for warmth and strength. The insulation was planned to protect against temperatures of $-80°$.

On this balmy, sunny day, with the temperature just below the freezing point, it was hard to realize that we would be living in darkness soon, in the silent, cold air of the Antarctic night. Winter was already drawing near; the camp must be finished in time, and all our preparations made. Antarctic winter, with the wind whistling in your face and threatening you always with frostbite, with the temperatures at unbelieveable low register— these are no days for men to struggle in the shifting snow to build their camp.

I saw two dark objects standing out in our little town, towering above the rest of the buildings. One, square and mounted atop four columns, was the aurora–air-glow observatory, from which observers would have an unobstructed view in all directions. The top of the observatory stuck thirty feet above the surface, and four plastic domes rose above the top providing vantage points on which to mount instruments and observe the phenomena above in any kind of weather.

The second strange structure was a ball-like building that reminded me of nothing so much as the Mosque of Omar, next to the old Wailing Wall in Jerusalem. This was the Rawin tower, a bulge of intricate radar instruments set to trace the path of weather balloons on their ascent high above the earth's surface.

These two buildings were as complete as anyone but the scientists themselves could make them. Around them, and scattered pretty much through the "town," were a number of masts—some of them forming an antenna system for general radio use.

Now that we were in the heart of the camp, Commander Elliott and I began our tour of inspection. First, we went to the generator room. Only one of seven generators was running. That meant we had power in only a few areas. The huge craterlike building in which we were to keep them was full of crates, cartons and boxes of all descriptions.

The radio room disorder was as bad. A transmitter was mounted on a pair of two-by-fours, and a receiver sat on a table. In the middle of the room wires hung from ceiling to floor; inconvenient, if not downright dangerous. No other equipment was working. I saw a chief petty officer sitting against the wall with the others and asked him why nothing was being done. The SeaBees had just delivered the equipment, he said. It would be four or five days before he had his communication system in order.

I knew then that we were in for a difficult period. McMurdo Sound, where task force headquarters was located, would want to know why they hadn't heard from us before that time. As long as the ships were at the edge of the ice we were all right, of course, but soon they would be gone and we would need to keep in touch with our Navy communication centers.

From the radio room we made our way down the main tunnel toward the galley, and along the tunnel we saw sailors putting up chicken wire on the cross pieces. On the outside surfaces they nailed burlap to keep drifting snow from seeping all through our camp. Bulldozers packed snow high against the tunnel's outside wall to give extra insulation. It was important to keep these tunnels open; they crisscrossed the entire camp and would give us access to all the buildings on days when it would be too cold, dark and windy to venture outside.

What amazed me and upset me most at this point was that we saw so few men working. Most of the SeaBees had returned to their ship, but what about my men, the men who were supposed to winter with me? They had all transferred from the *Wyandot* to the station by this time, I knew. Except for a few of my chief petty officers, I had seen only men from the ship's company of the *Staten Island*.

The framework was up in the galley passageway, but it had no covering. Inside it was pitch dark. I tried the light switches. Nothing happened. What a disgusting place this was! It was cold, too. No heat, no light, no men and nothing to see. Commander Elliott lit a cigarette lighter, and by its flickering yellow flame we saw rubbish scattered everywhere.

What a dismal place! What demon had got hold of me to make me volunteer to live here for a year?

We moved on. In the next room, we propped open the outside doors and let in enough light to see where we were. This was the mess hall. But what were the seating arrangements? Short tables, with four round disks bolted on for the men to sit on? I had always pictured only labor camps and prisons as having such crude and unfriendly furniture. Immediately, I made up my mind to change that arrangement and have the carpenter make benches, if regular folding chairs were not available.

Huge steel boxes blocked the passage between the dining hall and the galley. I recognized the huge galley range in one. Others held bake ovens, proof boxes, cabinets and sinks. None of the equipment was in place. Obviously, we would have to eat in the dark, dull Jamesway huts for many weeks ahead. At least, I noticed ruefully, the light fixtures were up, and the snaky arms of a jet heater twisted in and out of the roof stringers overhead. As we moved on to the next building, I wondered if any heat would ever come out of that stove.

Of the two bunkhouses for the enlisted men, only one was heated. Everywhere we found confusion and rubbish from the packing boxes. In the administration building I groped my way to the place I had selected for my own room. It was crammed with steel cabinets, barely a foot of space between them.

Back in the welcome daylight of the uncovered tunnel, we went to the main head.* There were no lights there, either. The whole water system, including a snow melter, stood in cases on the floor, an inch-thick layer of ice on part of it. Rubbish and half finished work was everywhere.

In bunkhouse number two we found a small space heater running; otherwise, it was full of rubbish. The recreation building was just a shell, filled with rubbish and spare parts scattered around in confusion. Only the main tunnel was built completely. The side tunnels were either unfinished, or uncovered, with wire and burlap outside. Out in the open, acres and acres of ground were covered by rows of material that should have been inside the tunnels for protection. Bedding, cabinets, lockers, recreation gear, heavy machinery, and household supplies were stacked everywhere, and were now partly covered by snow. If a blizzard struck suddenly we would lose most of the material and have to bulldoze for it.

From the main section of the camp, we walked some 300 feet to the two aviation buildings. The tunnel that was to connect them with the camp was only partly completed. The buildings were unheated, like the rest. The floor was stacked with piles of green rubber tile, far more than enough to cover the floors of every building in camp. Commander Elliott asked me if he could take some tile aboard his *Staten Island*. Even later on, after we had covered all the floors of all the buildings, we still had plenty left over.

It was the same with everything. We had enough equipment and enough basic supplies for three units as large as our thirty-nine–man force that would stay the winter. We had many tons of beer, enough to last us eleven years (in round figures, 3,600 cases); a good quantity of liquor; and enough food, I thought, when I looked it over, to see us through four to six years of heavy eating.

My worry was the state of the camp. After our inspection, Elliott and I agreed that the work was about sixty-five or seventy per-cent complete. We checked with two of my chiefs who were supervising the work. They agreed that sixty per-cent was a fair figure. Later, however, I revised my estimate downward quite a bit. I don't believe the camp was really much more than half finished at this time, and I knew there was nothing to do but accept it as satisfactory, so the *Staten Island* could pull out and join the *Wyandot* for their run to the open sea.

Of course, the building of the station had not been Commander Elliott's responsibility. I knew how hard he and his men from the icebreaker had worked on this camp—harder than the SeaBees by far, although the Sea-Bees were assigned to the job, and the *Staten Island* men were simply pitching in for an emergency caused by the late arrival.

------

*Washroom and toilet.

44

Many times during the unloading operations I went to the building site between unloading chores, just to see what was going on. Very seldom did I see many of the SeaBees working. I was always told they were sleeping or eating, no matter what time of day or night it was. The galley was always packed with them.

Later, I learned that as soon as the ship's crew came to help, the SeaBees thought that their job had come to an end. They decided to work only as supervisors. So in the end, more than half the work was actually done by the sailors who had come just to help. If the SeaBees had pitched in, the station would have been much further along. The officer in charge of the construction group had difficulty pushing his charges beyond normal output. Coffee breaks had been frequent and long.

Actually, the lack of modern conveniences did not matter so much to me personally—I had been in far worse circumstances in the Antarctic —but the utter disorganization was staggering. In this circumstance, my responsibility for the thirty-eight men who were spending their first year there did concern me, but there was no use crying about that at this late date. Now I had a difficult decision to make—one that might involve the safety of all thirty-nine of us who were going to spend the winter here.

As we drove back to the *Staten Island,* we could see the masts and stack of the *Wyandot* in the ice, to the east of us. She had been there, stuck, since the night before. I could almost see the always congenial and highly able Captain Gambacorta fuming out there in the bay ice because the delay in moving out might jeopardize their chances of getting home this year. I could imagine, too, his feeling toward McDonald for not coming over immediately to pull the *Wyandot* out of the ice, and I knew that McDonald was just as concerned. All of the men aboard were eager to get back to warmer and more friendly climates. The only amusement here, watching seals and penguins and killer whales, offered little solace to restless sailors.

Lunch was ready for us when we came back on board the *Staten Island* and entered the skipper's cabin. McDonald was there, waiting, and he asked me if I would accept the station as it was.

The pressure was certainly on!

I knew all the SeaBees were back on board the *Staten Island,* and now all the ship's working force had been ordered back aboard, too. Obviously, unless I wanted to create a real uproar, I had no choice but to accept the camp in its unfinished state. Even if I did not take it, I knew the estimates of the degree of completion were subject to every kind of interpretation. There was no use making trouble all around, so I told Captain McDonald I had no choice, seeing that all the crews had gone back to their ships.

McDonald was sympathetic and apologetic because the station wasn't complete. The officer in charge, a lieutenant commander, had just not known his job. This officer's ignorance and refusal to listen to even the most elementary common sense was to create a good deal of trouble for us later. It had been a cardinal mistake to face the station in the direction he had, because of the prevailing winds. We would have trouble with meteorological work and communications because of it. I had stressed this when it was being done, but without any success. He let me know that it was his responsibility—and he knew better.

But at least the lunch was excellent, so I enjoyed myself. There was no point in worrying about what was done and what had to be done. We would have to live with the mistakes, and as for the undone work, we would just have to settle down and do it.

While Commander Elliott and I were still at the table, Captain McDonald went out to dress and leave for the station. He wanted to have a small ceremony in turning the station over to me. All the men in my wintering party were already at the base, and I would join them in the Jamesway huts as soon as I had put my affairs in order here.

I took a hot shower. Since examining the state of the water system and heating plant at the station, I didn't know when I would get another. Then I mailed off the last letters to my wife, Jackie, at the ship's post office, collected my personal belongings and set off in a weasel for the camp.

Chief Albert Spear had managed to build a crude wooden flagpole about twenty feet high. An American flag, given to me by Commander Elliott, was flying on top. All the officers, chiefs, IGY civilians and men were lined up in a **U** formation around the pole, and McDonald and I stood in the center, next to the pole.

McDonald was obviously in a hurry, and I can't say that I could blame him—with a ship stuck out in the ice and the weather beginning to turn nasty. There were threatening clouds in the south and the temperature was dropping.

He made a little speech. He explained that the men had been a long time on the ships because we had come to an area where ships had never come before, through uncharted waters. Except for my flight over the ice shelf in 1947, nothing was known of ice conditions in this area of the Antarctic before we came to the Weddell Sea. The pack ice, we had found, was the heaviest we had ever encountered.

All that was explanation for the delay in building the station. Then he came to the point and turned the station over to me, wishing us a "pleasant and adventurous year" in the Antarctic.

My mind was spinning. McDonald had said the station was "operative," and all I could see in my mind's eye was acres of material and the dismal look of every nook and cranny of our new home.

There was dead silence for what seemed like minutes. Finally, words started to trickle out of my mouth in a slow, very determined way. I was scarcely sure which word would come out next.

I talked for a minute about our choice of site. This location was the best we could find under the circumstances, I said. Although we had hoped to establish our base much farther west, at a more sheltered spot on Bowman Peninsula, we had taken this place. At least, I said, for the benefit of the scientific work, we should be able to carry out the full program under IGY here. Had we located at Atka Bay, where we had been ordered, we could not have carried out all the work.

Then I gave my first order to my newly appointed executive officer, Lieutenant Commander Charles McCarthy, USNR—twenty-four hours of leave to all hands to get themselves somewhat organized and so they could rest up for the big job of putting the station in working condition.

Captain McDonald, Commander Elliott and I went along the line, shaking hands with all the men, none of whom had ever wintered before. The ceremony was over.

We went back to the Jamesway huts where long tables were set up and beer was served to all hands. I took one sip, but it tasted like mud to me and I could not finish even half of the can. After a few minutes I accompanied McDonald and Elliott back to the *Staten Island* for the last time. They loaded our weasel with extras, even including some champagne which I had purchased in Chile for use at special celebrations. I thanked McDonald—we had been friends for many years. He had done his very best for us, now there was nothing more he could do. Knowing Mac, I think he would have liked to stay with us. Then we said our final good-byes, and McDonald went up on the bridge to join Commander Elliott.

The officers and the men of the *Staten Island* lined the decks as the gangway was taken in and mooring lines were cast off. I stood on the edge of the barrier with Edward Thiel and Hugo Neuburg, two of the IGY civilians, watching the impressive maneuvers of a ship's crew trained to clocklike action. Finally, only two small mooring lines held the *Staten Island* to the ice, and they asked us to cast them off. Both were secured to the "dead men" that were buried deep in the snow. The knots were frozen, so one of the IGY men took a tiny pocket knife and cut the securing line allowing the hawser to slide free. The second line was cut, and *Staten Island* was clear; probably the first ship ever freed with such a small implement.

The overcast was heavy as the icebreaker began to move east, plowing steadily through some eight inches of new bay ice that had formed around her. We took pictures until she rounded a small ice tongue about a mile away, and moved out of sight. Then the three of us got into the weasel and the larger Sno-cat and drove back to the station, with a mutual feeling of let-down.

At the station there was no sign of life. The men must have crawled into their sleeping bags in the Jamesway huts for the needed rest.

I walked over to my quarters in the administration building and found them just as cold and dismal as the rest of the station, although the filing cabinets had now been moved out and I had some room in which to turn around.

The jet heater was not going. I tried to get it started, although I should have known better, because loose wires were sticking out all over it. I was determined to stay there, however and set about clearing up rubbish and moved all the equipment but one cabinet into the dispensary.

I borrowed a hammer, tore down the partition to the storeroom that had been built next to my quarters, and enlarged my own space so it would be thirteen by thirteen feet square. Then I moved my belongings over from the Jamesway hut, and the Chiefs Walter May and Albert Spear brought me a bunk and mattress, sheets and blankets.

I worked on the room until midnight that first night, putting a Navy locker in one corner and installing a table that had been made for me aboard the *Wyandot*. Except for a break at supper, I worked straight through. At supper time, I walked over to the Jamesway mess hall to eat. It was a rough meal, roughly served. We ate with plastic forks, spoons and knives, on paper plates and drank from paper cups. It was quite a contrast to what we had become accustomed to on shipboard.

Even the men were rough. They paid no attention to me. At one table the men eating would not even squeeze over to let me sit down. I thought, then and there, that separate meal hours for the men should be established. The IGY civilians, who had officer status, should eat with us. In earlier expeditions I had learned that too much familiarity breeds contempt, and I was trying to avoid the first breakdown in discipline.

After supper, I returned to try to make some order out of my quarters. Finally, at 11:30 I had the room under control. I knew where the furniture should go, had the bed in place, and was really tired after so much excitement on the first day ashore.

In a few minutes before I fell asleep, I turned the situation over in my mind. With both ships gone we were on our own until next year. As soon as those ships moved outside the pack ice, no outside help could reach us in any way. The pack ice would congeal into a solid mass, as solid as if it were cement.

We were deep in the Antarctic, on the edge of unexplored territory, and it was hard to know how ready we were for the long year ahead. It was a sloppy beginning for a tough year ahead.

CHAPTER 3

FRICTION

My first step, as far as the men were concerned, was to establish the procedure of my command. It was vital, I knew from three previous expeditions to the Antarctic, that the work begin on the right basis. Otherwise, we would have nothing but trouble. While there is certainly nothing new about troubles on Antarctic expeditions, I was optimistic and hopeful about ways of preventing or at least minimizing major difficulties.

That first night, in fact, even as the men were resting and I was trying to get my quarters in order, I called several of my responsible officers together to settle a few important matters. I asked Lieutenant Commander Charles J. McCarthy, Lieutenant Conrad Jaburg, Lieutenant Clinton Smith and Dr. Edward C. Thiel to meet with me in one of the Jamesway huts to settle the immediate question of bunking arrangements.

McCarthy was my executive officer—six feet of Irish humor and sensitivity, topped by a bushel basketful of hair and a black beard. McCarthy was also in charge of the aviation unit, but since he was second in seniority with sixteen years as a naval reserve officer, I had earlier made him executive officer of the party. Lieutenant Jaburg had come to the Antarctic as a helicopter pilot, but he would have to take on additional duties. I could see, even at the beginning, that this responsibility might not sit well on Jaburg's shoulders. The shoulders were broad enough—Jaburg was even bigger than McCarthy—and his young, round face and reddish beard made him look like a friendly bear.

Lieutenant Smith was our medical officer. He had been given the task —extremely difficult for a doctor—of administration of the affairs of the SeaBee detachment in the camp. The responsibility had been assigned him by the Task Force staff, as doctors at all the other stations had been appointed in charge of the station as well. It was a job that made him nervous from the first, and the nervousness already showed in the tall

49

doctor's face. Just out of medical school, he was already beginning to lose his sandy hair. But Smith, I could tell that, was intelligent. It was not his fault that his first trip abroad and his first important assignment would lead him into the ticklishly close quarters of the Antarctic.

Dr. Thiel I appointed as spokesman for the civilian IGY men and second to me in charge of the scientific work at Ellsworth station. He was the best educated scientist on the expedition and the only holder of a Ph.D. in our camp. He looked every inch the scholar: sharp facial features and thinning hair, medium and slim frame, and the low voice of an introvert. In my brief contact with the IGY men until now, I was satisfied with my selection of Thiel as spokesman for their civilian group. I might have hoped for an older man—Thiel was just twenty-eight—but I knew what difficulty the IGY committee had encountered in finding competent scientists to do the work in the Antarctic. Thiel's particular job, as seismologist, was to probe the subterranean layers of the earth's crust. In the case of the Antarctic, it was important to find out how far down the ice lay, what was under the ice, how old it was, and what deductions could thus be made about the land, its climate, composition and history.

Thiel's scientific job was difficult enough. I did not envy him the task of handling other civilians in a military environment. I was impressed with the way he comported himself in this first base meeting. He was careful about his remarks, and obviously thought things out well before he said anything at all. Here, at least, was one man who seemed mature enough for the work at hand, I thought.

The first meeting was over. We had settled the bunking arrangements, so that we would have no more than three men in a room. I went back to my cold room. The next morning, it was no warmer, nor were there any lights. I dressed, shivering, and then walked to the Jamesway hut where the temporary messhall had been established.

For breakfast, I had scrambled eggs, bacon and coffee. I looked around the messhall. Edward Davis and Richard Grobb, the two cooks, looked worn, ragged and unshaven. They had been working hard since we first landed, preparing 650 meals a day. They worked in their undershirts in the hot galley, a dark and miserable room. That would have to be changed.

Not that I blamed the cooks for their appearance; they had done a superb job for many weeks. This temporary messhall was completely unsatisfactory. The generator was not working, and the oil stoves were on their last legs by the time we took them over—after two short weeks. Constant and excessive heat on the stove caused the fire-box to collapse, and soot accumulation was always excessive. The small mess tables were crowded together in the hut, and the men had little room to move their elbows when they ate.

Moreover, the sloppiness of the hall had its effect on the men. That

50

first evening, I noticed the men just stared at me. They were not used to having a captain share the table with an apprentice seaman (one of them told me just that), and most of the men did not seem to like those close quarters with an officer. I was not a regular naval officer, so I fully intended to integrate with the men as much as possible. But we were a fairly large group with many dissimilar interests, and the atmosphere did not seem conducive to such a plan. But here we were, and the best course was to make it likable to all hands.

My first important assignment was to make the camp shipshape. While we had been discouraged by our hurried inspection, Commander Elliott and I had not quite realized how bad things really were.

McCarthy set the men to work at once; he gave the actual job of supervising the men to Albert Spear, a chief petty officer with sixteen years in the Navy and one of the original SeaBees first shipped out to build runways for attack on Guadalcanal during War War II. Spear was in his late thirties, short, plump and cleanshaven. His basic job in camp was to run the garage, or "public works department," but he was also the best man we could have found to supervise the rest of the construction job. When I went out for breakfast that morning, the men were lounging around the camp. When I went out for coffee in the afternoon, I found men working everywhere and getting the job done.

Little by little we got the station in order. I tiled my own floor, after Chief Spear spent a half hour showing me how. Early in the first week I had my green rug on the floor and a high fidelity record player hooked up. They sound like luxuries, but tiles on the floor get icy in constant subzero weather and the hi-fi was the personal recreation which I brought with me from home. I knew there would be numerous occasions when I would be condemned to the same life of loneliness as a ship's captain, and I had to find my own small pleasure to stave off the boredom.

The men had their own record players in the recreation hall. They did not have green shag rugs, but they made their own, almost immediately, from the felt packing of the crates, from rope, or from rags.

It was to be a far cry, certainly, from a couple of the expeditions I had joined in the past. Then we had lived in furs, slept in caribou sleeping bags in unheated buildings, killed seals to supplement our food, or subsisted on the basic trail diet of pemmican.

Now, just inside the door of my room, I had a full-sized bed with a Beautyrest mattress, white Navy blankets that covered white bed sheets and an upholstered chair. A typewriter helped me keep my daily log, and the wall behind my desk was covered—partly, at least—by the American Geographical Society's latest map of the Antarctic. Elsewhere I had the space to display an American flag, an Explorer's Club flag and pictures of Jackie and our six-year-old Karen.

My quarters were whipped together quickly enough. That was no problem, for I did the work myself, as was expected and demanded of all of us who were wintering together in this Antarctic station. It was a fine line that had to be drawn between maintenance of discipline on the one hand and pulling at least my own share of the tiresome housekeeping work on the other. The Navy detachment—seventeen men of the SeaBees and eleven men of an aviation squadron—were sent to the Antarctic to assist in housekeeping and other support. It is one thing to run a caterpillar tractor or a Sno-Cat across the ice, but someone like Chief Spear has to be on hand to repair breakdowns and improvise spare parts.

Spear kept the men hopping those first few days. The worst problem, as far as station operation went, was the SeaBee construction technician's failure to put the communication equipment into the proper working order before leaving. Chief Electronics Man Kenneth K. Kent reported that the crew had wired the radios incorrectly; one amplifier had already blown its tubes. Electrician James Hannah said it would be about ten days before the wiring in our buildings could all be corrected.

Spear with his crew of specialists began on the permanent mess hall, changing the improper wiring and correcting the errors in plumbing installation so the stove and snow-melter equipment could be installed. With the work under way morale took an immediate turn for the better. There is an old Antarctic slogan which originated with Roald Amundsen: "Keep the men busy and you will keep them happy." But the larger the complement of men and the fewer objectives, the harder this rule is to follow. Idleness created no problem at this stage.

The second morning when I went to the Jamesway hut mess hall, the tables were cleaner, the room nearly empty and the cooks were closing up. Baker Richard Grob, a small and very wiry fellow, made an exception for me, although he had closed the mess hall, and I had hot cakes and coffee. The men had eaten the same—some of them with the giant appetite the cold of the Antarctic brings on. One man, I heard, had eaten twelve hot cakes, sausages, a bowl of oatmeal and had drunk a big mug of hot chocolate for breakfast. That was all right. We had enough food for at least four years, and we planned to stay for only one.

As with the food, it was apparent that we had too much of everything; thirty-five tons of beer, which meant six cans per man every day for eleven years; seven thirty-KW diesel-electric generators, when we needed only two; medical supplies for a 1,000-bed hospital for six years, including a woman's breast pump. The surplus equipment on this expedition was unbelievable!

These tons of supplies were scattered all over the camp. Whether we used them or not, we could not let them stay out in the snow and cold over the winter night. They had to be moved inside, into the unused Jamesway huts, into the tunnels within the camp—wherever we could find storage space. The weather had not grown cold yet, but we were coming to the end of the summer period. A storm was already brewing, somewhere across the ice, and though the temperature was still around 28°, we could expect a sudden drop and a heavy blow any day now.

A storm of our own was brewing in camp. The second day Lieutenant Jaburg told me that the small OTTER plane was ready to take off on a long exploratory flight, and asked if I wanted to go along. I was amazed to learn of the flight plan. As commander of the base it was up to me to authorize any such flights, just as I would authorize any other movement off the station itself, or any unusual action. That matter would have to be cleared up with McCarthy at once. I knew he had said he was responsible only to the over-all command unit, another lieutenant commander at McMurdo Sound. But I had already told him I was responsible for the entire Ellsworth Station—including the air unit.

We could not have a split command; it could only result in chaos, and in actual danger to the lives of all the thirty-nine men in the wintering party. There is no room for oligarchy or anarchy in the Antarctic. Weather, the single enemy, has no respect for human emotion or ambition. The success or failure of our year's work depended on our ability to keep all components in the best working condition.

I held another organization meeting that night and made it quite clear that I was responsible and must be informed of all activities at the station. I put together an organizational chart for the occasion and showed it to all of them. Chief Spear had done such a good job of getting the men to work that I had McCarthy put him in charge of the entire construction and completion program. The civilians would have to work, too, I told Dr. Thiel. He agreed. Everyone could see that we had to complete the station before winter set in, in the interest of our own safety and comfort.

We divided up the work, acting as a council. That system is the one I hoped would work all the time I was in command at the station. The civilians would concentrate on the tunnels; others would build the permanent galley; and the specialists would get the equipment going. The aviation crew would work at moving all the equipment into the tunnels and Jamesway huts. McCarthy said he would have to concentrate on getting aviation supplies put away as soon as possible, but I reminded him that other things came first.

That night we made our first contact with the outside over our Antarctic communications system. We heard the British Shackleton Station calling, and I spoke with Dr. Vivian Fuchs, leader of the group. Shackleton was fifty-four miles east at the other end of the ice shelf, and between us was the Argentine's General Belgrano base, which was the closest station to us in all the Antarctic. Our own headquarters, McMurdo Sound base, was 2,000 miles away.

If we thought we were in trouble, the British, it seemed, were as badly off. Of eighteen flights they had planned to make to an inland station

(South Ice) some 250 miles inland, they had been able to make only six. They had to work fast to beat the weather. Dr. Fuchs asked that we have our weather reports transmitted to them every day, and I made arrangements to give them the surface observations we would make of temperature, humidity and barometric pressure. I knew, even then, that it would be a full month before our meteorological program was under way.

As we talked with Shackleton, the icebreaker *Staten Island* came in on the same frequency radio circuit and I had a chat with them. They were still on their way out of the Weddell Sea. Commander Elliott told me they had met heavy concentrated ice between us and the Argentine station Belgrano. It had taken them eighteen hours to make thirty-five miles. When they reached Halley Bay they ran into a storm with winds of fifty knots and zero visibility. They were in storm again as I spoke to them, about fifty miles south of Cape Norvegia. The weather, I could see, was beginning to turn. Soon it would hit us. We had to be ready.

Work was coming along as well as could be expected, but the next morning I saw that during the night we had had our first snow fall. It was a light one, luckily—only a couple of inches—but it was enough to cover up the supplies that were still outside. The men could see now that after two or three snow falls anything left outside would be lost forever. At that point there must have been 500 tons of supplies still outside. Every hand was turned to getting them in. The temperature had dropped to 25°, and the barometer was falling. With the wind blowing from the northeast, it looked as though we were in for a good lacing.

The men were at work at eight o'clock in the morning. Chief Spear was doing his job, and from the look on his face, I could see that he was pleased with himself. But the IGY men were slacking off on the job. Coming into the Jamesway hut we were still using for a mess hall one morning, I saw half a dozen of them lounging around. Some of them, I learned, did not even eat breakfast, in an effort to get an extra half hour's sleep in the morning. After three and a half months on a ship doing nothing but sleeping, they still wanted more.

The two junior aviation officers had turned to their own problems with the snow fall, but I had to step in to stop them from performing work with such inefficiency. Lieutenant Jaburg was using a fifteen-ton fork-lift to load aluminum frames that weighed only forty pounds each, lifting only one or two at a time, when a man could lift three of them on at once. I put a stop to that poor method of loading a sled, but when I next looked around for Jaburg he had disappeared. We didn't see him again until supper time. I worried about a number of the men with whom I felt there would be trouble before we were through.

The first indication of trouble did not come from the Navy men, but from the IGY civilians on the first day we moved into our permanent mess hall and abandoned the sketchy Jamesway huts to the housing of emergency supplies.

All hands ate at the same time although the officers and civilians had their own table. There was a great deal of confusion with so many men milling around—it was the first time all thirty-nine of us had eaten together. Our seating capacity was for only twenty-six men, so some were left standing. Others lingered even though they were through eating. The talk of the men was so loud and vulgar that it annoyed me. I noticed that the three Navy chiefs—Spear, May and Kent—had their own table, apart from the men. I was all for this segregation, because it gave the men a chance to argue and complain and not be influenced by the presence of officers, and this is exactly what the enlisted men themselves preferred. After discussing the situation with McCarthy and obtaining his concurrence, we set the officers' mess a half hour later the next day.

Yet there was much criticism of this arrangement. The civilians came to me to say they preferred to have their meals with the enlisted men. They wanted to be part of the enlisted group; they did not want to appear to lean more toward the officers than to the men. Each of the nine civilians felt the same way, although a couple of them confided to me that they had been pressed by Hugo Neuburg to go along and would much prefer the first arrangement.

This attitude astounded me. These were the fellows who had demanded officer status when they were in Washington. As soon as they got it they seemed to change their minds. On ship they had complained that they did not have quarters as good as those of the ship's officers. They had come into the wardroom in their undershirts in direct violation of Navy regulations and customs.

Among the IGY men, I could see the one who was complaining the most. His name was Gerard Fierle, a meteorologist with the United States Weather Bureau, a short fellow, with rarely a smile, but with an extensive command of profanity he had picked up as a weatherman in Alaska. Fierle had been sent along to install the automatic weather recording instruments for the Weather Bureau. He was the only civilian in the meteorology section, but he made up for both his loneliness and size by making lots of noise.

I had noticed Fierle's attitude every time I called the IGY men together aboard the *Wyandot*. He objected to every suggestion made. When the ship was unloading at the barrier edge, some of the other IGY men swung to and helped. Fierle, however, flatly refused to work on any but his own equipment. During the unloading period, he spent his time for the most part in his cabin or in the wardroom eating. He said he had been sent to the Antarctic as a government employee, that he had no agreement or contract with anybody to do anything but his own work, and that "no damn fool" was going to get him to do anything.

Now, when I went to the science building to speak to another IGY man about building a special passageway between the glaciology room and the radio-meteorology room in the communications building—since it was already obvious that these two departments would have a great deal of traffic—Fierle, who overheard the conversation, blew up. He said he would not bring weather reports to the radio room by any other routes than the one already worked out. If any other passage was made, he said, he would refuse to take weather observations!

At the staff meeting, Thiel more or less apologized for this man's behavior. Aboard ship, Thiel said, he had learned that there were troublemakers among the IGY men. In spite of the opposition from the civilians, which by now had slackened some, we decided then to go through with the idea of two separate messes in the interest of morale and discipline. McCarthy and the other officers were all for it. Thiel was noncommittal, but I had a feeling from previous conversations that he didn't object to the idea. Besides, there just was not room for all thirty-nine of us at one sitting.

I recalled only too well the stories of the morale problem Admiral Byrd had had with his men on the first expedition in 1928-30. At that time Byrd, who had just received word from Washington that Congress had advanced him in rank to rear admiral on the retired list, tried his best to be congenial with the men and wanted to be just like one of them. Everything went well for a while. But one day one of the men got into an argument with his chief. The young man's final remark was: "You may be an admiral to some, but you are just a pain in the ass to me!"

Obviously, being chummy with the men is difficult for a leader under the best of conditions. As Byrd had learned, it just cannot be done.

On the same expedition, Byrd involved himself in competition with the men in a game called "Indian wrestling." In this game two men sat across from each other at the table. With elbows on the table they grasped hands, then matched strength to see who could press the other's hand down on the table. After having watched the men in the bunkhouse show their strength for a while, Byrd decided to enter into the spirit of the game. He took on several of the men, each of whom pretended to exert his best effort. They all let Byrd win.

One day Byrd had approached Sverre Strom, a huge Norwegian, 230 pounds with arms like an ox and muscles like steel bands. The ring Sverre wore was so large I could slip two of my fingers through it.

"I used to be pretty good at Indian wrestling," Byrd said. "How about you and I trying it, Sverre?"

Sverre, who understood but a few phrases of English, understood *this* all right, but played dumb. "Hell," he said in Norwegian to another, "I'm afraid even to shake his hand. It may be so brittle it will fall apart." Sverre refused the invitation several times.

But Byrd insisted. Since he was the commander of the expedition, Sverre really had no choice.

Even as they sat down, the men could see that it was no contest. Byrd's arm stretched only part of the way up to Sverre's, so Sverre had the edge. At the signal, Sverre calmly stretched Byrd's hand down to the table, without strain, but so quickly that Byrd was startled, lost his balance, and with a yell, fell off the seat and against a brick underneath a leg of the galley stove, where he cut his eyebrow quite severely. It took eight stitches to sew him up.

Byrd never forgot the incident. Sverre had been the sorriest man on that expedition because of it. Although Sverre had years of experience in the Arctic, he never left Little America again after that mishap, except for one short mission on a supporting party.

The point there, of course, was that in trying to be a pal to the men an embarrassing situation was created, and the services of the most experienced man on Byrd's expedition were forfeited.

No Antarctic expedition can afford such luxury as personal vendetta. There are too few men, and the elements are completely inflexible. In our wintering party of thirty-nine men, each man had been chosen to do a specific job. Otherwise, that man would not have been at the station at all. But to avoid friction we had to establish precise lines of authority, and artificial social mores as well. If the officers were to merge with the men, there would be nothing but bickering. If the civilians wished officer status, and they claimed to want just that, they should conform to normal military procedure. While I was not responsible for the mixed status situation with which I was saddled, it was my responsibility to find workable means of dealing with it.

Being fully aware of the pitfalls of any leader, I decided to create a gap between the men and myself right from the start. I wanted no Byrd incident here. On the other hand, I did not want such a class distinction as had been drawn on the expeditions of Britishers Robert Scott and Ernest Shackleton. A razor-sharp line separated their enlisted men from the officers and civilian scientists, which even influenced their tragic return trip from the pole. Before their departure Petty Officer Evans, a member of the fatal party and a big man who required more food than the others, had tried to tell Scott that the food rations were not sufficient. Scott, a traditional officer of the British Navy, brushed the matter aside. History records that tragic mistake.

Already, both the civilians and VX-6—the aviation unit—had attempted to subvert my over-all command of the station. Even after Jaburg had told me about the OTTER flight, I learned later that the OTTER had taken off without authorization, and had flown 100 miles to the coast. I had given McCarthy permission to make proficiency flights in the immediate vicinity of the station only. If something had happened to the plane on that flight, I would have been held responsible, yet I knew nothing about the flight until later.

The chafing of the civilians under military restraint was more understandable, but just as obvious. Yet they had undergone a special training course before they left the United States and supposedly expected to live for a year at a base operated by the military. They had accepted these provisions before they arrived in the Antarctic.

Thiel, my deputy science leader, understood this, or seemed to. It was the junior IGY civilians over whom he had no real control who had already begun to cause friction.

The friction had to end if we were to do our work. Winter was approaching rapidly, and our camp had to be completed before the scientific work could begin. One of the great problems of the Antarctic is time. One might think it a soft life, in which the "mechanized explorer" does nothing but sleep and read and eat steak. At times they do. But for the most part this was not our experience. And at that particular time there was more work to be done than we could do. Only by taking advantage of every moment of favorable weather could we account well for ourselves.

The seismologists wanted to take some soundings to determine the depth of the ice shelf and the composition of the material underneath. This work would have to be carried out before the winter set in, for even two miles from camp is a long way when the winter winds blow.

In the Antarctic the only winds not carrying some degree of moisture are those from the south, directly off the continent. Except for a few mountain ranges about eighty miles to the east and some further to the southeast, the terrain around Ellsworth Station is flat and featureless. Icebergs and pressure ridges dot the surface of the frozen pack, and the pressure ridges rise on the Filchner shelf itself. Southward for fifty miles or more the ice barrier is filled with crevasses—very dangerous for survey parties under any condition and practically impossible to traverse in the winter night.

There are other difficulties in the terrain. The elevation of the ice shelf increases gradually—so gradually that you cannot notice it with the naked eye. At our station we were about 140 feet above sea level. One hundred miles south of our station the shelf is 700 feet above sea level. The entire southern area is covered with crevasses continuing west to Gould Bay. Other than that we knew little. We were fairly confident that there were telling features elsewhere, but we did not discover them until later in the year.

If the scientists were to go out alone, they would have to observe some rudimentary rules of discipline for their own survival. They would have to take two Sno-Cats, big caterpillar machines that could stay afloat on the snow. They would have to be careful of crevasses, and, when they reached the edge of the ice pack, careful of the slender killer whales that travel in packs, poking their buff-and-ochre–colored heads up through openings in

58

the ice. A man is as welcome as a seal or penguin to the killer whale in its search for edible material.

Unless one is working constantly when out on the trail, the surroundings bring on deep mental depression. Perhaps it is the isolation, the knowledge that this is the absolute end of the earth, and that there is no chance of seeing a strange face or a strange sight. The level ice barrier and air above both seem lifeless and extinct. Unless the wind is howling or some person is making a noise, the absolute silence of the ice is deafening. Distance and time fade away beyond your grasp.

It was not really cold yet. The mercury now hovered around 10° above zero, but one could still see his breath in the air. It would be a matter of days now until the weather turned, and finally, the sun would disappear altogether over the horizon. As I stood in the cold of the Antarctic and gazed into the unknown stretches beyond our vision south and pack-ice–strewn waters northward, toward home, I reflected on what the darkness was to be, spent among men, who had no conception of what we would have to go through.

Still protected by the familiarity of the conveniences they accepted as normal—such vast luxuries as washing machines, electric dryers, showers and unlimited electric current—these new men of the Antarctic were oblivious to the land as it really was. Mass production, the profusion of supplies landed by the Navy and underestimation of the difficulties ahead marked the "new" in the Antarctic.

I, who represented the "old," felt very much alone.

CHAPTER 4

RACE AGAINST TIME

O N SATURDAY, FEBRUARY 16, THE NORTHEAST WIND INCREASED GREATLY in strength, and while it brought higher temperatures, I knew any warming was simply a respite before the winter closed in on us.

I was worried because we were not nearly prepared enough for the winter night. Drifts of snow had already covered some of the equipment. Nothing had disappeared, but if we did not get the material inside soon it would be lost.

I ordered all hands to the job of bringing material into the tunnels, and what a job it was. We had more of everything than I had believed, even after my first inspections. In the radio room I noticed two large spools of heavy one-inch cable woven with fine aluminum threading on the outside. It was obviously quite expensive. When I asked Chief Kent, our electronics man, what it was for, he replied that we had needed fifty feet of cable for radio transmission. We had received two big reels, each reel holding 800 feet.

Waste was not the only problem: while we had too much of most things, we were short of two beds, and for a while it seemed that two men would have to lay their mattresses on the floor. It sounds like a minor difficulty, but in a camp of thirty-nine men, which two would it be? I know from past experience that a minor problem of status like this one could have a terrible effect on the morale of the entire station. Luckily the problem solved itself. We had a number of beds earmarked for the special team of the Air Force not due to arrive until the following summer. They would have no use for the beds for some nine months, so we took two of them.

In other ways, even in my personal gear, there was too much of everything. I spent one afternoon sorting out the four bags of Antarctic clothing issued to me at Davisville before we had embarked. I set two full bags aside unopened, and later returned them. Even the clothing I kept was not quite right. Although I had ordered medium size of everything, whoever had packed for me had given me small sizes and every item was heavily painted, in indelible ink, with the word RONNIE. I would have to live with the annoyance of a misspelled name for a year.

In addition to the problem of storage, we had great difficulty in getting our communications system ready. The radio room crew had worked hard to put the local transmission and receiving sets in order, but our general radio, for international voice transmission, was still not ready. This was causing some impatience in higher echelons, and our own mass of housekeeping and information messages were stacking up. But it could not be helped. Ironically, one of the first messages we received when the set did get working a few days later was a report from Captain McDonald, in which he indicated our station had been ninety per cent complete when the Task Group left. Two months after we had been left alone, with the men working all day every day, we still had not finished the job. How we wished then that the station had been completed when we took it over.

One day, in the middle of the stowage job, I skied down to the edge of the barrier where the ships had landed. Officially, I was taking a look at the helicopter which had not yet been moved from the unloading site, but personally, I wanted to look over the site. Everything was quiet and peaceful on the barrier's edge. New snowfalls of the last few days had covered the refuse and squashed snow which remained as an inevitable result of the tremendous unloading job involving two ships, 667 men and tons of equipment.

The beach area looked like a park after the circus had moved out. Debris was scattered on the ice for miles in both directions. Lumber and broken packing cases lay everywhere. The crevasse markers had not blown down nor had the flags on the edge of the ice been removed. But the flags were no longer on the edge. The pack ice had once been eight miles offshore; today it was rubbing up against the sheer ice wall, right where the ships had tied up.

Not far from the edge of the barrier, Lieutenant Jaburg and mechanic Ronald Brown were working on the helicopter. They worked feverishly, hampered, of course, by the constant cold and the problem of working in parkas, heavy boots and thick gloves. The helicopter had already given the aviation unit a great deal of trouble. Someone had taken his eyes off the oil-pressure gauge, and the result was a burned-out engine that had to be scrapped. Now they had installed another engine, but it was causing trouble, too. One problem, apparently, was that while Jaburg was a well-trained helicopter *pilot,* he was not so well versed in maintenance of these complicated aircraft. It was not hard to understand why. Jaburg had just finished helicopter school — fresh from Pensacola — when he had volunteered and was assigned to this mission. While I was there the mechanic got the motor running and the huge rotor-blades spinning. Slowly the 'copter rose off the surface and moved toward the station. Here the rotor-blades were removed and the 'copter covered with a tarpaulin for winter storage.

The helicopter had been brought along largely as a navigational aid for the traverse party we hoped to send out at the beginning of the summer. The men would have to travel on land, of course, but on the first leg of their journey the helicopter would give them a mountain-top view. With close co-operation by radio, the Sno-Cats on the ground should be able to avoid crevasse areas and difficult terrain, and achieve their objectives quickly. We would have a totally different approach to traverse than on previous expeditions; it was something new for me, too, even after all my time in the Antarctic.

Properly used, this new technique would be a great advance over our old sledging methods of the past. Actually, I had made my first trip to the Antarctic in 1933 as a dog driver and ski expert, so the change struck me forcibly. On March 1, 1934, with three companions, I had sledged south on the Ross Ice barrier for the first time. Ours had been a reconnaissance party to break trail for tractors which were to follow. We had been setting up the tiny camp that Admiral Richard Byrd would occupy alone for the winter. When we had sledged 190 miles, we were told by radio to return to the 100-mile depot, and in retracing our steps we had become entangled in a crevasse area that was honeycombed with deep canyons, some of them hundreds of feet deep and thirty feet across. Most of these crevasses were covered by snow—as they are still—so it had been impossible to detect them from the surface. Today a plane or helicopter could probably tell the danger from the configuration of the entire area. In our 1934 traverse we had broken through the snow crust often. Sometimes half our teams would be hanging over the edge until we could pull them back to safety. In the excitement of one such mishap a dog on my team had chewed through her traces, freed herself from the team and dropped so deep into the abyss below that it was impossible to rescue her. Eventually we reached our destination and built the tiny nine-by-thirteen–foot hut in which Byrd would live for the winter. Retracing our steps over 125 miles to Little America the weather reached −64°.

Helicopters and Sno-Cats now made a great change in our methods. They could not raise the Antarctic temperatures, but they could speed our work and shorten the distances we had to travel. Yet the old needs for efficiency and absolute order were as great with these new machines as they had been in sledging expeditions. In the early days it had been important that the highly specialized equipment be used properly and preserved. An error could mean some important article might break down or be lost. The result could be death by cold and hunger. With the new, mechanized equipment the need was the same; only the technology was different. The old Antarctic disciplines had not changed; just a few of the details.

As I stood watching the two men work on the engine of the 'copter,

Lieutenant Jaburg shouted: "Captain, I can hear the killer whales now." Sure enough, within five minutes I saw the whales, in packs of several dozen, poke their heads up through the ice floes. Their slender mud-colored underbodies with buff and ochre sprinkled in patches over their heads and upper bodies is a striking sight at close range. Even more impressive is their mouthful of sharp teeth and the snorting sound made by these wild beasts of the sea. I thought these man-eaters of the Antarctic would have withdrawn north to open water long before now, but instead they were to remain with us more or less all winter.

There was little sign of life on the ice barrier. A pair of Emperor penguins seemed to be making a career of examining each and every piece of rubbish on the barrier, playing among wooden boxes and garbage, waddling importantly in and out of sight. Jaburg told me he had seen a pod of killer whales passing in front of the ice cliff twice a day. In the morning they would steam east into the open sea, returning with clock-like precision shortly after lunch and heading for Gould Bay.

I skied back along the road that day, through the drifting snow that covered most of the trail markers, past the ragged, wind-whipped, orange-colored flags that looked so strange in the snow—the sole touch of un-natural color in an ocean of white ice. It was a beautiful day, about 20° above zero, calm, and not a cloud flecked the horizon.

It was a pleasant respite, these few hours alone on the ice, but it was not getting the work done.

As the days went by, the camp began to take shape. Furniture, tables, easy chairs, lamps and desks were moved into the rooms to make the men comfortable for the year ahead. The housekeeping work went faster than the preparations for the scientists. We were particularly behind on building the aurora dome, which would be used for our basic study of the aurora australis—those strange lights about which men knew so little.

Kim Malville, the twenty-one-year-old civilian scientist who would record the aurora, needed a protective entrance to his observation tower. We built a plywood frame around the ladder so he could have access to the dome as well. Further, it was necessary to build his magnetic hut, from which he would study the problems of magnetic reaction in the Antarctic. This building, still in the planning stage, had to be built some distance away from the other buildings so the magnetograph would not be affected by electricity and metal within the camp.

The study of the aurora was one of the more important scientific disciplines in the IGY Antarctic program. All through the winter night on the southernmost continent, the snow seems to be tinted red and green by the strange southern lights. In the air, brilliant clouds of luminous gas move and change in form and color.

Since man first saw the aurora australis he has wondered about it. Only within the past half-century have men had the tools and the knowledge to learn what causes the strange lighting.

As we began our study in 1957, we knew certain things about the aurora. The sun is responsible for these brilliantly colored gases through the phenomenon we know as sunspots—immense cyclones of hot luminous gas that rip the surface of the sun. Every eleven years the number of these sun spots increases to a peak we call the maximum of the sunspot cycle. The year 1957-58 was to be such a peak year.

During such a peak, vast clouds of charged particles are spewed into the emptiness of space. Positively charged protons and negatively charged electrons speed toward the earth at the rate of a thousand miles a second — 93,000,000 miles in little more than a day. But before these atoms have a chance to collide with the atmosphere of earth, they encounter the earth's magnetic field, an almost impenetrable shield that surrounds the planet, warding off the charged particles from space which bombard the earth constantly.

All around the earth the charged particles are deflected, but at the two north and south magnetic poles the particles are able to enter the earth's atmosphere. They enter the atmosphere in a spiral, and as they near the surface they continue to spiral in tight circuits around the poles. Thus the gas clouds, the aurora, are seldom seen outside the auroral zone, near the geomagnetic poles of earth. Rarely do they escape from that narrow zone.

When the charged atoms of oxygen and nitrogen from the sun strike our atmosphere they become luminous. As they collide with earth's own atoms, they string out in clouds of glowing gas which produce a train of light as much as 700 miles in length. This is far from ordinary light in appearance, as the rays often stand vertically in a rainbow pattern. They are yellowish-green and red and look like searchlight beams in the sky.

Although the aurora is one of the most beautiful sights of nature, that was not the reason we were to study it so eagerly. When these giant electrical clouds mass, they disturb the earth's magnetic field much as a short circuit would disturb the operation of an electric magnet in a laboratory. The earth's magnetic field then sets up a pulsation which sends the auroral rays fleeing across the sky. The disruption can be measured much as that of an electric storm, which causes a compass needle to waver alarmingly and sometimes to spin wildly.

During the IGY, American scientists hoped to discover a great deal more about the aurora at the six U.S. bases in the Antarctic. The immediate application, of course, would be to radio communication, for the same charged particles that cause the aurora also produce dead spots and fadeouts of radio waves. If we could learn the laws that govern auroral behavior, we could learn much about our own atmosphere and the problems of communication.

It was important that we hurry preparations for the aurora study. On April 4 Malville was to begin co-operative research with other sta-

64

tions—in which their measurements would be taken at the same time, from the different locations. We finished the wiring and installed a space heater before March 1. By March 10 he and another IGY man had put up the magnetic building, away from the camp, and by March 16, when there was an unusually impressive display of the aurora, Malville was able to take a full recording.

Here, in this first scientific work, the magnitude of the human problems we would face began to come clear. From the beginning of the expedition the IGY scientists had been reluctant to fit into the Navy's way of doing things. On the barrier, it had taken many conferences to persuade the civilians that we needed the help of every man to get the camp in shape, particularly since so much time had been lost in the ice. The civilians agreed to take over the ice watch at the mooring site, inspecting the cracks that developed at the ever-changing edge of the barrier and informing the officer of the watch of changes that might cause damage to one of the ships.

As over-all leader of the station I had to work out such matters. In Malville's case I relieved him of almost all extra duties, so that he could concentrate on his investigations. He had some difficulty, particularly in arranging the heating of his domes so the window surfaces did not ice up. The space heater, we found, was not adequate for the job, so we snaked two of the arms of the jet heater from the adjacent science building into the tower. When that did not do the job, we added two more. With four blasts of hot air coming into the domes, he had enough heat to warm Madison Square Garden. It did the job.

The electrical cable that led to the magnetic shack shorted out almost immediately. The magnetic work was not part of the IGY requirements for Ellsworth Station, but a program of Malville's own. Yet we were all anxious to do as much work as possible in all scientific fields, so within a few days we had the electrician lay off other repair work and get the cable repaired. Malville was then able to take constant recordings of the changes in the earth's magnetic field. The instrument was simple enough: a small magnet suspended by a very fine quartz fiber in the center of the tiny hut. The main problem, except for the cable, was to have the hut far enough from the station to eliminate interference, yet close enough to be accessible in any but the worst of weather. Malville finally put it 250 feet from the nearest building, and there his simple machine worked constantly.

The little magnet was fixed with a mirror to reflect light from a projector onto a moving strip of film. As the earth's magnetic field changed, the motion of the magnet caused the light to move back and forth on the film, leaving a fine tracing for later analysis. The only problem was to change the film every two and a half days, since the magnetograph ate film at the rate of forty feet every twenty-four hours.

Malville's aurora program demanded much more personal attention.

One of his most important pieces of equipment was an all-sky camera, an automatic movie camera equipped with a convex mirror that reflected the entire visible sky into the lens. Every aurora within a radius of 250 miles of the station would be photographed, weather permitting. Each day the camera had to be inspected and wound, the clock that automatically dated the film had to be calibrated. Every fifth day a new spool of 100 feet of Tri-X film had to be exchanged for the exposed film.

The actual light from the aurora, ranging from the usual yellow-green to blood red and blue gray, could be analyzed only by using an auroral spectograph—a prism-like instrument that split the auroral light into the segments of the spectrum. At the same time, this splitting was photographed by an extremely fast camera lens (f/0.6) on 16/mm spectroscopic film. A photometer measured the intensity of the aurora's light electronically and recorded split-second variations of the light.

Besides all this (and paying constant attention to the spectograph during an auroral display) Malville was responsible for a series of observations of the altitude, color, motion and form of all the aurora that occurred along the north-south meridian. On nights of observation he used a simple alidade to measure altitude of the aurora every fifteen minutes. The data was then transcribed to IBM cards.

Because the Antarctic has not been contaminated with dust from factories, automobiles and all the other implements of highly civilized human life, it is also possible there to study the cosmic debris and dust particles that enter the earth's atmosphere constantly from outer space. This study, too, was part of Malville's work. He carried out investigations by exposing glycerin coated slides to the air, well outside camp. The dust particles could then be examined more at leisure.

Malville had plenty to do, particularly in getting his routine established, so we left him alone as far as other duties were concerned, although it was understood that all the IGY civilians would help when needed in the messhall and other normal duties of the camp.

Busy as he was, Malville did help when we first started setting up the eighty-foot antenna mast for the ionospheric recorder and a shorter pole for the "whistler" program. That was all. He was excused from the other work.

There was more than enough work to go around and for the most part everyone pitched in where he fitted best to get the camp in working order. However, the annoying attitude of the IGY civilians toward team co-operation, was ill-disguised from time to time and continued to cause trouble. During the early days of setting up camp, Chief Spear took his assignment as boss very seriously. He told two of the civilians, Hugo Neuburg and John Behrendt to bring supplies of water to the galley, where snow-melters had not yet been placed. They came to me, protesting about being put on "water detail." I had already ordered that all civilians would be exempt from housekeeping tasks for the present time. And this order, in turn, did not sit well with the enlisted men. They began to call the IGY civilians "sandcrabs."

The tenuous three-cornered relationship between men, officers and civilians began to adopt a pattern. The civilians wanted to associate with the enlisted men more than with the officers, although they had theoretical officer status. The men, always nervous in the presence of officers, were not quite sure whether to accept the civilians or not. And the officers found the civilian attitude incomprehensible.

A basic reason for all the conflict, of course, was that the unit had not been selected in full knowledge of the job at hand. Most of the personnel just did not know what they were getting into or the full extent of the responsibilities they had undertaken. And once we were left on our own, we were definitely alone.

A close approach to a fatal accident came in these early days when we were setting up the eighty-foot–high mast for the ionospheric program. It was a ticklish job, hoisting the steel framework with the use of a fifteen-ton caterpillar tractor, pulleys and all the manpower available. The guywires were attached to "dead-men," anchored, we thought, securely in the frozen snow. But someone had been careless. One of the "dead-men" was not secure, and when the mast was almost in place, a guy-wire slipped and the mast came crashing down. It missed the fifteen-ton tractor by a very few inches. Inside the cab of the tractor Lieutenant Jaburg turned almost as white as the snow around him, when he saw how closely he had missed being crushed.

While some men were careless, others did more than their duty, and under trying conditions. John Brown, the ionospheric physicist, began having trouble with his C-4 recorder almost as soon as he assembled the instrument. Unfortunately there was no operational manual with the kit. Although he had sent for one, it did not arrive on the last mail, which we had collected in Punta Arenas, Chile. Months later, in radio conversation with an expert at Little America, he was able to track down the difficulty and get the recorder operating in time to do the work we were assigned.

As I became more familiar with the camp layout, it became apparent that many small details had been overlooked in the official plan. When I studied the practicability of the location and the relationship of the buildings, I knew then that the plans had been drawn and approved by men unfamiliar with the conditions. Architecturally the buildings were sound enough—except that they had been made without any thought given to the men who would use the station. The messhall, placed near one end of the long street, should have been centrally located. The toilets, instead of being thrown in where they seemed to fit, should have been built next to the quarters of the men who were supposed to use them. The communications building was placed on the wrong side of the station, as were the meteorological facilities. The meteorologists were to have serious trouble with their temperature recordings later in the year, simply because the smoke from the cooking stoves in the galley blew across the thermometers in the prevailing wind, and the heat destroyed the accuracy of their readings.

The aviation buildings and the site for launching weather balloons were on the wrong side. The meteorology, radio and glaciology sections were all lumped together, although the men all kept different hours on their work schedules. The result was that some men were tramping through the sleeping quarters while others were trying to rest.

Even as we worked against time to finish the construction according to the plans, we had to make changes in the plans, so we could be sure of carrying out the work.

As we worked, the temperature began to drop. Two weeks after we were left on our own, the thermometer dropped to $-9°$. The cold increased our sense of urgency; material kept streaming into the tunnels, and before long we had most of it inside. Some of the heaviest machine parts, of course, would have to be left in the open. We had no way to store heavy cable, bundles of tracks for the weasels and other spare parts which weighed a ton or more.

And what would we do with three safes?

Yes, we had three of them. Each one must have weighed between 500 and 700 pounds. One was for a postal clerk, although we had no post office—not even an Antarctic cancellation. No wonder it took 6,250 tons of supplies for this camp.

The great bulging surplus of supplies caused problems in a way one might not suspect. Lieutenant Commander McCarthy came in to see me one evening and told me he had called all hands together for a meeting, to warn them about stealing of tools and opening of supply boxes. Not that the men had ulterior motives. There was just so much material that they dug in where they thought they might find something they could use in their own work, or out of sheer curiosity. Without experience, they did not seem to realize that the part they took now could immobilize the entire camp if it were not available when we needed it.

McCarthy was concerned about this misappropriation, as any executive officer would be, but even as he served in that capacity, we began to have differences about his operation of the aviation unit.

He had planned to store the planes we would use the next spring in a three-sided hangar with a layer of wood on top of them. Knowing that the snow drifts and sticks at the highest point at which you build anything, I urged him not to build revetments or protective fences high in the air, because if he did so, during blizzards the entire station would be buried many feet deeper than necessary. Nor was it sensible to build a

68

three-sided hangar, for the blowing wind would pack the snow inside so tight you would need a pick and shovel to dig the planes out. Only if the planes were strong enough to take a tremendous load on the wings and fuselage should he so protect them. Even so, they would be buried, and possibly crushed.

Then I outlined how we had done it during our 1939-41 expedition. We left the plane in the open. The snow swept around it all winter, but not a bit of damage was done to the plane. On my own expedition, in 1947, I had staked our Beechcraft and Norseman planes out in the open. The Beechcraft had picked up some snow, under one wing; the Norseman not a bit.

I asked McCarthy to consider my plan before he went ahead with his own. He replied that I had nothing to do with the airplanes, which were his responsibility, and he reported only to the chief air officer in the Antarctic, not to me.

I said I had brought up this point as commanding officer of the station, for I was responsible for government property. He would not listen.

"I have already thought out that plan. And that's the way I will do it," he said.

My fear was for the airplanes, which would be needed to support the traverse party the next spring.

There were so many pressing personnel problems shaping up in every direction that my desire for harmony with McCarthy outweighed my better judgment. There was no doubt in my mind about the chain of command which he questioned. His orders and those of the other officers specifically stated that they report to the Ellsworth Station for duty. Although they probably should have read "report to the commanding officer at Ellsworth," I considered this an unfortunate administrative technicality.

While I felt he was making a mistake regarding the storage of the planes, I also reasoned that my fears for the safety of the planes might prove to be unfounded. So, in the interest of harmony I decided to let him do the storing of the planes the way he wanted.

Although the aviation unit was doing a little flying, in a few days the planes would have to be "put on ice" until spring, for it is impossible to fly in the darkness and wind and snow of the winter night, when blizzards rise from nowhere and lash the flat Antarctic plain in frozen fury. It was already apparent, at the end of February, that winter was coming in fast. Although we still had total daylight, it was getting darker toward midnight. In another few weeks we would have early evening, and dark nights, and then a complete darkness.

Weather, of course, was not the problem for us that it had been for explorers of the past. I remembered that in 1934 at Little America, the thermometer in my bunk room had registered —28°. If we wanted to be warm before breakfast, we had to struggle out of our bunks and fight with the icy remnants of the night before. In 1957, on the other hand, the fact was that I had been too hot in my room, even with the thermometer below zero outside. With the oil-fired jet heaters, operated by individual thermostats, we had to worry more about overheating than cold.

Yet even this early in the year, cold had become a problem. With the warmth inside, the men had a tendency to forget the unforgiving cold of the Antarctic. Early in the game, someone left water in the large storage tank in our number two laundry room, and then let the fire go out in the heating unit. With all our surplus equipment, we had no spare parts for this vital unit, and no replacement. Worse, we had a fire in the galley. The bake oven caught the floor on fire because no insulation had been put around it when it was installed. The damage, luckily, was not serious, and the oven could be repaired. I shuddered when I examined the damage, for fire was our worst enemy. We could survive cold, and boredom, and even complete snow-in; we could not survive if our special equipment burned. And no one on earth could help us if our camp was destroyed in the depth of the winter.

Examining the camp, I found that the fire traps we were supposed to have to prevent fire from spreading were not yet in place between the tunnels. Immediately, I had Chief Spear break out the fire extingushers and place them everywhere around the camp, in easy access for emergencies.

I also began a project to furnish a complete emergency camp, and store it in the unused Jamesway huts where the original camp construction unit had stayed. We would have a cache of food, fuel, stoves, medical equipment, sleeping bags, emergency radio, and all the supplies we would need for survival if our camp burned down.

Temporarily, we had settled into a routine—one that would suffice until we had finished the camp construction work. At the end of February it was easy to notice that the sun had moved below the horizon to the south, because around 10 P.M. the tunnels were quite dark and hard to navigate.

We maintained a rather strenuous schedule in our hectic attempt to get all the work done before the winter set in. The men worked very hard, with only breaks at meal times, and fifteen or twenty minutes for coffee in the morning and afternoon. For the enlisted men, the schedule started in the same way every day—including Sundays. (We had decided we must work seven days until the job was done.) Between 6:15 and 7:00 the men had breakfast. If they were late they went without, for the cooks were already preparing the second round, for the officers and civilians, who ate between 7:15 and 7:45. At 8:00 sharp there was a muster for all hands in the main tunnel. Lieutenant Smith, the medical doctor, who was in charge of the construction unit, handed Spear the work list every morning in accordance with the decisions my staff meeting had made the night before. Spear handed out assignments to the men, to the IGY civilians who had no pressing scientific duties, and to the junior officers.

Except for the coffee break there was no letup until lunch time; then back until supper at 5:30 for the men; 6:15 for the officers. At 8:00 every evening there were movies. We had 150 different feature films with us, which meant we could show a different movie every evening of the winter. It was interesting to note that the seven Antarctic bases had forty per cent of all the Navy's movies during this period.

In the beginning, relatively few of the men attended the movies. Many of them were too tired, after the hard physical work in the cold, day after day. Some preferred to sit around in their quarters and drink beer, rather than join the rest of us. Others seemed to be having a little trouble getting acclimated to the Antarctic.

As the only old hand in the station I was constantly shocked at the lack of knowledge with which these "explorers" had been prepared for their work.

Paul Walker, the assistant glaciologist, came to me early in the game and asked if he could go down onto the sea ice, three miles away, during the winter to make periodic measurements of ice thickness and accumulation of snow. I told him I had no objection, but asked if he knew the problems involved.

He had not considered the problems. He did not see that there were any problems, since each reading would take no more than an hour a day. So I had to list the hazards confronting him:

a. *Darkness.* The complete darkness we would find ourselves in for at least three months meant that he would have to work as though he were working at home around midnight in December.

b. *Low temperatures.* He could expect the thermometer to drop down to around $-60°$ or $-70°$.

c. *Frequent blizzards.* Liable to arise without warning.

d. *Overcast with zero visibility.* Sometimes he would be able to see little but his hands before his face at close range.

e. *Danger from the ice itself.* Constant wind might blow the ice loose from the shelf, and carry him out to sea. The shifting pack ice creates leads and rifts. He might fall through one of these and freeze in the water, even before he could drown.

f. *Presence of killer whales.* They are always lurking in the pack ice, even in winter time.

This outline gave him a little additional light on the problem. I asked him to think it over some more, and consider a party of no less than three men each time he wanted to make a measurement, that he take the skiff along, just in case one man might be marooned on the ice, and that they take emergency equipment, to protect them in case of a sudden blizzard.

By the first of March, we knew winter was almost on us, and the tempo of the work became even faster. Some of the equipment was completely covered by drifts now. And as we brought more and more inside the tunnels, the waste and amateurish planning again was impressed on my mind. I counted no less than a dozen twenty-foot ladders stored in one passageway. McCarthy brought me a wall-type pencil sharpener one evening. There was sixty of them stored in a large case, enough for the needs of a big business enterprise for ten years.

When we reassessed the work to be done, we realized we would have to begin our scientific program before the camp was finished. We still had to install some antennas for radio, complete the tunnel system, and cut in the extra generators to assist the single one we had running. We had to complete a second lavatory, and do what we could to repair the broken pipes, burned-out motors and debris that reminded us of the price of carelessness.

We were to build a recreation hall—so far only the shell was up—and a hangar for McCarthy's airplanes. Three Jamesway huts had to be hauled to the rear of the science building, two for ship's stores and a third for "an enlisted men's club," where the men could get completely away from the officers and civilians, and shoot the breeze and bitch about everything and everybody in the world. It wouldn't be an expedition unless that went on.

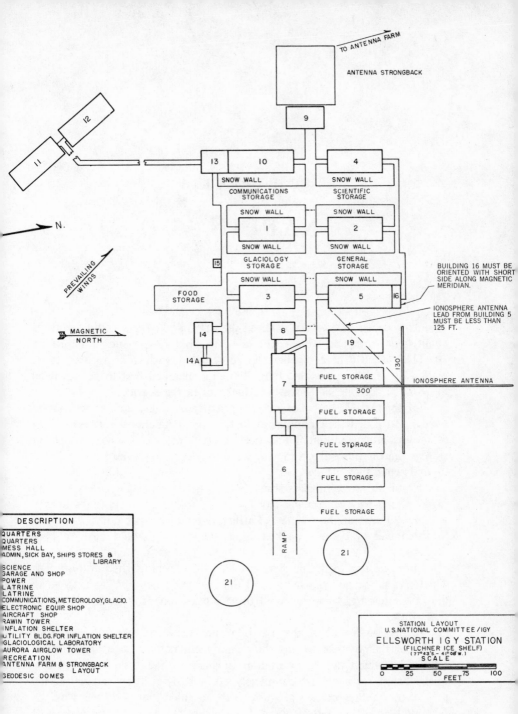

TO ANTENNA FARM

ANTENNA STRONGBACK

9

13 | 10 | 4

SNOW WALL SNOW WALL

COMMUNICATIONS SCIENTIFIC
STORAGE STORAGE

SNOW WALL SNOW WALL

1 2

SNOW WALL SNOW WALL

GLACIOLOGY GENERAL
STORAGE STORAGE

15

SNOW WALL SNOW WALL

FOOD
STORAGE

3 5 16

14

14 A

8

19

7 FUEL STORAGE

FUEL STORAGE

FUEL STORAGE

6

FUEL STORAGE

RAMP

FUEL STORAGE

21

21

N.

PREVAILING
WINDS

MAGNETIC
NORTH

MAGNETIC
NORTH

BUILDING 16 MUST BE
ORIENTED WITH SHORT
SIDE ALONG MAGNETIC
MERIDIAN.

IONOSPHERE ANTENNA
LEAD FROM BUILDING 5
MUST BE LESS THAN
125 FT.

130'

300' IONOSPHERE ANTENNA

DESCRIPTION

QUARTERS
QUARTERS
MESS HALL
ADMIN, SICK BAY, SHIPS STORES &
LIBRARY
SCIENCE
GARAGE AND SHOP
POWER
LATRINE
LATRINE
COMMUNICATIONS, METEOROLOGY, GLACIO.
ELECTRONIC EQUIP. SHOP
AIRCRAFT SHOP
RAWIN TOWER
INFLATION SHELTER
UTILITY BLDG. FOR INFLATION SHELTER
GLACIOLOGICAL LABORATORY
AURORA AIRGLOW TOWER
RECREATION
ANTENNA FARM & STRONGBACK
LAYOUT
GEODESIC DOMES

STATION LAYOUT
U.S. NATIONAL COMMITTEE / IGY

ELLSWORTH IGY STATION
(FILCHNER ICE SHELF)
(77°43'S - 41°08'W.)
SCALE

0   25   50   75   100
FEET

73

CHAPTER 5

SNAPPING TO

As the camp began to take shape, the scientists grew anxious about their work and were eager to begin. Before the end of February, Dr. Thiel asked if he could be relieved of camp work to begin his seismic work. He and his assistant, John Behrendt, planned first to go down on the edge of the barrier to test the thickness of the sea ice.

For three days, the seismologists pried into crates, unwrapped instruments, and tested their equipment in the communications building. Most of the scientific equipment had been moved into the science tunnel for storage, and it was quite a job for them to sort through the piles of boxes to find what they needed.

It took the seismologists some time to get started. First they wanted to go a long way out on the bay ice, but I told them they ought to stay within 400 feet of the barrier. Farther out the ice was covered by five to seven feet of densely packed snow, which they would have to chip through.

After one trip to the barrier, in which they accomplished nothing, Dr. Thiel said he needed the services of three of the other IGY men to make the first sounding, so we excused these others, too, from camp construction work.

Finally, on March 2, the five IGY men drove off toward the barrier in one of the weasels, towing their equipment behind on a sledge. The road, over which thousands of tons of supplies had been hauled a few weeks before, was almost completely covered by drifting snow, but the tops of the marker poles still stuck forth, to guide them on their way.

Just before they left, I asked Thiel when they thought the first shots would be fired. Chief Spear wanted to go down to give his expert advice on the first actual use of the dynamite charge, and I planned to go just to be sure the work was progressing well.

Dr. Thiel was very vague. "About eleven," was all he could promise.

"Unless you are certain of the timing," I told him, "Spear and I will be down on the ice shortly after lunch."

That was the day we were finally raising Brown's ionosphere mast after the first near-fatal attempt. We had relieved *all* the IGY men from responsibility for this task, since Chief Spear stated that he had found the IGY men spent so much time arguing about how it should be done that he would rather do the job with the Navy men alone.

By 11:00 the mast was up, and at 1:00 P.M. Spear and I were down on the barrier cliff. Ahead of us we could see the tent, about a mile and a half out on the ice. It was a bright, clear day, ideal for the job at hand. We could see a herd of seals lying near the edge of the ice. Apparently the killer whales were not about, for when those monsters made an appearance, thrusting their long, dorsal fin out of water, both seal and penguin flee to the safety of the inner ice.

Although it was two hours after the time for the first sounding, there was no activity around the tent the IGY men had pitched. Even though I had warned him, Thiel had made it nearly impossible to take any kind of sounding.

From the station, it took us fifty minutes to move out to the tent, Spear driving the weasel, and I "ski-kjoring" along behind. As we reached the edge of the ramp leading down to the bay ice, our weasel opened up a crevasse about four feet wide. We stopped the tractor, and Chief Spear walked the rest of the way, while I skied, with a line between us for safety.

It was a warm day, and I could not understand why the men had pitched the tent. They certainly did not need it for protection from the weather. All of them were dressed in protective Arctic clothing, parkas, heavily lined trousers and sealskin mukluks that had' been tested for warmth in —50° weather.

It was only when we were within 200 feet of the tent that I learned why they were inside. First I heard voices raised in argument. They were having a bull-session! Chief Spear and I waited for about five minutes, but it gave no sign of ending, so we walked up to the tent. Outside, nothing had been done. No cables were in sight, nor any instruments; just the sledges, and they gave no sign of having been touched. As we approached the tent, I called out to ask how the first shot had gone off.

John Behrendt was the first to reply. He did not come out of the tent; indeed, it was no mean feat for him to unfold the raw bones of his six-feet-four-inch frame in a tent. One of the men had compared him to a St. Bernard dog already, for even in a few weeks all but eyes, nose and forehead above his collar was covered with long, shaggy hair. Usually, Behrendt seemed even-tempered enough, but today he replied aggressively and nastily that they had just arrived at the site about twenty minutes before. Chief Spear and I had had the tent in sight for forty minutes without a glimpse of life or movement.

Paul Walker, a twenty-two-year-old blond glaciologist, said they were just too tired after their walk. Hugo Neuburg, the other glaciologist, and another six-footer, said they had been pulling so hard at the sledges they didn't realize how much time had gone by in the tent. Thiel, the head of the party, agreed with that statement, mildly enough. But the beefy, red-faced Nolan Augenbaugh, a geologist, was very nasty.

"What the hell," he said. "We have to eat, too."

I ignored the last, and began to ask a few questions.

"Wouldn't it have been more efficient if two of them had made lunch, while the others set up the instruments for shooting—stretching the cables, made the distance measurements, and arranged for the dynamite blasting?"

It was my responsibility, I told them, to be sure they *did* the work, and to give them every facility to do the work properly.

Neither Chief Spear nor I felt like wasting any more time that day, so I told the IGY men I would make arrangements for them to have breakfast by 7:30, so they would have an early start the next day. They should leave camp at 8:00 in the morning, and get some work done. Then Spear and I left.

That night, when supper was over, I asked Thiel and Neuburg to come to my quarters to review the work. In six days of preparation they had not made a single shot.

The next morning, when I arrived at the messhall I found Augenbaugh there, eating steaks, his wild beard straggling around his face. By 8:30 the party had not left; at 8:45 the last man, Walker, straggled into the weasel and they set off for the barrier.

I could not go down to the ice and nurse-maid the civilians again. The weather cleared nicely around noon, so five of us, including Neuburg, who would be the driver of one of the Sno-Cats, flew over to Shackleton in the OTTER plane, to see what modifications the British had made to their Sno-Cat for scientific traverse work. It was still slightly overcast, but the day was good enough to see the horizon, and we had good depth perception—always a problem in the dull sameness of the Antarctic wastes. We flew over the seismic camp, but saw no signs of scattered snow that would indicate they had made a sounding shot.

At Shackleton, Dr. Fuchs and his crew greeted us with a cup of coffee. They had made sixteen flights to their advance depot inland, where four men were staying, and had three more supply flights to complete before the weather turned, Dr. Fuchs said.

Like our party, except at three times the distance, the British were planning a traverse over land to gather information about the area, so we compared notes and laid tentative plans to gear our trip so as to avoid duplication of effort.

76

When it came time to return, we had difficulty in starting the engine. The plane had been sitting for an hour and a half, and since the oil was not diluted, we had to use their heater for fifteen minutes before McCarthy, who was piloting the plane, got the OTTER'S engine to catch. Again we flew over the seismic tent, but saw no sign of action.

That night, Dr. Thiel told me he would not need as many men as he had been taking to the seismic site, so I asked him to leave Augenbaugh behind to help with the wiring of the tunnels, so we would have light during the coming long night. Dr. Thiel was quite amenable, but after the movies that night, Augenbaugh jumped me in the galley, using the most abusive language.

He had not come here as a common laborer, he said. He had a contract as a geologist and assistant glaciologist, and was not going to do anything else.

Thiel came over later, to apologize for Augenbaugh, but also to ask that Neuburg be left to do the work around camp, since the latter had volunteered.

That issue was settled, but the seismic work still went far too slowly. Finally, Dr. Thiel realized that they were working too far out in the ice, and decided to try to lower the dynamite charge into the open water leads along the barrier edge—a suggestion I had made much earlier.

On March 4 Thiel and his party got off after breakfast. It was windy. and the temperature was −5°; consequently it was very cold and uncomfortable. An hour after they set out from camp, Dr. Thiel came to my quarters, where I was working.

"We can't get across the lead this morning because of open water," he said. Further, there were schools of killer whales playing all around the open leads. What did I suggest?

When he told me the lead was ten to fifteen feet wide, I advised him to get the skiff out, put a line on each end, and haul the men across as quickly as possible; to be sure they had long poles with them to push the ice aside, and when they were through to drag the boat well away from the water, lest the ice bear down and crush it, leaving them stranded.

Dr. Thiel said they were not afraid of the killer whales, but I warned him to look out for them. The seismic party, luckily, did not encounter any killer whales that day, although they were around. Ensign Sumrall, the junior aviation officer, flew over the area that day, and saw packs of the drab beasts. As usual, the penguins and seals had fled to the safety of the inner ice. As McCarthy put it that day, it seemed that the penguins had more sense than the scientists—at least about the immutable laws of survival in the Antarctic.

The seismic work dragged terribly. The men were careless with their instruments and the expensive equipment that had been provided them. One night I stumbled over a sledge in the science tunnel—one just dropped there by the seismologists. When they returned the tent from the ice, I found it, cooking utensils, sleeping bags, stove and blow-torch, lying out in the tunnel, instead of put away where the equipment would be safe and available for use the next time needed.

Dr. Thiel was attempting to learn the character of the land under the ice-cap. He wanted to trace the inclination of the rock structures, by reflecting sound waves off the land, and recording them. These waves would be produced by setting off dynamite charges, which pick up the sounds and transmit them to the recording machinery. The record thus obtained is a tracing on a long sheet of graph paper.

When we began our work, only the outer edges and surfaces of the Antarctic glaciers had been studied. So little information was available that the scientists did not know whether the glaciers in the Antarctic were advancing, retreating, or remaining in dormancy. Nor did they know, with a few minor exceptions, the rate of flow of the complicated glacier systems.

Before winter came, the seismologists were trying to complete their work along the barrier edge, so when spring broke and they could travel over land for long distances, they would have no need to remain in camp.

So even as they experimented on the ice, to find the best ways of making their shots, Dr. Thiel and Behrendt began to prepare for the trip that they would make the following spring.

The most important part of their preparation was installing their delicate instruments in the Sno-Cat—the over-sized tractor they would use as basic transportation and laboratory in the field. Besides radio, batteries and all the normal supplies, they would take a gravity meter, to measure the force of the earth's gravity at various spots, a seismic camera, seismic amplifiers and other specialized equipment. The installation was no mean job, for it meant completely reworking the inside of the truck-like "cat."

By March 19, they were beginning to get some positive results from their sounding shots, but on March 21, Dr. Thiel drove off in a weasel to look for a ramp leading down from the high barrier, so he could take the Sno-Cat onto the bay ice. I told him not to go more than four miles away—since I knew he would be safe within that area. Instead, he drove the weasel about eight miles. As I had feared, he fell into a crevasse, but luckily the two men with him were able to pull him out. The weasel fell in a crevasse, too, but only with one track, so they were able to haul it out safely.

By March 26, the Sno-Cat had been in use for several days, and the team was bringing it to the sounding locations regularly.

One day, while Augenbaugh was driving the Sno-Cat, the machine began to lose power. He shifted to a lower gear. After a while the "cat" lost power again, so he shifted to a still lower gear. Finally it would not move at all, so he went outside to take a look. He saw smoke coming out of the clutch housing; the clutch was burned out.

Thiel came back and asked that I send a man out to fix it. Again the IGY men showed how little they knew about conditions in the Antarctic. It was −25°, a twenty-mile wind was blowing with drifting snow, and they wanted a man to come out and work on the tractor, as if he were dispatched from a service station in the U.S. to fix a balky car. Under these cold conditions, a mechanic can not even touch tools with his bare hands. They freeze to the fingers, like an ice tray suddenly removed from the freezing compartment of a refrigerator—only much more strongly. I would not think of sending a man out to work in the open in such weather, and I told Thiel just that.

He sent Neuburg out in a weasel to tow the Sno-Cat back. Then, we sat down to assess the situation. The IGY men had been instructed how to drive the Sno-Cat at the factory over a period of two weeks, but they had picked up some bad habits from the SeaBees in the early days of our expedition. Instead of starting the "cat" in its lowest gear, they were always in a hurry, so they started in the next, or fifth gear. This treatment had the same result that one would get by starting a heavy truck in second gear over a period of time. But in this case it didn't take long. The Sno-Cat, brand new, had only 110 miles on it when it was broken down.

Under normal treatment the Sno-Cat could have been expected to go smoothly for the entire year with simple maintenance in Chief Spear's garage. But now it needed repair, and despite tons of unusable objects we had no spare clutch in camp. Nor did there seem to be any chance of getting a spare until some time the following year. It was true that the Air Force team would fly in early in the spring. But the clutch-assembly weighed around 50 pounds. We could hardly ask the Air Force to bring it in for us, in planes that were already loaded to the last ounce.

What would happen to the important overland traverse we had planned for the following spring? The program called for using the two Sno-Cats together in the field. At this moment, it was anyone's guess.

Nor could I concern myself too much with a problem so far off. We had the entire winter in which to solve the problem of the Sno-Cat clutch. Now, in the late fall, I had trouble enough, lately with the psychological adjustment of personnel, to keep me from worrying about something more than six months away.

One of my problems, at this moment, concerned the station doctor. Like practically all the others, he had not really known—or even suspected —what he was getting himself in for when he came to the Antarctic to winter over.

His many personal attributes, unfortunately, did not include the specific qualities needed in the man who had been chosen to do the very difficult job his superiors had given him. In this instance, the whole original concept seems to have been muddle. In my own experience, the last man on earth I would choose for a key administrative post on a polar expedition would be a medical doctor. The qualities that make a good doctor: compassion, curiosity, and interest in individuals—are qualities that may not make a man the best leader. Nor do doctors (or scientists, for that matter) want to be burdened with detail of administration. But the doctor was charged with the administrative duties involving all but the aviation unit and the IGY civilians in camp. Had I not come as leader, and the doctor confirmed it, he would have been one of a triumvirate, trying to work out their destiny in the frozen southland.

Even before the *Wyandot* had sailed from Davisville the doctor told me that he had tried to discuss the problem of command with Captain McDonald, in the hope that he might somehow be relieved as Officer in Charge of Detachment Bravo, as they called the SeaBee unit he led. McDonald would not even discuss it with him. There was no alternative possible; it was far too late to select another officer to run the SeaBees, and he had told the doctor he would just have to stick it out.

We had not been two weeks at the camp before the doctor asked McCarthy to help him secure my acceptance of his resignation as officer in charge of the SeaBees. He wanted to concentrate all his efforts on medical matters, and forget the many unpleasant duties connected with handling enlisted men.

As a human being I could sympathize with him, but as a commanding officer, I was finding the situation somewhat difficult to resolve.

On shipboard, the doctor had asked me if it would be allright for him to cut out a panel of the wall in the dispensary when we established the camp, so he could build a cooling room in the snow outside. There he planned to conduct some experiments with volunteers to discover some of the factors that influence metabolism in the Antarctic. He had all the equipment he needed, and a research project already in mind.

I told him that would be perfectly all right, since we were all here on the same mission—to discover all we could about the earth, the Antarctic in particular, and man's reactions to his environment. I was particularly interested in the latter, for I have long felt that men need to spend much more time and effort in preparing for trips to the cold continent than any expedition has yet spent.

Expeditions of the past, including my own, did all they could in this regard, in consideration of their limited resources. This expedition, I had reason to fear, had paid precious little attention to the human factors. The Antarctic was just another mission, to be accomplished by shuffling ships, men and materiel around.

For that reason, I was quite disappointed a week after our arrival when I asked the doctor if he still planned to renovate his dispensary to include a "chill-room."

"No," he said, "I have decided to make a cooling room out in the tunnel later."

I did not continue the discussion. I wondered what the outcome would be, but I was afraid I already knew. There is something about the quiet, the sameness, and the feeling of unlimited time in the Antarctic that leads men into fits of lassitude—unless they are driven by dedication to the work they are doing.

A more serious problem, from the standpoint of men's morale, was the foul-up in the examinations the men wanted to take to advance their rating. This unfortunate incident undoubtedly contributed to the "medic's" growing discouragement. Before leaving Davisville, he had done his best to get the examination papers aboard the *Wyandot* so that the men would have the chance to take the exams aboard ship. When he carried the examination material aboard nearly two weeks before the *Wyandot* sailed, he asked that it be placed in the ship's safe for security. However, the "one-in-charge" of that department refused custody of it unless it was received aboard by registered mail. The doctor's only alternative was to haul all the material back to the SeaBee office and mail it registered via Fleet Post Office, New York. The end result was that this particular mail failed to reach the ship prior to her sailing or at any port of call as she progressed southward to the Antarctic.

The men were bitter and blamed the doctor. Despite the fact that I explained to the enlisted SeaBees the true sequence of events as I knew them, they continued to hold the opinion that the doctor somehow had failed them. The men were given make-shift examinations in allied fields but felt they had not passed them. When the correct papers finally did arrive aboard the incoming ships the following year the men had no warning, nor any time to brush up on their specialties. Consequently, most of the men who did take the examinations felt certain again they would fail them. It was a sore point which plagued us the entire year.

As administrative officer for the base unit, the doctor was in charge of the men's records, and of such extra activities as the ship's store, where the men could buy candy, cigarettes, shaving cream, and other niceties of civilization. Within a few weeks he asked to be relieved of that duty. We agreed in self-protection, so the men could buy something when they wanted it. Ensign William Sumrall took on the duties as ship's store officer and he was a very efficient and competent one.

Perhaps having seen me busy with a hammer on my quarters in the administration building had its effect on the doctor. My quarters, of course, also served as my office, and it was necessary for me to have at least room to put a desk and some chairs inside, as well as my bed and chest.

The doctor was supposed to bunk with McCarthy in the other end of the administration building. Instead, he took over the sick bay which was supposed to hold four bunks for ailing men. As a result, we ended up without a sick bay. And as for his quarters, he spent some three weeks hammering and moving things around until he got them the way he wanted them.

By that time, the doctor was in bad with some of the men. He had been in several squabbles with three of our Chief petty officers, and his hospital corpsman, Mathis, had asked to be transferred to a cook's job, rather than work in the dispensary with the lieutenant. Since we needed an extra hand in the galley, I made the change with the doctor's and McCarthy's concurrence.

But by far the worst problem with the doctor was his slowness in getting the dispensary ready for medical service. This I also attributed to the unique conditions we were living under and the gradual disappearance of the sun that caused the ever-present lassitude among many of the men.

Very little was done to get the instruments and equipment in order. Once, in March, the doctor placed a large bucket of instruments in a solution, and then set the entire bucket outside my door, in the open air. Snow fell, the instruments and bucket were completely covered, and still he did nothing. Finally, I told him to get them inside. Later, I learned that these instruments in the bucket represented the entire supply of medical instruments at our station. Had they been lost we would have been in serious trouble.

Later, that same bucket showed up in the washroom, still full of instruments; finally, I saw to it that it was taken into the dispensary where it belonged.

The entire dispensary looked like a junk-shop for weeks. Packing cases, paper cartons, rubbish—all were mixed in with floor tiles and glue. Chief Spear made a long table with drawers for the medical instruments and equipment, but the doctor spent most of his waking hours making tape recordings of records in the recreation hall, painting, making ship models, and getting into charged discussions with the enlisted men.

As is often true in cases of early disillusionment, eventually we would witness a radical change in the young doctor's self-confidence. But first, the situation would get worse before it got better. As events progressed, the doctor would be one of those who found himself in trouble involving the "ham" radio operations, but at the moment, he had not discovered this facet of Antarctic life.

Radio, of course, is the one single direct link with home. It becomes increasingly important, day after day, as men who winter in the Antarctic realize the extent of their isolation from their own kind. We had an amateur radio station, for the use of all personnel. In the beginning, Chief Kent was unable to get any contacts at all—which was not too serious because we were still fresh from civilization, and no one had begun to worry seriously about relatives or loved ones.

Of course, two of the IGY men, Neuburg and Walker, began making nuisances of themselves about the use of the radio at the very beginning. Neuburg nagged Chief Kent constantly to try to reach a "ham" station in the New York area with which he had arranged a schedule. But in the beginning, our signals apparently were not going out at all, for Kent could not get a single response from any point in the world.

Within a few weeks the station's radio was working. Most of the men then started to send messages to their families and friends and some messages were even received, before I wanted to take advantage of the facility. It was mostly as a morale-builder for the enlisted men, that the amateur radio station was installed in the first place. Finally, on March 1 I gave Chief Kent my first message to relay to my wife, Jackie, and daughter, Karen, who would be celebrating her sixth birthday on March 5. It was received by an amateur station in Texas, which acted as an intermediary for Sam—our contact just outside Washington. She got it about a week after her birthday.

There were several ways we could keep in touch with home. One was through messages relayed by the "ham" radio stations, whose operators have always seemed to me to be touched with the patience of Job and the goodness of a saint. Another, more personal direct way, was to establish a "phone-patch" by way of the amateur radio station. We would reach an amateur radio operator who had a phone-patch attachment connected with his receiving and transmission set. He would then call the long-distance operator who would call the home of the individual asked for, just like any other long distance call. All transactions, of course, would have to go through the amateur radio station who would monitor the conversation. Thus we could speak to anyone we wanted in the United States, limited only by our ability to spend the money necessary for the personal contacts at long distance rate from the "ham" station to the city desired.

Almost immediately, of course, we ran into the problem of priorities and service on the messages. Chief Kent, naturally, was primarily responsible for the dispatch of messages of official business, and on the official short-wave radio for Washington and other Navy stations. It was McCarthy's job, as executive officer, to straighten out such priorities, but before he was through they were to give him more than one headache.

Early in March, one of my anchormen displayed his one great weakness—an inability to keep from over-fraternizing with the enlisted men. Shortly after we arrived on station, he went over to the enlisted men's bunk house about five o'clock, and never did show up, either for dinner or for the regular evening staff meeting we were holding to lay plans for the camp construction on a day-by-day basis. Drinking, of course, made the fraternization easy, and we had far too much beer and liquor available for my liking. That was a considered plan, made by someone higher up in the command setup who felt that the men needed to be able to get roaring drunk if they wished, to relieve the tension of living together in the endless snow.

I could not have disagreed more, but my man found himself right in line with such policy. Again on this particular night, he did not show up at all in my quarters, before I went to bed at midnight.

His failure to appear made both my position and his that much more difficult, for the men knew he had not come to dinner nor to the staff meeting as planned. Perhaps his military training had been limited; but one would assume that after years of active duty, any officer should know that you cannot drink with the enlisted men as a usual thing and have their respect, too.

One result of the fraternization, of course, was immediately noticeable. The men slackened off in their work. For about ten days very little was accomplished. Part of this, of course, could be attributed to the natural running down, after a sustained period of hard work. But more important, the men, without my knowing it, had been given to understand in the States that the normal rules of discipline would be suspended while they were in the Antarctic. They would not receive punishment of the same nature or severity that they would have gotten had they taken the same action while aboard ship or at a shore station. Higher commands had ordered even that the officer in charge of the SeaBees (in this case the doctor) was not to mete out normal punishments at all.

Obviously, under such conditions, with split commands, and the most tenuous kind of authority in my own hands, I needed all the help I could get from my officers and the responsible men around me. It was a sad disappointment that some of my assistants proved to be so ill-equipped for the jobs I had hoped they would handle. Had I known them only casually in civilization such faults in character would have been also known to me or probably overlooked. But in isolation your relationships are not casual affairs—they are closely knit family affairs, minus the customary loyalties.

It was not their fault, certainly, but the beginnings did not speak well either for the process of selection used by the personnel selection board or for the future of the expedition. Each time one of my officers or one of the men I trusted failed me, it made my job harder, and our chances of doing all the work we had come to do that much less.

The day after several of the officers had spent the night carousing with the men, I had come to the conclusion that another bunking space had to be found soon for Lieutenant Jaburg and Ensign Sumrall. Because of a lack of bunking space in the administration building where McCarthy, Lieutenant Smith and I had our quarters, we assigned these two younger officers a corner room in number one bunkhouse, which we thought would give them sufficient privacy from the enlisted men occupying the rest of it. That was part of the trouble—but not all of it. I took matters in my own hands—which I should not have done since I did have an executive officer—but I wanted to show all concerned how seriously I regarded this problem.

When I happened to pass through the enlisted men's bunkhouse at 10:30 A.M. that same day, I found an officer still stretched out in his bunk, tired from having been a part of the carousing the night before. All hands knew that he had not been up for breakfast. Since the executive officer was asleep and not available to do it, I called all the younger officers to get on with their duties of supervising the construction of the three-sided hangar which McCarthy insisted on building and which responsibility they had shied away from.

This was a particular bad morning, and I also had a ticklish problem to resolve with Hugo Neuburg, the civilian glaciologist. Chief Spear called my attention to the fact that Neuburg had snatched a door from another building and put it on his room which was located between the met-office and the radio room, where no door was scheduled. Except for a couple of spaces inside the building shells, heavy green draperies had been supplied for the openings of all the cubicles to afford the men privacy. Spear pointed out that if Neuburg got a door, everyone else would want one, too; and that was exactly the trouble. The door had not been in place an hour before several of the other men had already complained to Chief Spear and demanded their "rights."

Unfortunately, there were only about six doors inside the entire camp and all were being used or destined for more important functions. In order to squelch that item of contention, we had to eliminate Neuburg's door and let him use draperies the same as the other men.

When Chief Spear took the door off, Neuburg was outraged. He came to me and made some nasty accusations, then he lost self-control completely and showed such disrespect I was forced to put him in his place.

While I recognize there are a few men who can be reached by appealing to their higher instincts, my past experience has convinced me of the realism in the piece of advice I had been given a long time ago about dealing with any divergent group of men.

"Don't waste your breath on appeals to patriotism and duty. The fear of punishment and the hope of reward are the only two forces that move most men. A good method is to dangle the hope of reward, the fear of punishment to be held in the background."

My problem at this time was that I did not have such control. I could not reward the civilians, they were already highly paid, with special allowances for hardship in coming to the Antarctic. The only way I could punish a civilian for infraction of law and order was by hauling out the Uniform Code of Military Justice. It had been decided before we were left alone on this ice cliff that the civilians were under the same code as the military. This, of course, they were aware of—and held many discussions on that subject. I had no idea how far I would be backed by my superiors. These "back-home" directors had never been faced with these disciplinary problems—I knew they seemed to think there were few problems of discipline or morale in the Antarctic, and these not their responsibility.

I could punish the other men only by threatening them with minor disciplines which I did, and then always with the concurrence of both my executive officer McCarthy, and Lieutenant Smith. I had no authority to administer any type of judicial acts. We had no brig—we could not afford to waste the services of a man unless he committed some heinous crime.

I could not reward the service men at all, except by complimentary letters in their service records. For aside from the confusion about the examinations for advancement, the men learned very early that all the service personnel had lost their per diem allowance. The Navy men got no more for Antarctic duty than for any other, it turned out.

Reward and punishment—certainly these are the fuels for men in large groups. But in my case, I should have to work some new kind of reward and punishment to fit the problem at hand. It was apparent that it would take every ounce of command power I possessed to keep the men in hand during the year of wintering—and I sorely needed the support of the administrative council.

CHAPTER 6

FLYING WEATHER

Suddenly, in March, the beer-drinking problem became so severe I had to crack down. Every night for weeks the enlisted men in number one bunkhouse, across the way from my quarters, had been drinking half the night. Consequently they were not worth much at work in the morning. Equally as bad, their outbursts and continuous talk kept non-drinkers awake. By orders the men were to have beer if they wanted it. I have always been opposed to drinking anywhere in excess and drinking at all in the polar camp, except on special occasions; far too much is at stake. But orders were orders—and the men could buy unlimited quantities of beer. They bought it three and four cases at a time, and it cost them only eleven cents a can.

The first indication of the tension they were creating came when First Class Mechanic Walter Davis came to me to ask if he could move out of the bunkhouse and sleep in a corner of the garage. He did not drink himself. He worked every night until 10 o'clock (at this point he was helping with the construction of the washrooms) and he needed sleep. I spoke to Lieutenant Commander McCarthy, just to keep matters within the chain of command, and within a few hours Davis was moving his gear.

The second incident occurred on Sunday, March 10, when I was awakened early by voices in McCarthy's room at the opposite end of the building from my own. It was Chief Spear and one of the enlisted men, having an argument.

Later in the day I heard the entire story. Lieutenant Jaburg, the helicopter pilot, Donald Skidmore, the twenty-eight-year-old ionospheric assistant, and a group of enlisted men wanted to have a party in the science building.

They held their party, all right, and most of them got to feeling high! They were singing and yelling in the main tunnel until four o'clock in the morning.

Some of the men had it in for Spear, who was quite a proud and efficient Navy disciplinarian and who had been working them hard on camp construction. So they woke him up.

They also woke up Hugo Neuburg, Lieutenant Smith, and a great number of others and kept them from going back to sleep.

Unfortunately, some of my officers were involved in the party. Chief Spear and Chief Walter May, the head of our weather section, were both hopping mad about it, but they could do nothing when the men were supported by the officers. And one of the worst things of all—McCarthy and some of the others had gotten on a first-name basis with the men, so the control over them was diminishing.

Spear and May came to see me about the incident. My first action was to order Spear to put up a small one-room bunkhouse adjacent to the administration building, where McCarthy, Smith and I were located, for Jaburg and Sumrall to bunk in. All five of us would utilize the same entrance passageway which would be labeled "Officer Country." I hoped this would be a deterent to the late carousing with the enlisted men. Second, I directed the two young officers Jaburg and Sumrall to move out of the enlisted men's bunkhouse as soon as Chief Spear had their room completed, a move I had been considering since the first major incident.

After lunch, I called the IGY civilians together and urged each one of them to support me in my effort to eliminate any further incident similar to those we had already experienced. I particularly appealed to the civilians who had participated in the rumpus and reminded them again that they were here to do a job.

Then I called Lieutenant Jaburg and Ensign Sumrall over to my room and talked to them about their responsibilities. I let them know I was disappointed in their behavior, that I expected them to set examples of character, and initiative for others to follow.

I did not make much impression on Jaburg, a Florida boy who had been in the Navy since 1951. He had come up through the ranks, serving his four years as an enlisted man, had received his commission after taking pilot training, and while he might be a good pilot, I had my own reservations about some of his actions.

Ensign Sumrall was a different fellow. He was a slender twenty-one-year-old from Mississippi, impressionable, friendly, and although he enjoyed sociability he was an abstainer. He had been flying for about two years, in fact had scarcely been in the Navy longer. I blamed him less than the others, but I wanted to have a talk with him for his own good. Among other things, since we had been ashore, he had been one of the officers passing up breakfast every morning, because officers paid for their food, and by skipping breakfast every morning they could save twenty-five cents a day. Consequently, at lunch time, they were ravenously hungry.

He was a handsome boy with sharp features and a kind of "growing-up" look about him which belied the fact he was a crackerjack pilot.

He took the advice I gave him in good grace, and promised, among other things, to eat breakfast in the morning. I felt that my talk with him had cleared the air, and it added strength to our friendly relationship.

It was remarkable, in fact, how the incident helped restore discipline. The next morning—Monday—all hands were up bright and early. Skidmore, the IGY civilian, was the only one to miss breakfast, but even he made it for the morning muster at 8 o'clock.

The IGY civilians had a guilty conscience for their part in the affair, I felt. They seemed to be considerably subdued, but with this incident matters had come to a head. Where before there had been a certain amount of confusion, now there was open opposition to my command from the civilians.

Skidmore, strangely enough, was the one who told me about it. From time to time I had played at darts with him in the evenings. (He was the best dart-thrower in camp and constantly beat me.) He was a strange young man, a graduate of a small northeastern business school, and the father of five children. He was medium sized, inclined to carelessness about his personal appearance, and a curious mixture of great energy and great slovenliness. He had with him a coin collection, and confided in me that he had written two chapters of a book on coins. He had been a merchant seaman, a male nurse, a machinist, and a college student. When we first arrived, he and Augenbaugh were the only two IGY men who had unhesitatingly volunteered to move ashore and work at base construction with the enlisted men. Skidmore was quite good at electrical work, and had been very helpful in repairing and installing wiring around camp. Yet he was also resentful of authority, and inclined to complain a great deal over minor matters. He was definitely deficient in the rigorous requirements for a real Antarctic IGY representative, but in many ways an admirable and extremely likeable fellow.

In the beginning, I knew, both Skidmore and Behrendt stood up for me in many of the IGY men's griping sessions. Augenbaugh, the chubby one, was the principal fire-eater then. I found out that he had been a Marine, had detested the Corps and the discipline, and had sworn when he got out that he was never going to take orders from a "lousy officer" again. The fact that I was a four-striper just made things worse as far as Augenbaugh was concerned.

When I learned these things, I replied that I had hoped to get to know the IGY men well and be on a friendly basis with all of them. Obviously it was impossible to do so now, and I intended to let them strictly alone, except as far as their work was concerned.

But it was just not me, or the Navy, Skidmore confided. The civilians were not getting on well among themselves. They resented everything, including my appointment of Dr. Thiel as deputy scientific leader (an appointment which the IGY suggested I make because of his superior education and status as a scientist). Thiel, they said, had no idea of leadership. They neither followed him nor listened to him. By this time I was becoming convinced that they would neither follow nor listen to anyone.

At this point, the three most unhappy and most resentful were Gerard Fierle, the eldest and least educated of the civilians who was a Weather Bureau employee; Augenbaugh, the geologist, and Walker, the glaciologist. Walker, however, I did not consider so much trouble, since like Behrendt, the junior seismologist, he was just a youngster.

Several of the civilians were unhappy about their treatment by all the military personnel. They did not believe the military was giving them adequate support, especially as far as use of tools was concerned. Chief Spear was in charge of tools, and he took great care to see that they were not ruined. A practical man, he hated to lend tools to the theoretical IGY men because they did not bring them back, or if they did return them, usually the tools were broken.

But the dispute with the IGY men would have broken out over something, I am convinced of that, no matter what the military men had done. From the time we arrived they were determined to have things their own way. It began with the interminable discussions of messing arrangements, and their request that we act as one big happy family.

No one would have enjoyed this better than I if it had been possible to do so. The main difficulty was the lack of messhall space. At the other bases, no doubt it was possible with only eighteen or twenty-two men, but with thirty-nine men it was another story. Then, the few times we all did mess together the enlisted men appealed to me to separate them from the officers and the IGY civilians, so they could be on their own. As one first-class technician expressed it: "Captain, I just don't feel the same; it is not right to rub elbows with a commissioned officer." Lots of thought had gone into the final decision and McCarthy, the exec, was all for it.

Several of them were unhappy with my decision to separate the officers and civilians from the enlisted men. Then they began a rumor campaign: They were happy to perform household duties and do such jobs as mess duty, but the Captain would not let them. This rumor caused lots of trouble, for some of the Navy men who were doing mess duty had as much as sixteen years of naval service, were specialists in their fields, and did not come to the Antarctic to wash dishes any more than some of the twenty-year–old civilians. When the enlisted men began bitching, I had a long talk with Thiel about mess duty. Thiel objected to doing it. He said they had not come to the Antarctic for that purpose, it was below their dignity, and while if ordered to do it they would, still he wanted to know if the officers would do mess duty, too.

When I suggested mess duty for a specific date, he said all the "scientists" were busy with their own work. So that ended that discussion, for a time.

The IGY civilians were busy by now, almost all of them. By mid-March the camp was nearly completed, and the various scientific studies were well begun.

In the beginning, Hugo Neuberg and Paul Walker, had helped Dr. Thiel get the seismology program going, because later in the year they would need some help from the seismologists to do their work. But after the first reflection shots were finally taken, and the graphs made, Neuburg and Walker got down to their own work.

I had heard of Neuburg before. He was a figure around the Explorer's Club in New York. In order to get on the IGY expedition, he had switched to work in a new branch of science. Only recently had he specialized in glaciology, particularly in the summer of 1956 before sailing, when he flew to Greenland and Alaska to get checked out on glacier formations in the North.

One of the first jobs Neuburg undertook in the glaciology program was to set out a "stake-system," which covered an area of several square miles. He set down stakes, about eight feet long, in a pattern laid out geometrically from a base line (a point or line from which a start is made by the survey method, as a basis for computation). The stakes formed into various diamond shapes, the legs measured up to a mile in length, each stake with the aid of a surveyor's transit, to form parallel lines that were measured within a fraction of an inch.

At each stake the accumulation of snow was measured once a week all through the winter. The heavy winds beat down on the surface and gradually ate away the snow, changing its depth in some areas. The data from the glaciological measurements was collected, then shown on a curve or a graph. From it, the scientists could tell whether an area was accumulating or losing snow.

Then six months after the stakes were put out, Neuburg and Walker would re-survey the entire system, checking every point, and noting the smallest deviation from the past figures. That way, they would find the trend in the movement of the ice shelf on which were were living.

Actually, we were floating on the water of the Weddell Sea in our camp, although we were two and a half miles inland. The ice and snow at the station site was about 760 feet deep, but the distance to the bottom of the sea was 2,600 feet. We were sitting atop a massive chunk of glacial ice that was moving into the sea, ever so slowly. Before the winter night, we measured our geographical location, and found that we were at Latitude 77°, 44′ South, Longitude 41°, 07′ West, and 139 feet, eight inches above sea level. (Our location was later slightly corrected by Chapman of the Air Force as indicated in Appendix.) How far would we move in a year, if at all? That was one of the questions Neuburg and Walker had come to answer. The second part of the glaciologists work was the study of the structures of the snow and ice, and their relationship to each other. Once each month, the men would take core-samples for study, samples that were gotten from shallow pits dug into the ice—about six feet deep, six feet long and three feet wide.

Along the sides of these pits, were inserted small steel tubes about three inches in diameter. They were spaced in a vertical row on the wall, about six inches apart from the upper edge to the bottom. Each one contained a core sample, which was then tested inside in a cold laboratory.

The third job would be to dig a deep pit—more than 100 feet deep, straight down into the ice. Through the year, Neuburg and Walker would go down into the pit to dig, discarding all but their lightweight clothing even when the temperature was $-60°$ on top of the surface, and study the composition of the ice at nine-foot intervals. The digging was hard work and made them warm up quickly. They examined the layers, the location of snow grain and ice crystals and their angles to the slopes of surface they had fallen on, perhaps many hundreds of years ago.

The core samples they took in the deep pit would be packed in special containers, and stored in the ice laboratory where temperatures always were around $0°$. Eventually, they would be shipped in the deep-freeze of the *Wyandot* to the Ice, Snow and Permafrost Laboratory at Wilmette, Illinois, for further examination of density and structure.

Later, Dr. Thiel would use the deep pit to make some gravity measurements, but at the moment he was still trying to complete his depth soundings of the ice barrier, and be sure his equipment was in working condition for the spring overland trip he still hoped to take if we could repair the damage to the Sno-Cat.

We were deep into the fall. It would not be long before we would have to secure all the outside equipment, especially the aircraft. Before we put the planes away, however, I wanted to make a few reconnaissance flights, if possible recheck some of the areas I had first sighted on my expedition in 1947.

On January 28, I had made a flight in a 'copter piloted by Lieutenant Newell of the icebreaker *Staten Island*. We had traveled about fifty miles south of what was now our station, and I had seen the heavily crevassed area that surrounded the station. Also, before we turned back, I had seen a huge rift in the shelf about three miles wide and fifty miles long with ice-masses jumbled together 150 feet below the surface of the ice shelf. And fifty miles or so farther to the south there were the high snow banks that formed the eastern bank of higher land (which I had also observed on a flight in 1947). Later, I determined that this land was an island.

Early in March, with McCarthy as pilot I flew south of Gould Bay again and saw the high land once more. Ensign Sumrall was along with us also, as co-pilot and navigator. It is one thing to navigate a plane over normal terrain, where at least an occasional feature will tend to straighten you out if you fall in error. But in the Antarctic, you must know at all times your actual air and ground speeds, your drift and wind's velocity and direction. Sumrall, I learned, soon showed his efficiency in the knowledge of these navigational tools.

And on March 16, McCarthy and Sumrall flew me due south as far as the escarpment of the continent, some 200 miles away from camp, then east, where we encountered the mountains the Argentines had first seen. More recently the British had named them Shackleton Mountains, after the great explorer Sir Ernest Shackleton, and, incidently, after their camp as well. During the summer of 1955 the Argentines sighted these mountains and huge glaciers. In the small Beaver plane, piloted by General Hernan Pujato, they flew to 83° south where their plane was wrecked. Some of these same mountains were later seen, in January, 1956, by a U.S. Navy flight crew under Captain Trigger Hawks, including the Pensacola Range and Dufek Massif.

At our due south point, along with these, I sighted other high mountains southwest, too. This was our first long flight—about seven hours. I took Thiel and Neuburg along as passengers, because they were both to be members of the five-man traverse party which would make a surface trip the following spring. I knew they were anxious to see as much of the land as possible first from the air; especially the crevassed area through which they would have to thread their way overland. Later, I would have to work out a safe course for their overland traverse party, so that they could get to the high land I had seen, but I hoped they would be able to make some observations of help to themselves in coming months.

Thiel and Neuburg sat in the back of the plane, one on each side. Admittedly, they did not have very good vantage points. But on several occasions when I walked to the back of the OTTER, I called their attention to the heavily crevassed areas everywhere beneath us.

"Where are they? We haven't seen any," they answered.

The power of observation of the untrained eye is not very great over Antarctic terrain.

That flight ended our flying weather except for local flights. But before the end, we had enjoyed a visit from Dr. Vivian Fuchs and four men from his British Shackleton Base. They had been scheduled, on the day of their visit, to fly the 250 miles south to their advance base, but when weather closed in in that direction, they decided to visit us instead. Dr. Fuchs was particularly anxious to have us turn on our radio beacon when he made his inland flights. Then, if the weather turned foul and he had difficulty in returning to home base, he could land at our base instead.

He was worried all the time he was with us. The flying weather had been terrible for about ten days. Eleven days before, he had landed two of his men twenty-five miles short of the advance base to do some geology work on some rock outcroppings. The weather closed in. Twice, they flew over the area hoping to pick them up. But they could not see the ground. They did find the spot where they had landed the two men, but they were no longer there.

It was a very ticklish situation. The men had a radio receiver but no transmitter. They could hardly navigate through crevasses in zero visibility. Worst of all, they had food for only ten days, and this was the eleventh day.

They had been trying to reach us for several days by radio without success. They discussed us with their compatriots at Halley Bay, but Halley Bay did not know our frequencies either. Halley Bay had an idea, though.

"Why don't you try Mirny?" they asked. "The Russians should know Ronne's schedules and frequencies."

It was a tribute to the Russian curiosity, if not their intelligence system. But Dr. Fuchs decided to come over instead.

This incident pointed up one of the problems of the Antarctic, even during the IGY. No expedition can take the time to monitor all frequencies on the radio dial, so unless you know someone else's sending system and the frequencies he does watch, you might as well be across the earth from him, instead of a few hundred miles away.

Then and there we established a regular radio schedule with the British. And I offered them all of the facilities here at the base if Fuchs wanted us to join in the search for the two men. I spoke to McCarthy who thought we could have an OTTER plane ready in a matter of two hours, if need be.

Two days later we learned that they had found the men who were left in the field—safe and sound. When the weather cleard the morning after they left us, Dr. Fuchs took off at 4 A.M., landed near the spot where they had been left, and found a note that said the two had begun walking toward the advance base two days before. The plane took off again and followed the trail, until they found the men a few miles from their advance station. It was a happy end to a story that might have been tragic, a reminder that Antarctic conditions are basically intolerable to man unless he observes the most careful safety precautions at all times.

During the British visit, we were visibly reminded how well our government provided for our welfare, even at the cost of waste. The British were delighted to see that we had steaks on our menu, and one of them ate four! He said he had not tasted steak since he left London on November 1, 1956, and did not expect to taste it again until his return in the spring of 1958.

This lesson might have had some effect on the morale of the men and civilians, but it did not. The rumor mill seemed to be working overtime these days. Latest was a false report that the Recreation Building would be declared out of bounds for the enlisted men. It probably stemmed from my crackdown after the tunnel drinking party. But the result was that the enlisted men quit working to finish up the Recreation Building in their spare time. It took me several days to straighten that one out.

On March 17, we held memorial services for Admiral Byrd, who had died on the twelfth of the month. The Recreation hall had just been completed, so we held the services there. John Brown, our ionospheric physicist, was a lay reader, so he conducted the simple religious services, reading from the Bible, and delivering a prayer. With deep emotion and sincerity I made a short speech about Byrd's sudden death, and the great name he had made for himself in Antarctic exploration. I had known him for nearly thirty years.

That same day the most serious breach of discipline we had yet suffered was to end in a frightening incident.

I was sitting in my usual place in front of the projector in the movies, when Dr. Smith came alongside.

"Captain," he said, "I have bad news for you."

"What's that?" I replied.

"One of the boys got drunk and drove off in a weasel about forty minutes ago. We've been searching around the camp for several weasel tracks but no one has found any. We don't know where he's gone."

Hearing this, I ordered the movie stopped. I told everyone to get dressed in outside clothing and meet here in the messhall, just as quickly as they could.

On the way over to my own quarters I met McCarthy. His face was full of frost from having been out in the wind searching for the young fellow, along with several other VX-6 men. They had found no trace.

I went to my quarters and dressed heavily, ready for a long search, and went back to the messhall. I had been gone only ten minutes, but it seemed as though every man was there ahead of me—all of them serious about this sudden emergency.

For the search, I divided the area into four quadrants, North, East, West and South. I put Lieutenant Jaburg in charge of the Western group with five men. He was to drive a weasel to the crest of the hill and search along the inlet for tracks. The Southern group, under Ensign Sumrall, would search south, but would go no farther than four miles, because of the danger of crevasses past that point. I put Hugo Neuburg in charge of the Eastern group, since that was the area in which he had been setting up his glaciology stake lines, and he knew the lay of the land. I took charge of the Northern group myself.

When we started out, we fanned out, careful to keep within shouting distance of our own party, and in contact with the other three parties by walkie-talkie radio. Two men stayed on in the messhall to relay communications, too.

My group was working its way down toward the old ship's landing on the edge of the barrier when we saw a weasel coming in full speed, right through the crevasse area, very close to the place where the dynamite and blasting caps were cached. He was heading west, with his headlights on.

Since we only had three weasels in commission and two were in use in the search party, I knew we had found him. The Western group was informed by walkie-talkie of his approach to that sector. Lieutenant Jaburg raced his weasel toward the missing machine, cut it off and finally forced it to stop. Jaburg then ordered the man into the back of his weasel and brought him back to the messhall.

When the young man stepped out of the weasel, his face was cut, he was frostbitten, and badly shaken. We got him inside and poured hot drinks down him. Then he began to revive, and in a few minutes was acting as though he was the hero of the occasion.

I went back now, and ordered the movie reinstated. Afterwards, I called McCarthy, Dr. Smith and Dr. Thiel together and we discussed the entire chain of events. Dr. Smith had the story. Although still very young, our runaway had been an eager indulger. He had come to the messhall in the afternoon, waving a beer can in one hand, in a bellicose mood.

When Dr. Smith told him to quiet down, the boy said: "Go to hell."

That, of course, raised a serious charge. Yet, we were in no position to take any legal action at our station, and it had already been made quite clear that the men were to be treated with kid gloves on this expedition.

Besides, I did not blame the man for this as much as I did those who had fraternized in drinking with the men to the point that they had lost respect for officers.

Dr. Smith was unable to quiet him down. One of the cooks tried to shut him up—told him to go back to his bunk and sleep it off. The boy finally wandered out, mouthing something about how he hated camp life, and especially work around the messhall.

But after supper, he told Walter Cox, our photographer that he was fed up and was going for a ride over to Dr. Fuchs' Shackleton base. Twenty minutes later, when he did not return, Cox became worried and put out the alarm.

Something had to be done in order to stem the lawlessness and general disrespect for authority. McCarthy noted that he had orders which showed he had authority over the men, too. We would have to settle that later, after we decided first what to do with the youthful offender as an example to the men. But first, it was essential that we make sure no such incident could occur again. This time it was not too serious. The temperature was only at about zero, and the wind was only about fifteen miles an hour. Another time, in extreme cold and with heavy wind and no visibility, he might not have been found until he was frozen stiff. Actually, this was our first emergency when a concerted effort of all hands was needed. The officers and men responded enthusiastically in the grim night, and they carried out the search in a very efficient manner.

The next morning we issued a new set of camp regulations. The weasels were to be put away in the garage for the winter. Night watch was to be tightened up. We would keep a tighter eye on beer-drinking and on use of the Recreation hall during daytime, since that was where the drinking party had begun.

After lunch, we had a meeting, and McCarthy decided to take some disciplinary action against the boy. I agreed.

This time, since it was a first offense, we gave him two hours of extra duty every evening for fourteen days. The extra duty would be served between 8:00 and 10:00 P.M., which also would mean he would miss the movie for two weeks.

Later in the afternoon McCarthy brought the young fellow to my quarters. He told the youngster he had endangered his own life, but not only his own life. He had endangered the lives of some twenty men who went out into the night to search for him, too.

The boy was obviously sober and sorry. I told him he ought to look ahead, get interested in something positive, and quit drinking. I did not want to see him drinking beer again, and he promised me not to touch it again without my permission. As for the rest, I let McCarthy take care of it. From my point of view the young man had been "put upon"; the system was not without blame in this case. He had for some time been doing more than his share of mess-duty.

Handling the affair thus, I did not settle the question of authority over the men—the question McCarthy had raised from time to time. This was no time to settle that most complicated problem. There were just too many letters of authority floating around the camp, and too many separate commands that had been created by different branches of the Navy and the IGY.

The incident was scarcely settled when the civilians began causing trouble again, undermining my authority throughout the camp, by what they did and what they said.

During the long survey flight on which I took Thiel and Neuburg, Augenbaugh had expressed himself very loudly to the men at camp. He told them how free he felt when I was out of camp, and how he despised anyone with authority—that no one was going to tell him what to do. Then Skidmore and Lieutenant Jaburg showed up at lunch carrying beer cans. While there was no written law against it, they both knew they had no business bringing beer into the messhall. After lunch that day, I saw to it that there was a rule against bringing beer to the galley and messhall, except during the showing of movies in the evening.

CHAPTER 7

ANTARCTIC FEVER

On MARCH 21 THE TEMPERATURE FELL TO $-34°$ AND WE KNEW WINTER was approaching rapidly. The camp was now about ninety-five per cent completed; all that remained to be done was complete the various tunnels between buildings so we could move back and forth during the long night without having to venture out into the bitter cold.

It was good that we were so far along, for we were beginning to have intermittent—although light—snowfalls. Most of the men continued their work. Spear's builders were putting the finishing touches on the bunkhouse and the junior officers had already moved in. In another day or so their tunnel-entrance would be finished. After walking over to the aircraft buildings through the long tunnel I saw that the aviation group had not made any effort to keep the drifting snow from seeping in. At one point, the clearance between roof and snow was only three feet, so I had difficulty getting through the shallow opening. When I reached the first building, I found Lieutenant Jaburg sitting in front of the space-heater with two enlisted men, deep in a bull-session.

The scientists were all hard at work now, but they displayed really enormous ignorance of their environment and carelessness in the handling of all the equipment. Sometimes it seemed to me they could not have realized that we were alone here until the spring, and if something was broken and we had no spare, we would just have to do without for the rest of our time here.

A few days before, Dr. Thiel, who was using the second Sno-Cat for his sounding work, lost the cap to the gas tank. Snow got in, of course, and before we were through they had ruined the fuel pump. Luckily we had spares.

The scientists were so preoccupied in their work they did not seem to notice the change in the weather. On my way to the aviation building

I had stopped to talk to Chief May, the meteorologist, about his work. He said he was going to help Neuburg get some of his stakes out that day, rather than do his own work. Thiel was going to do the same.

But coming back from the aviation building, I noticed how hazy it was. I could not see 200 feet in any direction because of the low layers of cloud and fog. It was hardly a day for surveying. The glaciologists would have a tough time completing their stake system when the visibility was so poor not even the telescope of the theodolite could penetrate the dense fog.

By this time we had two generators on the line and in operation, which increased our work load a great deal. We had to have a man on watch at all times, to observe the load and balance of each generator. In that respect, it was apparent that we were short of men in the Bravo—or housekeeping—detachment, although we seemed quite long in the aviation detachment with three officers and eight enlisted men, who hadn't much to do now.

The shortage of maintenance personnel also made itself felt in our radio communications. I was quite embarrassed when Dr. Fuchs visited us, because when they were ready to leave, he asked us to call up Shackleton to get a weather check before they took off, but our radio operator did not seem to know how to do it.

Chief Kent, the senior man in charge of radio at our station, was more of an electronics man than a radio man, and after we had been there more than a month he had still been able to arrange only a few phone-patches and sent out a handful of "ham-grams."

We assigned the first-class radio man Haskill to the nightwatch, to the relief of Kent, who was needed during the daytime on the important job of hooking up our fire alarm system.

Since winter was here, it could not be long until we would go on a winter routine. That change ought to help morale, I thought, and we needed some help at that moment, for the enlisted men were showing signs of restlessness. Some of them came to me complaining that they did not like to serve anyone at the table, when they were on mess duty. They also thought that officers and IGY men ought to have mess duty, too.

I asked one of them if he had ever seen a lieutenant or a commander serving meals to a third-class radio operator or seaman. Then they had to laugh, and admit that it did seem a little strange.

These were trivial matters, but they had to be settled promptly to keep morale from collapsing. We were still feeling the effect of the officers' ill-timed fraternization at the big party. The men were not doing their jobs as they were told in many cases. One morning, they were told to bring their extra clothing bags to a Jamesway hut, so we would have plenty of extra clothing in case fire destroyed the main camp. Instead of complying, they began to ask a lot of questions about the necessity of such a move and thought it best to leave the clothing bags where they were. Two of the men were told to tile one of the heads. One did not go in at all, and the other laid only a handful of tiles in his first day.

I had no sooner solved that problem when I found that the aviation people were warming up the airplane without my knowledge. I had to lay it on the line for McCarthy; there were to be no flights without my knowledge, and that I was responsible for the safety of the entire camp and mission. While he agreed to all these matters in our discussion, he kept reminding me that his *verbal* directive from Chief of VX-6, was that Captain Ronne had no jurisdiction over operations of the planes and, that he, Lieutenant Commander McCarthy was responsible only to Captain Cordiner in this respect. That was all very well, except that Cordiner was now some 10,000 miles away in Washington, D. C.

The next day, I had Lieutenant Smith see to it that the clothing bags were moved to the Jamesway huts—no questions asked! Right after morning muster they moved the bags, in record time, and without argument.

For some time the men had been bitching because of a fear that when the new head was completed, the officers would take it over. The tiling finished, the head was done, and the men had bigger and better washing facilities than the officers and civilians. It was turned over to them, with a warning that if they abused the equipment they would have to do without. That time, at least, the item went off the gripe list.

It was immediately replaced by general complaint about the continued need for mess duty. Some of them brought up remarks by Admiral Dufek that the men did not have to do mess duty. Who was going to do it then? We had no mess stewards.

The closest to a mess steward was Mathis, the hospital corpsman who had asked to be transferred to the galley from the dispensary. But now we found he got along no better in the galley than he had with Dr. Smith. He turned out to be resentful of everything, he worked under protest at all times, and he contaminated the other men with his complaining. Dr. Smith was concerned, he told me, lest Mathis break down before the winter ended.

Dr. Smith had a long talk with him, worried because Mathis was enjoying his beer sessions in the recreation hall too much and was complaining constantly. The doctor hoped to be able to persuade him to take some educational courses, both to learn something and to advance in the Navy. Mathis wanted no part of it. He told Dr. Smith he hated the Navy and was getting out as soon as he could.

Why he was ever sent to the Antarctic I will never know. I was going through the requirements for enlisted men, and the more I read the more I could not understand how this station complement was ever put together. In the first place, all the Antarctic winterers were "volunteers." But a volunteer for transfer in any service is often a misfit. His boss is

100

likely to give him a good character, just to get rid of him, to pass him on to another command. Further, the selection rules said, the volunteers should not have signs of abnormal responses to discipline, inappropriate laughter, anxiety, sulkiness, depression, discontent, resentment, suspicion, or dirtiness of person or language.

After less than two months it seemed to me that at least a fourth of the men were selected because they had an abundance of the bad characteristics listed. The language of the enlisted men was the foulest I have heard in nearly thirty years of exploration and Navy life. I had already called several of the men down for this misuse of language, but it continued, more or less, all the time we were in the camp.

Others have struggled with the question of what constitutes proper conduct in the polar regions. I recall, Elisha Kent Kane, a Navy Medical Officer sent to the Arctic in search of the Franklin expedition in 1853 met a similar situation head on. In his book *Arctic Exploration* Kane states:

Ten of our party belonged to the U.S. Navy, and were attached to my command by orders from the Department; the others were shipped by me for the cruise, and at salaries entirely disproportionate to their services; all were volunteers. We did not sail under the rules that govern our national ships; but we had our own regulations, well considered and announced beforehand, and rigidly adhered to afterward through all the vicissitudes of the expedition. These included—*First,* absolute subordination to the officer in command or his delegate; *second,* abstinence from all intoxicating liquors, except when dispensed by special order; *third,* the habitual disuse of profane language. We had no other laws.

There is still much to be learned from the old explorers on whom some of our modern ones look so disdainfully.

Morale was suffering from something over which we had no control at this late date: Poor radio operation. Whether it was the fault of the operators, the equipment, or atmospheric conditions, we were having a desperate time maintaining communication of any kind.

For several days late in March we were unable to raise *any* outside station—even in the Antarctic—either on code transmission or voice. It was exasperating, for we could hear other stations talking back and forth and talking to the United States. We could hear both ends of some conversations, but still we were off the air.

One problem, I knew, was that there were too many fingers in the pie. Unauthorized men, military and civilians wandered in and out of the radio shack, changing settings on the receivers and fiddling with the transmission equipment, apparently at will. Finally, McCarthy had to put up a sign at the radio shack telling unauthorized people to keep out.

The weather was beginning to close in now, which meant that radio would play a more important part in our lives than it had been when we had more work to do outside. On March 26 it was still —34°. The next day the temperature fell to —37°, and felt much colder, for a nasty, eighteen-mile-an-hour wind accompanied the change. That is a light wind for the Antarctic, where wind velocities are often well in excess of 100 miles an hour and have been clocked at around 200 mph (Siple). But any wind in these temperatures is dangerous, for it speeds frostbite. Almost every man who put his nose out of doors in this weather came in with tell-tale white patches on his face, the beginning signs of severe frostbite.

The change in weather meant something else, too. Outside scientific work, except the work that could be conducted right around the camp, was about to come to an end. Dr. Thiel wanted to take a few more shots on the bay ice, but I was doubtful now if he would be able to make them, particularly since it meant moving southeast toward the Shackleton base, and the weather was turning so rapidly it would be remarkable if he found enough good days to do the job.

The ending of outside work did not mean we were to sit and twiddle our thumbs all winter. Indeed, one of the most important disciplines at Ellsworth Station was meteorology, which required no movement from the station area at all.

We had parallel meteorological studies at Ellsworth. The Navy had sent Chief Walter May to conduct weather study. He was a heavy, rosy-cheeked bachelor of forty-two, seventeen years a Navy man, and an expert in his field. Like many of the men he sported some kind of beard—his was a sharp goatee, which he kept well-trimmed. The IGY had sent Gerard Fierle, a Weather Bureau recorder, to conduct vaguely parallel studies. But from the beginning it was obvious that Chief May was the man in charge, who knew what he was doing.

By the end of March, the meteorology program was fully underway. Chief May, Fierle, and three enlisted men had begun to take regular observations. The critical part of the program, the use of balloons and RAWINDSONDE equipment, had been tried twice on a trial-run basis; both times successfully. For the trials we had used bottled helium, but for regular observations we were to make our own gas. The program could not begin until the gas-producing building, or "inflation-shelter" was completed. This was done just before the end of the month.

The RAWINDSONDE system of measurement was quite complicated. It took four men to use this equipment, and measure weather conditions in the upper air.

A RAWINDSONDE system consists of a balloon-borne radiosonde, a receiving and tracking unit, and a recorder. The radiosonde unit transmits specific information about pressure, temperature, and humidity. These are amplified in the receiver so they can be recorded, and the recorder puts them in graphic form for permanent study.

The entire radiosonde unit is contained in a light-weight plastic box about six inches square, and, of course, it is sacrificed every time a balloon is released into the upper air.

On March 26, the meteorologists began their RAWINDSONDE observations, following a balloon up to more than 100,000 feet. Immediately, the station layout began to pose problems for the meteorologists. The balloon field was located south of the station. Unfortunately the prevailing winds were from the southeast, so the men always ran the danger of hitting a building with their balloon before it could get clear. This point had been made, quite strongly, to the SeaBees construction group; but they had paid no attention. Consequently, our balloon release program suffered. When winds were greater than twenty-five miles per hour, we lost many balloons, either in the buildings or tangled in the radio wires and lead-ins that dotted the station area. Eventually, we solved the problem by installing side doors in the inflation shelter itself. The aerologists could release the balloon by walking away from the station obstacles, such as antenna wires, ventilators and heating stacks before letting the balloon go. By the time it drifted over the station it was high enough not to get entangled. Under Chief May's supervision, the Navy aerologist's work day was twelve hours on and twelve hours off. They kept to this schedule for the entire time on the ice. The first break came only when the relief ship came in. They successfully completed 740 soundings with an average height of 89,000 feet.

The day after the successful RAWINDSONDE launching I was flabbergasted when Dr. Smith and Chief Spear came in to my quarters to ask if Spear could help Hugo Neuburg get the big D-5 tractor *out of a crevasse* down at the edge of the barrier. I had not known that it had fallen in a crevasse.

Despite all my preaching, the IGY men were still going directly to the men to get things done. I called Neuburg in to have a talk with him. Did he think, really, that he could get the big, fifteen-ton tractor out of the crevasse without my hearing about it?

He said yes, he had hoped to.

I reminded him of my warning when they had first taken the big tractor out, to tow the clutchless Sno-Cat down to the edge of the barrier for observations. At that time I had told him to be sure they had a long towing line, of some 400 or 500 feet, so the D-5 would always be able to stay far back on the barrier, towing the Sno-Cat at an angle. Neuburg also knew the area was full of crevasses, for I had opened one up for him one day. What he did not seem to know was that the commander of the unit should be kept informed of everything that occurred.

I let Spear take complete charge of bringing the tractor out of the crevases and back to camp. The IGY men were to take orders from him. Spear knew enough to stay away from the crevasses with any other equipment, and to use long cables of 150 feet or more, to hoist the 'Cat out of the hole.

Seismic operations had been limping along for some time, and as far as I was concerned, the tractor episode would just about put an end to them for the winter. The civilians had made far too many unnecessary mistakes and had cost us dearly in terms of time and material. The temperature was hovering in the mid-twenties below, and the cold wind continued to blow.

Spear and the others went off in one of the two thirty-five–ton tractors to try to rescue the D-5. About 10:00 o'clock that night the chief reported back to me. He had gotten the D-5 to the surface, out of a crevasse that was about five by seven feet wide, but they had no sooner started driving the thirty-five–ton tractor across the area than other crevasses began opening up. So they had left the Sno-Cat down on the barrier for the night—we were in the short period in which there is both day and night in the Antarctic—and would bring it back when it grew lighter the next day.

On March 30 the thermometer stood at −36°, and while Neuburg and Walker went out that day to do some surveying, it was getting pretty chilly to continue work outside. I met with McCarthy and Dr. Smith in the afternoon to work out some of the problems of changing over to winter schedule. It meant a greatly changed way of life. I appointed a recreation committee to take responsibility for the Recreation hall and manage everything within it. I also got the IGY men going on making a science building library and conference room. This involved relocating a few walls, and cutting a bit of space out of some of the sleeping quarters, but we all agreed that we needed the extra reading and meeting facilities. We had about 250 books and magazines for the library, but we intended to store office supplies and machinery there, too.

Winter schedule would give the men a great deal of time to kill, so it was important that we have all the facilities possible for their amusement and education. We laid plans to change working hours, meal hours, and just about everything else. The periods of light were growing shorter every day. Soon we would be living by the clock, in a world of constant night. It took some doing to cope with the drastic change in conditions we would face.

One problem we would have to solve immediately involved the use of the generators. Although five generators were installed in the same room, we could use only two of them because the large water tanks were blocking off the air supply to cool the other three. If we had to make use of the other three generators, we would be forced to move the big tanks—and that was quite a job. Worse, we had generator trouble. The governors did not work properly all the time, and sometimes one of the two generators seemed to be carrying all the load, and pulling the other as a motor. This caused violent fluctuations of voltage, from 110 to 280 sometimes—and the consequent burning out of equipment. My own record player burned out a condenser and an amplifier even before winter began. Radio tubes burned out often. Malville's aurora camera in the tower burned out one day when the voltage shot suddenly to 240. To control this, we would have to cut down on our use of electricity. There was one simple way to do it—stop using so many lights. In each tunnel we had five 100-watt lamps, when two would do. We would have to eliminate those extras, and more.

After my meeting with McCarthy and Dr. Smith, we decided to put winter schedule in effect on April 1. The meal hours were delayed an hour or so for both men and officers. On Sundays, instead of having regular meals we would serve brunch from 8:30 in the morning until noon, then supper as usual. To keep the camp shipshape, we would carry out a regular weekly inspection on Saturday mornings at 11:00.

We would keep the Recreation hall open twenty-four hours a day—as a trial. But curfew in the bunking areas was to be set at 11:00 P.M. If a man could not sleep, he had to go to the recreation hall to amuse himself, not to bother the others in his area. The generator watch would continue, twenty-four hours a day. In addition, we would have a sergeant-at-arms, who would carry an official badge, who would patrol the camp from 11:00 P.M. to 7:00 A.M. to enforce the sleeping rules.

We were to have work details as usual. The Bravo detachment would take care of the water details, filling the snow-melting machines every day. The VX-6 aviation unit was responsible for the fuel supply in the various heating units throughout the camp. As soon as the temperature had fallen to $-20°$, the fuel consumption of our jet heaters had doubled. Before, my own heater has consumed five gallons of oil every day, now it consumed ten gallons. The aviation men would have to spend three and a half hours every afternoon, rolling the fifty-two–gallon drums out of storage and filling the heaters from jerry-cans. We had no fuel problems, for we had no less than 6,000 drums of fuel, and even in the coldest weather were using it at the rate of about eight drums a day, or a yearly average of about three drums a day. Our supply was enough for five years.

Dr. Smith, who was in charge of the recreational program, began getting out the gear and study courses for the men. If they applied themselves, they could prepare for examinations that would let them rise in grade. The winter night certainly was the best time for a man who seriously wanted to advance himself, for he would have more uninterrupted hours for study than at any other time in his service life. The men were already beginning to study, even before the winter schedule officially became effective, for with the decrease in daylight hours and the virtual end of construction they had plenty of free time.

When Dr. Smith began to unpack the recreational gear, we found that the Navy had forgotten nothing for the entertainment of the "explorers." We had a wrestling mat, boxing gloves, weight-lifting equipment, even baseball bats and balls. We had tape recorders, record players and at least 1,000 records, from the finest operas to the latest songs of Perry Como and "hill-billy" music.

This array seemed to open the eyes of some of the prime complainers around the camp. One of the IGY men, Paul Walker, who until now had been loud and frequent in his complaints, came to me for a little chat.

"You know," he said, "when I think of all the small things our group was griping about aboard ship and after we got to the station, I can see how foolish it was. We have a finer set-up that anyone could dream about. Everything we need and still more. And your advice to us came through. The camp is all under cover. No more outside work. So the temperature can go down now, and the wind can blow."

I was gratified. It seemed that gradually they had begun to learn.

We were already getting involved in the things we wanted to do over the four months in which we would be in total darkness. After the movies every evening, Neuburg and Grobb, the baker, were playing German lessons on a record player. Dr. Smith was studying Spanish the same way. McCarthy started a course in typing, besides a heavy load of Navy courses he was taking for advancement. We had a large supply of kits in which you paint by numbers, and they were very popular. I had already painted a waste basket and a dinner plate, and had a tray in my quarters to start on. Besides, I had a project I had started in 1940 when I wintered over on Stonington Island—some small model dog sledges of hickory and rawhide. They were scaled down versions of the actual sledges I had used on all of my long sledge trips in the Antarctic.

We had no specific problems in establishment of a winter schedule, except the handling of religious services. We had seven practicing Catholics with us who would hold their own services. The rest would attend the non-sectarian services conducted by John Brown and Chief May, who was also a lay reader. We had no chaplain at the station; it was considered too small to justify such services, although second in size to Little America which had one. But we had a plentiful supply of religious records and devotional material.

When the winter schedule was posted, I saw more smiles around the camp than before. The cooks, in particular, were pleased with the schedule for it cut down on their long and difficult hours. They did not have to get up as early as before, since breakfast had been advanced nearly two hours. Altogether, as we began the "wintering in," the future looked somewhat brighter than it had in the first few weeks of adjustment by thirty-eight men new to conditions in the Antarctic. I was hopeful that we would get through the winter months without serious friction.

CHAPTER 8

WINTER ROUTINE

W HEN WE CAME TO THE ANTARCTIC IT WAS PLANNED THAT WE WOULD carry out our preparations for winter and our outdoor work in the fall—February, March and April. We would spend the winter night indoors, doing only those jobs that could be done without danger to ourselves or our equipment. Then, in the spring (perhaps in September) we would be able to begin working outside again, as the weather cleared and the light began to return. Since the pack ice will only permit ships to come and go during the summer season, this plan has always been adopted over the years by the continent's periodic inhabitants.

Under the best of conditions, life is different in the Antarctic. Every aspect of normal daily routine living processes require infinitely more thought and time. In slight drift, tools that one places on top of the snow will be completely buried within two minutes. Drifts around tents and buildings blow so high that it is necessary to shovel your way in and out of the entrances.

Your camera shutters stick. Motors and equipment develop bugs and sudden stoppages. Oil must be thinned or it will not flow at all. In —45° temperature, kerosene gets as thick as molasses.

Quite often, especially in the winter, men want to sit around a pot-bellied stove and relax unless they are next to one of the jet-heaters. Despite much hard manual labor, men probably have more time to relax, chat, sleep, read, or work on hobbies in the Antarctic than they will ever have in their lives.

Men eat up to 6,000 calories a day, about twice the amount of the usual military diet of 3,200 calories. Your diet is limited to those foods which will stand freezing without deterioration.

April 1 was the first day of our winter schedule. Everything seemed to work out well. The enlisted men were out of the messhall on time and the officers and IGY men were in. As usual, Skidmore did not get out of bed before I came into the science building. I had him over to the administration building for a short and private talk about his behavior. He set a poor example—which was important because it affected the behavior of the enlisted men.

But Skidmore was not the only one at fault. Within a few days the IGY men had slackened off so much that I had to call Thiel, Brown and Neuburg over for a discussion of the IGY men's work habits.

Thiel could see why it was necessary for the IGY men to follow the code, but Brown could not. All the civilians had been passed on by their respective IGY chiefs, back in the States, he said. Why couldn't the military leave them alone?

We had to have some kind of order. I told them that if they would not get up on time, I would put them on mess duty. Each man would serve three weeks—and that meant he would get up at 5:30 every morning. I had every right to do so, for Hugh Odishaw, the IGY executive secretary had indicated by written directives that the IGY civilians were to do their share of the housekeeping, including messhall duty.

Thiel wanted to be sure that would include all the officers, except McCarthy and myself. When I told him it would be, he was satisfied.

The result of this meeting was temporary improvement.

As April began, the sun was not entirely down. Although we were on a winter schedule, Thiel had some hope of continuing to take a few seismic shots before the weather closed in. When the temperature was $-24°$, we did not feel the cold at all, we had become so used to the mercury in the $-30°$s. But April had hardly gotten started when the wind began to blow. It hit 35 miles an hour in the beginning. As a result, all the entrances to the doors and tunnels were beginning to drift within hours. This particular day the temperature was only $-16°$, but it was far too cold and nasty for anyone to work outside.

This was not a real blow. Had the camp not been completed, we would have survived. But I was grateful for the luck that had let us finish the camp before even this "mild" winter began.

When the weather turned, we opened the science library, which gave the men a chance to read up on the reason for being in the Antarctic during this year. The recreation hall, immediately, became the center of activity of the entire camp. Pool, ping-pong, and bowling took the place of outdoor work. Those who were not playing games were listening to records, reading or building models.

McCarthy mentioned again that the VX-6 group would like to set up their own "lounge" in one of the Jamesway huts.

"Sure," I said, "why don't you have them move one of the small huts to the rear of the rec-hall for easy access?"

The "fly-boys" had the Jamesway relocated the next day. Here, they enjoyed all the recreation gear provided and used it frequently during the entire winter, particularly for weight-lifting and some boxing. Other than VX-6 personnel, only our cook, Davis and corpsman Mathis, who very seldom watched the evening movies, probably used it more than the others for a nightly workout.

For some reason or other, our radio was still not working at the beginning of April. Something was wrong with the transmitter and the tuning of the antenna. While Chief Kent worked hard at it, he had difficulty finding the trouble. As always, this made everyone edgy, for messages were piling up. More, in the Antarctic, where radio is the *only* link with the outside world, the word that there are bugs in the system puts every man on guard.

It's as if the lifeline had a frayed strand.

Life was even more complicated at this particular time, because Chief Kent, our communications man, also had the fire alarm system to install.

Kent had been given the job two weeks before. Still it remained undone. Rather, when his schedule was changed from night to day, he complained. I had not realized it at the time, but the problem was a simple and typical Navy problem: Kent just hated change.

Dr. Smith was Kent's immediate superior. He had informed the chief of the change after we had decided on it in our staff meeting. But apparently, Dr. Smith had not used the greatest of tact. He had told Kent of the change *in writing*. It sounds like a small matter, but Kent read something ominous into the written orders. He balked. First, Kent complained, the note did not specify any time off for lunch, and he had no other authorization from Dr. Smith to have a meal in the middle of the day.

It was the most childish kind of thinking, but it affected our lives, immediately and seriously. In two weeks, Kent worked on the fire alarm system for about four hours, and did nothing else.

At the end of two weeks, we had Kent in to the administration office to see what was wrong. He had no excuse: He said he had underestimated the time necessary. I gave him seventy-two hours in which to have the system installed and be ready for a fire drill. We also had to provide him with written instructions that he was entitled to have a meal in the middle of the day—just like everyone else.

That same day we had to face other problems of discipline and camp management. Cox, the photographer, was upset, because the ionosphere and aurora men wanted to develop their own negatives. He had asked me to be sure he was allowed to do *all* the photo work. Since this was a ticklish problem, I decided to sit on it for a while, and see how the present system worked out, with Malville and Brown using Cox' equipment in the photo-lab. So far, it seemed to me that the two IGY men had cooperated fully with Cox.

Apparently Cox brooded on the problem, and decided he was being mistreated. Late one night he burst into the administration building and created quite a fuss. He wanted to see McCarthy, but McCarthy would not talk to him until he was in a calmer frame of mind.

The same day that we handed Kent his ultimatum on the fire alarm system, McCarthy banned Cox from the movies for two weeks.

Then, we had to solve the problem of the washing machine.

Machines had been placed in the enlisted men's head and in the civilian and officers head. But the enlisted men were very careless. Within two weeks after our arrival they had let their machine break down. Chief Spear had taken our *only* spare and installed it in the crew's head. With all the thousands of tons of supplies, it was strange that we were so short in the housekeeping equipment that would receive the hardest wear, but that was the way it was, and we would have to make the best of it.

The men did not seem to care. Spear told us they expected to use the machine in the officer's head if theirs broke down, so a notice was installed in the men's head:

Notice: The only spare washing machine we had is now installed
         here. If this machine breaks down like the first one—
         through misuse—please note—each man will then launder
         his clothing by hand. No other spares available.
4 April 1957

Strange order, and strange form for an order for the first time in the remote continent's history. But regardless of its newly acquired luxuries this was the Antarctic where little problems suddenly became immense, as the winter night closed in.

With the end of outside work, the men turned their entire working day into a long coffee break. So we were forced to limit them to one twenty-minute period in the galley in the morning and a similar time in the afternoon. Otherwise, the galley crew had no time to wash up and prepare meals.

And finally, within a week after we began our winter schedule, the men had turned the recreation hall upside down. McCarthy ordered them to clear out the beer cans and trash, and to put an end to the constant drinking parties in the room. This had gone on almost every night for the past four weeks.

The weather continued to be spotty. Some days were good enough that the scientists could get out and work. Thiel was able to make a few more of his sounding shots.

Brown and Skidmore had been experiencing a great deal of difficulty in getting their program started. First was the incident of the eighty-foot mast, which nearly caused a casualty. Once the mast was guyed in place, I could see that its supporting wires were not strong enough to guarantee

110

the mast against snapping during the winter winds. It took Brown some weeks to install the proper strengthening cables.

Most disappointing was the shortage of equipment for this particular program. Some of the parts were not even ordered, so Brown improvised. No sheathing material was supplied to bring his antennas inside from the high pole, so he used a stovepipe, and it worked.

The failure to include an operating manual for the ionospheric recorder was by far the most serious problem. For hours, Brown studied the machine and tried to figure out how to make it work, but he could not. Matters were complicated further by the erratic performance of our radio communication with the outside world.

Before the first of April we had all the equipment in place, but the recorder would still not operate. We had tried to arrange a radio voice schedule between Brown and Hans Bengaard, the ionospheric specialist at Little America, to see if he had the technical advice we were missing. But while I kept after the radio man three times a day to arrange the contact, we seemed to miss each time.

Finally, Brown prepared a long message which was dispatched to Bengaard, stating the specific difficulties. We were able to get this out and a few days later received a reply. As a result, Brown was able to put the machine in operation. Then, the machine itself offered us a new difficulty. Every fifteen minutes, for fifteen seconds it blacked out our radio shack. We could neither send nor receive. Fifteen seconds does not sound like much, but it forced us to work around this time constantly, and added another hazard to our already tenuous radio operations.

We had to do two things to shore ourselves up against such difficulties: Keep a sense of humor, and remember all the time that we were down in the Antarctic to accomplish specific missions. If we could keep those in mind, we would be all right.

One trouble, of course, was that many of the men did not have the slightest idea what all the scientific work was about, and were not interested enough to make an effort to find out.

Everything about the ionosphere, I must admit, scared most of the men off in the beginning. The very term sounds complicated, and its concept has worried men since that day more than three-quarters of a century ago when the British physicist Balfour Stewart suggested that somewhere in the upper atmosphere there was a layer of air that conducted electricity—and thus caused the earth's magnetic field to fluctuate each day.

Little attention was paid to Stewart's suggestion until 1924, when a pair of British scientists found and definitely located the ionosphere. In 1925 scientists of the Carnegie Institute in Washington and the U.S. Navy sent short pulses of radio waves straight up into the atmosphere, and caught echoes of them miles away on an oscillograph. This was the first use of the principle of radar.

111

Scientists found that the ionosphere is a thick mantle of ionized air, which consists of four different layers, in the region from forty-five miles to 200 miles above the ground. Its electrical properties come from free electrons and ionized atoms and molecules, the ionization caused by ultraviolet radiation from the sun.

The ionosphere behaves something like an ocean, responding to the gravitational tugs of the sun and moon in the same way. Occasionally it is beset by great storms, and by other disturbances that disrupt communications, for radio waves are carried and reflected by the ionosphere.

The instrument used to explore the ionosphere is called an ionosonde —a radio pulse transmitter and a receiver that picks up the echoes. The echoes are shown on a cathode ray oscillioscope and photographed.

During the International Geophysical Year, the major emphasis in the ionospheric program was placed on systematic ionosonde recording, at a number of stations all over the world. One project was to measure the ionospheric absorbtion of radio waves. There was to be a station at the South Pole, but our station, too, was an important link in the internation chain.

The fall weather was treacherous, and none of us went out alone, if we were moving outside the camp area. Early in April, Lieutenant Commander McCarthy, Dr. Smith and I took a skiing trip down to the old ship's landing, for the purpose of getting some exercise and to take a look at the ice conditions at the landing site as the winter night drew near. It was a mild day. The thermometers registered 15° above zero, and the meteorologists told me that the night before the temperature had gone up to 24° above zero, but that within a few hours, it could conceivably fall to −35°. Chief May would let me know—and he was usually accurate.

On our trip to the barrier edge the overcast turned into a "white-out," a condition of glare and atmosphere in which we could not even see our own ski-tracks. On the way over the hill and down to the landings McCarthy fell twice, because he could not see ahead. Only a handful of the old trail flags and the hawsers tied to the buried "dead-men" gave indications that once there were two great ships with hundreds of men unloading on the ice edge. About 200 feet from the shelf ice edge, we did see what we thought was a seal, on the edge of the sea ice. Beside him a ten-foot–wide lead of open water zig-zagged toward the open sea, but except for a few leads, the entire cove was frozen over.

I had brought my camera along in hopes of photographing the pressure ridges that rise alongside the barrier, but the wind had been from the south pretty steadily, and the pack ice had been pushed about two miles north, off-shore. There was nothing particularly spectacular to photograph. Since the skiing was both unpleasant and dangerous under these conditions, we retraced our tracks as best we could, and made our way back to camp.

The first Saturday after we started the winter schedule we began the regular Saturday inspection. Our routine was so relaxed that if we did not maintain this rudimentary measure of orderliness we should soon have found the camp a shambles.

The military men all showed considerable respect for the "Captain's Inspection," and stood at attention when McCarthy, Smith, and I came into the barracks. Even the civilians straightened out their belongings for the occasion. All the building spaces were clean and orderly and most of the accumulated trash had been taken away. Both bunkhouses were in good shape, and the galley was spotlessly clean.

But the military atmosphere was not complete. When I came into the galley for breakfast, I found only three men there. In the science building I found all the civilians in their bunks. Some of the IGY men had misunderstood the Saturday morning routine, and thought it was a holiday. But Dr. Thiel assured us it would not happen again.

For the good of the individual, as well as the entire complement, it is imperative to fight the lethargy which begins to overtake many at the outset of the winter night.

After inspection Saturday really was holiday routine.

At that time I took my weekly bath—a real luxury compared to the old days with Byrd and even on my own expedition. Then we used a small basin full of warm water to sponge ourselves. Now we had a regular shower with hot and cold running water.

From the snow-melting plant in the washroom and "head," water ran through a pump which forced it into two spigots over the sink, two outlets for the automatic washing machine, and into the shower, too. It was just like home—except for a few things.

Every time I went to take a shower, I had to first chip an inch-thick block of ice off the shower drain with a hammer, and then pour steaming water down the opening of the pipe far enough to unfreeze the drain. The head, just like everything else, was built on top of our 800-foot–thick ice shelf. There was no way to keep cold air from backing through the pipe when the shower was not in use. But by winter we had a real luxury, a wooden grill on which we could stand. Before, we had stood on the bare sheet metal shower floor, exposed to the huge sno-pit underneath— and that was pretty cold no matter how hot the water got.

This Saturday, like every other, I undressed completely in my room, put on a lined parka and felt or sheepskin flying boots and rushed across the "street" to the head. The temperature on this Saturday was −25°—a little chilly when you are not wearing many clothes.

Then I went to lunch, and afterward, McCarthy and I played a game of pool. That was all the activity until evening when we had our daily movie.

This particular Saturday night we had a minor incident. Greaney, the aviation electrician who showed the movies stood up before the screening to make a little speech.

He said he was tired of catching hell from the cooks in the galley because of the mess that was left after the showing, by a certain group—he obviously meant the civilians and officers. If the messhall wasn't cleaned up after each showing, he added, he would quit running the projector!

On Sunday, now that we had started religious services, I was interested to see how many men would turn out. Only six or seven of the Protestants turned up for the services conducted by Mr. Brown and Chief May, but all the practicing Catholics—seven of them—attended special services of their own in the dispensary.

But if the church services were badly attended, the beer mess certainly was not. One of the men showed up on Sunday morning sporting a really terrible hangover. When I asked him if he had drunk too much beer he said yes, that he had drunk plenty.

"I always drink plenty when I want to feel good," he said.

Thirty-six cans of beer! How they could pour that stuff into their bodies is more than I can imagine. But at least we had enough of it with us. One whole side of a fuel tunnel was stacked to the top, so was an entire side of the main tunnel, and we had an entire Jamesway hut full of beer.

Sundays were really rest days for the men who felt up to doing anything but sleeping. Excepted, of course, was the weather unit. But on Monday we got back to our jobs. The weather was fine enough for us to get one of the planes in the air on a local flight for two hours just to keep the pilots in trim. It wasn't necessary for flight time. The Navy waived the monthly requirement beginning April 1, so the men would not be penalized during the night hours, when it would be impossible to fly.

By April 8 the sun was getting so low we could tell we would be in total darkness in a few days. Dr. Thiel took his last seismic shots of the season, and we put his Sno-Cat away until spring. I told them to pull the 'Cat into the garage with block and tackle, but instead someone got the idea that it would be easier to push the 'Cat in with the big D-4. The result was a puncture in the cabin, which meant we would have to weld a plate on the outside of the cabin to seal it, if the IGY men were to use that Sno-Cat in the inland spring traverse that was planned.

After the Sno-Cat had remained in the garage overnight, we finally got down to taking the clutch apart to see what damage had been done weeks before when the IGY men burned it out. The IGY men did the job themselves. Davis, the mechanic, told them how to do it, but by 6:00 P.M. the job still was not finished.

Finally, the clutch came out. It was badly burned. The discs were burned out beyond further use, so were the finger guides and roller bearings. What we needed, Davis said, was a new clutch. That meant a load of fifty pounds for someone.

Major Lassiter with an Air Force unit consisting of two C-47 airplanes and a crew of ten would be coming in, but I hated to ask him to bring the clutch because of his own weight problems. Perhaps it could be sent to McMurdo next spring, and be flown in from there, "when and if . . ."

This was a sticky problem that IGY authorities in Washington would have to solve. We had two Sno-Cats for the traverse party, but Neuburg's glaciology crew had first priority on the second one, and Neuburg was violently opposed to transferring the clutch in the brand-new 'Cat into the machine fitted up with the seismology instruments. And I could not blame him.

It was no crisis at the moment, but we would have to come to some agreement by spring. Thiel could not do any more seismic shooting with the Sno-Cat in its present condition. He would have to be able to drive it, without having a fifteen-ton tractor pull him around as he had in the fall. There were just too many crevasses around the area, and in the spring they would be covered with fresh falls and drifts of snow. I could not risk the tractor and the life of the driver.

The radio—at last—was beginning to operate normally. That night I was able to send a radio message to Washington explaining that unless we had delivery of a new clutch by air the traverse would have to be curtailed. We were beginning to establish communication with other bases and Navy stations on a regular basis, and our "ham" station was beginning to get messages through to the United States. As soon as Chief Kent finished his fire alarm system, he planned to go back on the night schedule and spend most of his time operating the ham station, to keep the boys in touch with their families and friends.

He had the fire alarm system completed by Wednesday, April 10, luckily, for early that morning a fire broke out in the men's head.

The hot water heater blew up, and started the fire. Luckily the alarm box was straight overhead. The heat from the fire gave the signal to the generator room, where the man on duty could tell immediately the exact location of the fire, by the number of the tab that fell down. He ran over and put out the fire with an extinguisher.

Unfortunately, however, no one thought to secure the washing machine. Someone came in later and started the machine. When the hot-water heater had blown up, the snow-melting system had stopped working, so there was no water at all. When the washing machine began running, it burned out the pump.

It was a serious accident, but not as serious as it might have been. We had other hot-water heaters, and it was possible to repair the washing machine pump. Within twenty-four hours both were back in operating condition.

Less than two weeks after we went on winter schedule the weather

115

became totally unpredictable. One day the temperature was −35°, and the next it was 5° above zero. At the same time, we could feel lucky we were not at the South Pole, with Paul Siple and his party. When it was 5° at Ellsworth Station, Siple reported a new record for cold in the Antarctic — −84° —and this was not even winter!

With all the recreation equipment in the world, our problems of keeping the men happy seemed to grow worse instead of better. The enlisted men were hardest to satisfy. The trouble was that they had so much of everything and so many conveniences that they seemed to be lost. They were living two and three men to a room; some of them even had single rooms. Electric lights were on twenty-four hours a day. They had a recreation room, indoor toilets, hot and cold running water, and the best food in the world. Yet the complaining was far more severe than it had ever been in my first wintering over, with Byrd at Little America, when we had none of these luxuries.

The movies were not as much help in keeping up morale as I had hoped. Most of them were Westerns, and it did not take long for them to become tiresome. As interest waned, the men stopped showing up. Instead, they got together to play cards in the evenings in their bunkhouse recreation areas, and even when they were sitting around drinking beer and working on model kits—during working hours—they complained.

In mid-April the men had their monthly "whisky" party on Saturday night in which they drank eleven bottles, issued by the doctor. This was a common procedure especially established for those wintering at the Antarctic bases only. Otherwise, liquor is not permitted aboard naval ships, but due to our severe and isolated location an exception had been made. An uncounted amount of beer was also consumed at the party. Beer, of course, is a regular Naval Exchange Store item, and for sale at all Antarctic bases as it would be at military installations everywhere.

I stayed up until 2:00 o'clock on Sunday morning in the radio shack trying to get a phone-patch to talk home. The reception was good and I heard a station in Arlington, Virginia, coming in clear. When I went to bed some of the men were still at it in the recreation hall.

In the galley for breakfast the next morning, I found that only three men had been there before me. It was 9:30, but the settlement was as quiet as if it has been 5:30 A.M. It must have been a big night.

Later that day, I talked to one of the men on mess duty, when the subject of morale was raised.

"If there is no bitching," he said, "it is a sure sign that it is not a good ship."

If that's the criterion, I thought, we were in the best and healthiest camp in the whole Antarctic!

CHAPTER 9

ON ICE

T HOSE WHO HAVE NEVER WINTERED IN THE ANTARCTIC OFTEN HAVE the idea such isolated expeditions act as one big happy team in order to survive. Actually, individuals are quite often extremely selfish and will corner the market on specific items of community property. The smaller the group, the better the chance for harmony since each individual becomes more dependent on the other fellow for the attainment of his work and comfort. With thirty-nine men, Ellsworth Station was the second largest IGY station, Little America being the central control station.

Little America having the top Naval officer in the Antarctic, Càptain William Dickey, had the power to bring violators to court and give punishment. He did that during the winter, and as a result there was much more respect for law and order and they did not have the same disciplinary problems as at the other smaller bases.

April was not very far along before it became obvious that Skidmore was going to become a personal problem. He was doing a good job, and was quite capable in his work. In the beginning, he had been of more help than many of the Navy men because of his electrical experience and his willingness to tackle some difficult jobs of construction. But Skidmore had an unfortunate faculty of rubbing men the wrong way. Before many weeks were up he had been in serious arguments with several of the IGY men, and some of the Navy personnel.

He had already been spoken to several times about staying away from the enlisted men's mess where he had made a nuisance of himself while they were eating. He had a habit of monopolizing the hi-fi record player in the Recreation hall, too— although this was not much worse than some of the officers, who made off with camp equipment to their own quarters and took the best model kits for their own enjoyment.

There were men, however, who were strong and mature enough to

117

resist the more obvious human frailities. Chief Walter May kept the meteorological program going continuously without interruption. He had a good sense of humor, and was among the best liked in the group. I spent many pleasant hours in his company, learned to know of his experiences and his ambitions for the future.

Chief Albert Spear was another example of the typical Navy Chiefs, who as a group were by far the most stable men in our community. With his pleasant personality, Spear was always willing to assist wherever possible. He did more than his share of work at the station and ranks among the top expeditioners I have known during my lifetime in exploration and four winterings.

First Class Photographer Walter Cox did a particularly good job covering all of our activities in both still and movies. Where action was expected, he was always on the go—day and night regardless of the low temperatures. His colored movies taken at the penguin rookery were superb and copies of them were much in demand. One of his stills of a mother penguin cuddling her chick later appeared in Life Magazine.

One of the two who passed the Chief's examination was our Commissary steward Edward Davis. In his quiet, serious hard-working way he provided us with a good variety of food three times a day. His more lively partner, Richard Grobb, one of our avid participants in the Saturday night "jamborees," furnished us with a plentiful supply of bake products to satisfy even the most sophisticated taste. Both men retired early in the evening because they had to be the first on their feet in the morning. Their assistant Melvis Mathis, the hospital corpsman-turned-cook, was the sea-going lawyer type with a legal mind and view about everything that went on. For a while he seriously considered suing Dr. Smith for some infringement he claimed against him. Mathis used the legal terms of a criminal trial lawyer and hoped to study law upon return. He will be a good one.

The second man to pass the Chief's examination was Walter Davis, our versatile mechanic. He held forth in the garage where he could be found working to midnight on many an occasion during the latter part of the winter. He was a sturdy citizen, dependable and had a good sense of humor. Davis had much to occupy his long working days. Twice daily, during the roughest weather, with temperatures and wind that would force many a seasoned polar man to seek shelter, he drove the fifteen-ton tractor over the station area, filling the snow-melters. To my knowledge, he did not miss filling snow for the melters a single day; and he is a man the Navy can be proud of.

Electrician James Hannah was a quiet fellow, part Cherokee Indian, who worked conscientiously to keep the generators, the life-blood of all our activities, humming. The ping-pong games I had with him in the Recreation hall were always spiked by keen competition and only on the week-end nights did he join the "jamborees" for a spree.

118

Utilityman James Ray also bordered toward the sea-going lawyer type. He was willing and capable of tackling any discussion that arose. He performed all his work very well and looked forward to his impending retirement from the Navy when he planned to go out on his own.

Then there were others whose steady devotion to duty kept our camp maintenance repair functions at a minimum.

There were many nevertheless who gave me constant headaches.

One night in mid-April I heard it blowing hard all the night long. The next morning I noticed that several of our tunnels were filling with snow. The machine-equipment tunnel had a wide crack in it. I called a meeting of the IGY men and asked them to shovel the snow out of their own area before it became deep and dangerous. Thiel said they could not do it. They were all too busy.

I am afraid I got hot under the collar at that. I told them that every man at the station had specific housekeeping duties, including night watches, while the IGY men stood around trying to appear busy. Then I used the single weapon I found to be effective with them. I threatened them with three weeks of mess duty. So far, I had not tried to force it on them, because they were unwilling and because I wanted to help their scientific efforts as much as possible. But we could not have a total breakdown of discipline at the station. If they would not co-operate in the management of the camp, we would have to take more drastic steps.

They shoveled the snow that day, complaining every minute.

Despite the irresponsibility of the IGY men—and partly because of it —I felt it necessary to do something to assure success of the overland traverse planned for the following spring. Unless we wanted the trip to fail, fall and winter was the time to take action—not during the few days of spring, just before it would be time to start the trip.

We had several alternatives. If the clutch for the Sno-Cat could not be flown in, the men could take a weasel and a large sled to haul their supplies. But if they did this, they should get rid of the huge ten-man tent they were now planning to use. Only five were scheduled to go on the traverse. Why they had a ten-man tent I will never know. When they used it on the bay ice it must have weighed 300 pounds with frost on it. Not only was it bulky, and heavy, but it was extremely difficult for the men to handle in the wind.

We would have to make a five-man tent for them in the camp if they wanted to make a change. That could be done, if we were given adequate time. In the event it should become desirable, I made a drawing of a tent for the traverse group based on the available tent-material we had in camp. Thiel seemed to like the idea, but Neuberg sneered when he saw it.

There was still a possibility we could get a new clutch. We had radioed headquarters to consider having Lassiter's Air Force group bring it down when he came. Secondly, we would try to barter with the British in the event they had a spare clutch since all the 'Cats were the same kind. The third possibility would be to institute a special plane flight from Little America as soon as the weather cleared. Each alternative presented problems. The Air Force group would be setting out from the United States with a full load of equipment in their planes. On long over-ocean flights, an extra forty or fifty pounds of weight can be very important. It means just that much less gas.

The British, even if they had a spare clutch, might feel they ought to keep it. What happened to us might happen to them, too.

Little American could well refuse to send a plane over on such a mission. Airplane gas was scarce. In all the supplies brought down, we did not bring an adequate supply of high-octane fuel. Already a request had gone out on the radio for an additional 1,000 drums of aviation fuel to be brought in by the supply ship the following year.

After my warning, the IGY men seemed to show some improvement—but not very much. They would shovel their own snow, and they would do work that definitely concerned them. But they would do little for anyone else, or for the common good. The tunnel into my quarters connected with theirs, and they shoveled to the connection with the main tunnel—not one foot farther. I shoveled my own. Further, since no one else in camp seemed willing to do so, I shoveled off the walk to the Recreation hall. It was dangerous. Ice had formed there, and someone might fall and break a bone.

Easter Sunday, April 21, the sky above us was clear, but the horizon was completely closed in by heavy clouds. The days were so short now they hardly existed as such. On April 25, according to Hugo Neuburg's calculations, the sun would disappear for the winter, to remain hidden until August 22.

I had been worried about the way McCarthy insisted on storing the airplanes, and walked over to the aviation buildings to take a look. No damage had occurred so far, although the planes were bedded in drifts of snow that had packed inside their revetments of boxes. The men had dug the snow off the tops of the wings, so there was no strain on them yet.

High, hard snowdrifts had moved in all around the camp. April 20 we still had not had a real blow. From the south side, it would appear that the entire station was underground, for the drifts were steep. From any point one could walk up a ramp of snow to the roof of the buildings.

My regular work day began now when I got up at 8:20 in the morning: Breakfast for officers and civilians began at 8:30 under the winter schedule. Before going to bed at night I would look at the room temperature which hovered between 60° and 65°, and set the jet heater down to 50°. In the morning, inside temperatures had almost always fallen below 50°, so the jet heater was on. I dressed quickly and went directly to the galley after getting up. Usually six or seven others were ahead of me, sitting glumly at the long mess tables, all in heavy beards save Brown and Thiel.

I would say "Good Morning," but seldom got a reply, and then go to my usual spot at the end of the table. Breakfast for me consisted of some citrus juice, oatmeal, scrambled eggs and a special, strong cup of coffee the cooks made for me. Others ate steaks, and hotcakes, and eggs for breakfast, but I tried to keep my eating habits in check.

After breakfast I stopped by the Radio room to see what radio traffic had come in, then back to my own quarters where I brushed my teeth from the gallon thermos jug of water I kept there. After that I worked in my room until 12:50, then to lunch.

Every Monday, McCarthy and I had the washing machine for our use. I didn't have enough laundry to justify using it alone every week, and neither did McCarthy.

After lunch, McCarthy and I usually played pool or ping-pong for a half hour, then back again to work in my room. In the room I listened to fine music—O My Beloved Father, by Puccini, the Habanera from Carmen, O Star of Eve from Tannhauser, Intermezzo from Cavalleria Rusticana.

These melodies along with others came from records in the Recreation hall. I recorded them on my own tape machine, and could thus play for hours without changing record or tape. Under the isolated and morose conditions in which I found myself, spending so much time by myself, music helped to pass the time.

The life of a leader is a lonely one. I certainly experienced that loneliness to the fullest, particularly because none of the men with me were selected by me, nor were any of my age and temperament.

With the background of music, I worked on camp affairs again until 3:30, when I went to the messhall for coffee and cake, an old and pleasant Norwegian custom. The others had coffee time for twenty minutes at 10:30 and 3:00 each day. I tried not to go out at their time, so I would not put a damper on their "breaks."

After my afternoon break, I went back to work again until 5:40, when I got ready for supper. At 6:10 we usually went to the Recreation hall for another game of some kind, and then I went back to the room until 7:10 when they called me for the movie. At 9:00 I might stop by the Recreation hall or the science building for a while before coming back to my quarters. Then, I took an evening trip to the galley and radio shack, usually between 10:30 and 11:00 P.M. From 11:00, back either to work or play records until 11:30 or 12:00, and then to bed.

We began to be plagued by the kind of minor and relatively unimportant shortages that seem so important in the Antarctic. Chief Spear was seriously concerned about the great rate at which our lightbulbs were going. I told him to find all he could around camp that were not actually

121

needed and confiscate them—thus cutting down on extra bulb use, too. On top of the wooden slats across the roof structure in Skidmore's room, Spear found cartons of lightbulbs, which someone said had "accidentally" been placed in Skidmore's belongings.

Then we learned that we had burned out all the exciter tubes for the motion picture projector. Neuburg and Greaney managed to solder a small flashlight bulb to the socket, with a mirror behind it to provide the sound and it worked fairly well. It was not as good as the real thing, but we had to make it do.

With the careless smoking habits of most of the men, I became seriously worried about the danger of fire. I made a sign and warning notice about fire, and asked McCarthy to post it on the bulletin board, for we could not be too careful on that point. I also gave him a memo, and a request to clear the gear out of the main tunnel, so the passage would be totally unobstructed.

On my way to lunch that day I looked for my notice about the fire hazard on the bulletin board, but did not find it. I was mildly annoyed with McCarthy, for I thought he had failed to put it up. But when he came into the messhall he said he had put it on the board. Someone had removed it. And the only reason they could have taken it was sheer malice. I prepared another notice.

At this period, I noticed a kind of passive resistance creeping into the camp, and it troubled me. It reminded me of a phenomenon with which I was only too familiar from my earlier expeditions into the isolation of the Antarctic. We had given it the name of "Antarctic Fever" for that was pretty much what it was. After being isolated for some time with the same people and in the same environment men will become listless in their attention to duties, will want to sleep more than is necessary and will find grievance in the smallest thing which goes wrong. I suppose this is as true of expeditions any place where the same conditions prevail.

The first example of this came in the clearing of the tunnels. I pointed out to my officers that the tunnels were a fire hazard and that all of them should be cleared. McCarthy and Smith agreed. I told McCarthy to get at the main tunnel and the meteorology tunnel, where equipment was stacked high along the sides, and the passages were often obstructed. McCarthy said he would have it done, but days went by and nothing happened. He had agreed, but did nothing. I asked Lieutenant Smith to get the job done. He, too, agreed but again nothing happened.

It was the same with the problem of the photo lab. Malville, the aurora man, needed film development facilities. So I told Dr. Smith to get Davis in there immediately and complete the plumbing.

This lassitude bothered me, until I found a logical explanation for it.

The men of the Navy party were bogged down in the monotony. There was nothing to stimulate them in their work at the station. They had no program of exploration, no plan of which they were a part. All they were supposed to do was "support" the sluggish IGY men in their work. The whole set-up was just not practical, from the standpoint of relationship between military and civilian personnel.

Even our radio installation was not completely hooked up. I had asked Chief Kent to begin working the transmitter we had hooked up for the fifteen-meter band, but the Chief said he did not have the aerial up yet. Night after night Kent had been sitting up playing his bag-pipes, working on ship models, copying poetry—doing anything and everything but completing his radio installation. It would seem that everyone was falling prey to "Antarctic Fever."

Finally, I had reached a point where something just had to be done— and quickly. On the morning of April 26 I went to Chief Spear myself and told him I was on the war-path and wanted some action on the tunnels right that minute.

"Get me the men," Spear said calmly.

I said I would in five minutes, and went out to look for them. I began ordering them out of their bunks.

By 10:00 o'clock the work was well in progress. Spear got all hands going in the tunnel clearing that morning, and by afternoon we had the job done. We took one break, at 11:00 o'clock, when the sun was on the horizon, ready to dip for the last time not to be seen again until the latter part of August. All hands went off for their cameras and shot pictures before lunch.

The sun had actually dipped below the horizon the day before. What we saw was a reflection, or mirage of the sun. Through a smoked glass it appeared that there were three horizontal lines. The lower line was the line of the sun, the middle was the true horizon, and the upper line was also a mirage, similar to the lower line.

Those of us who braved the temperatures of the middle sixties below with an eighteen-mile wind sweeping the surface witnessed a most beautiful sight. The whole northern half of heaven was aflame in crimson colors ranging from red to bluish-red. We were now encased by winter's cold and severe storms or blizzards except for a few hours of twilight the first week or so.

The main trouble was that the officers were equally affected by the "Antarctic Fever" and appeared to be falling down on the job. We could not get much out of the enlisted men if the officers did not first snap out of their lethargy. It was not setting a good example for officers to sleep until noon when they expected the men to be on the go at 8:00 o'clock.

There was some protest about my abrupt action. Dr. Smith came wandering into my quarters while the men were clearing the tunnel and asked that we stop moving his medical supplies. He wanted to do it himself "later on." I had had enough of these "later ons" and rejected the request. He had made no move to get the supplies out of the tunnel for weeks. Now we would get them out for him. I found a space for the supplies and told the men to get them in there.

During the clearing of the tunnel, we found the ten-man tent the IGY men were planning to use on their spring traverse—frozen into a misshapen and unmanageable bundle. The IGY men had obviously thrown it together after they were through practicing with it in the fall, and had dumped it, wet, into the tunnel. What a mess it was.

I told Thiel to get the tent into the garage, hang it up, melt the ice and let it dry; and inspect it when it was dry to be sure there were no tears in the fabric.

"Where are we going to store it then?" Thiel asked.

"I don't give a damn where you put it!" I told him.

How those scientists would ever get into the field—let alone survive there—was a wonder to me. I had never seen such impractical men in all my years of exploring.

Finally, after much conversation, Thiel, Neuburg and young Behrendt dragged the tent toward the garage. That was all I could do about it, so I went back to overseeing the men.

We were now well along on the winter IGY program in all departments. Davis had taken the tractor out to erect the Whistler mast, which was about thirty-five–feet high, made of wooden poles bolted together in three parts. The Whistler program was to be conducted by Brown, the ionospheric physicist, and Skidmore, his assistant.

Whistlers, a relatively newcomer in our knowledge of the world around us, are special low-frequency radio signals traveling in space. They are hard to track because of their low frequency, but they are believed to be caused by energy from lightning flashes in the northern hemisphere. Their power ranged from 1,000 to 1,000,000 volts, and they traveled along the lines of the earth's magnetic fields. After striking earth at the Antarctic, the energy is reflected back, it is believed, to the point of origin—along the same track. During the travel the energy gives off audible whistles.

The job at Ellsworth Station was to record signals that originated at a matched point in the Labrador area, both points being equidistant from their respective geomagnetic poles.

There was nothing mysterious about our program of work with the Whistlers. . . . It was our station's job to record them, on equipment that amplified them 1,000,000 times and then record them on magnetic tape. Ellsworth was chosen as the only Antarctic station to record the "whistlers" because of its specific location to their point of origin—the northern hemisphere origin at Nova Scotia, or even New Hampshire.

At the end of the IGY program, recordings at Ellsworth and recordings at the northern Labrador station that were taken simultaneously would be correlated and the interval of time in travel would be determined. Previous experiments at Alaska and New Zealand proved that the strange, melodic whistling sounds do bounce back and forth. The actual time in those experiments was recorded as 2.2 seconds for the wave to bounce from almost one end of the earth to the other.

Our scientists were studying another phenomenon, too: Audio-frequency radio waves that did not appear to originate within the earth's atmosphere. These were known as the "dawn-chorus," for they were strongest at local dawn. They sounded very much like the phenomenon known as "spring peepers" in New England. Our physicist thought there was a definite connection between Whistlers and dawn-chorus sounds. A strange pair of noises—I found when I listed to both. The "Whistlers" were melodic, starting high and ranging up and down the scale. The "dawn-chorus" surely did sound like a whole group of singers.

Brown was the chief ionospheric physicist, but Skidmore took a proprietary interest in the Whistler program, while Brown's chief interest was ionospheric recording with the sounder he had struggled so hard to put in operation.

All around the station, the scientists probably did their best work during the winter period, for the strangeness of Antarctic life wore off a bit, and they had fewer distractions than they had either in the spring or fall of the year.

Brown spent a good deal of the day at the ionospheric sounder, a complicated instrument that stood six feet high, four feet wide and three feet deep. It weighed 2,700 pounds, and was so heavy the floor of the building had to be strengthened to carry it.

An old grandfather's clock hung on the wall behind the sounder, electronically tied to the Sounder's timing device, to control the timing phase, and let the operation of the recorder be controlled by time signals sent out nightly by the National Bureau of Standards. The two men, Brown and Skidmore lived in a room just off their laboratory, in double bunks tucked along the end wall, with Navy lockers, a writing desk and boxes of personal belongings on the floor. What they could not store on the floor was shoved atop wooden slats across the building stringers.

The other civilians lived under similar conditions, and all of them bunked as close to their work as we could put them.

The radio room, glaciology lab and weather central were directly across the street from the Administration building. They received by far the most visitors during the winter, as the men came to and from the radio room, visiting Chief Kent, and radio operators Robert Haskill and Charles Forlidas.

Most of the work of the radio people was routine, and consisted of sending messages and typing out messages they monitored on the official Navy circuit. But what all hands were interested in was the amateur radio set-up we operated, for they could use this to keep in touch with home. McCarthy was among the first to become an addict. He would spend hours in the radio shack at night, sitting with the headphones on, working the "ham" radio, and trying to contact various amateur operators in the United States, to relay messages and pass on gossip. We found our best radio contacts to be Clark, New Jersey and Syracuse, New York, but at our station, contacts were good only for two or three hours a day, in the fifteen-meter band during the late morning and early evening, and around midnight on the twenty-meter band.

Next door to the radio men, the glaciologists concentrated on their deep-pit. Neuburg, Walker and Augenbaugh walked out 200 yards every day, and dug in the snow with ice axes. From the bottom of the pit they sent the snow up in a wooden box on runners, hauled up the fifteen-degree slope off vertical by a weasel using a block and tackle. Men could not hoist the box by hand. The tight-packed snow under the surface was heavy. Each box full weighed 700 pounds.

The weathermen worked underneath the mosque-shaped weather-dome at the end of the station. Chief May and three enlisted assistants did most of the work; Gary Camp, Thomas Ackerman and William Butler. Gerard Fierle, the civilian weatherman, confined himself as much as possible to the activities outlined by the U.S. Weather Bureau before he came down.

The weathermen chemically produced gas in the inflation shelter and set off their balloons regularly to test the upper air and gather information for weather mapping.

Not far away, Thiel and Behrendt began to analyze the results of their fall seismic shots, or soundings under the ice and snow. But their major winter work would revolve around Neuburg's deep-pit to get a better idea of the contour of the bottom of the ice barrier and the bottom of the sea that lay beneath.

Malville's aurora program probably took the most effort of all in these days. On clear nights, when the Aurora Australis was bright, he got little sleep, photographing the aurora and measuring the time intervals and speed of the waves, and, from a bunk set eighteen inches below the ceiling, watching from the plastic dome through fieldglasses for meteors that probably were seen nowhere outside the Antarctic.

Malville also supervised his remote magnetic hut, and changed the recording film regularly, sometimes struggling through blizzard and drifting snow in the dark, to do his job. He was near the top of the satisfactory half of the men, civilian or Navy included who gave little cause for concern during the winter night. He was a good example of what happens when a person is sincerely interested in his work and kept so busy there is little time left to either complain or get into bad habits.

Around May 1, discipline became a problem. Cox, the photographer, had the gall to tell me he objected to having the men assemble, and then wait, perhaps a minute while someone came to my quarters to tell McCarthy and me the movies were ready to go on.

126

It was a blessing that we had plenty of reading matter in camp. We had not only one library—but two. The one for the use of all the men in camp was located in the hobby-room in the recreation hall. These books were mostly paper-backs and the men could come and help themselves. Usually, when they had read them they were brought back to the library again or passed on to someone else.

The science library, on the other hand consisted of books of a more permanent nature and some quite valuable. They were purchased by the IGY for use of the scientific staff; but no man in camp would be denied the pleasure of reading all the books in this library, so we made it open with an adjacent reading space. To insure that no book would be lost, I directed the men to read the books there. However, any book taken out would have to be registered. This would also insure that the IGY men could put their hands on any book in a few minutes for immediate reference. Otherwise, I knew from experience they would be lost and stashed away some place and never be seen again.

Skidmore was obviously violating the rules by letting books out from the library without filling out a charge card. While I was discussing the matter with Thiel, Skidmore came into the library. He readily admitted taking liberties with the books but then immediately blew up and spoke very roughly to me.

It wasn't the first time. A few days before he had a run-in with Dr. Smith, over recreation equipment. Skidmore had wanted some leather-working tools from the recreation supplies. But in order to keep matters from getting out of hand, Dr. Smith had divided the supplies into groups, and opened new batches only on specific dates. We were not to get into leather working until the middle of June.

Skidmore did not like being crossed, and got quite nasty with Dr. Smith. I felt sorry for him, but I also felt it was now time to get tough and bring Skidmore into line for his own good and ours.

The next day, I called Dr. Thiel and Skidmore into my quarters and told Skidmore what he had done. He had to learn to get along with others, I warned him. For his past actions, I denied him the Recreation hall for two weeks. He tried to argue with me—but he had spoken with such disrespect that I told him I had nothing more to talk to him about. Both of them left.

That same day, after I returned from the movie at about 9:00 P.M., I found a knife pinning a message to my door in Treasure Island fashion. The message, apparently written in blood, read: "The Phantom Strikes."

At this point I was beginning to realize there would be few dull moments from now on. Something unpleasant happened nearly every day.

The next morning, the unpleasantness concerned the washing machine. It was Monday, the day McCarthy and I had use of the washer and dryer. When we went to use the machine, we found that someone had broken two electrical connections and disconnected one of the hoses, so the machine would not work. It was not an amateur job, for the way the connections were destroyed, it took someone with a thorough knowledge of electrical wiring to do the job.

Later, I discussed the matter with Dr. Thiel, and he told me he believed the washing machine damage had been done by one of the IGY men. No one else could have done it except Hannah, the electrician, and he had no reason to make himself extra work.

As if that were not enough unpleasantness for one week, the very next day I had trouble with Fierle, the Weather Bureau man, about helping Chief May and the Navy meteorologists with the weather program. At first Fierle refused to have anything to do with it. He had plenty of work of his own, he said.

That was understandable, but to carry out the RAWINDSONDE program, the Navy men needed Fierle's help from 9:00 in the morning until 9:00 at night. It actually amounted to only about five hours' work, but he would have to be available for call during that period. Fierle protested, began swearing, and said he would do nothing at all unless ordered by his chief, who was located at Little America.

I made up a message to Chief Meteorologist Humphrey telling him about Fierle's refusal to do the work, but I did not send it. I kept it to discuss with McCarthy, and then, to see if Fierle would change his mind overnight and help the others in the morning.

Fierle's stubbornness was very strange. The Navy and the IGY program were exactly the same. Yet Fierle insisted on working entirely on his own, duplicating the work of the others, and not helping in the balloon launching which was the most important single part of the job. He was most unfriendly and most unco-operative—but I still hoped he would change.

To make matters worse, that day Dr. Smith had some trouble with Cox. He had tried to get a work party together to seal holes that were developing in the tunnels. The men, led by Cox dragged their feet. I had another talk with Cox—this time in the favorable atmosphere of my quarters, and gave him a bit of friendly advice—to the effect that what he did in the Antarctic would remain on his record. He tried to convince me that he *was* doing a good job, and I knew that in his own field of photography he certainly was.

To cap it all, I talked to Dr. Smith that day about an incident with Greaney, the movie projectionist. When the movies had started the night before, he had the sound turned up so high it hurt everybody's ears, particularly in my place in front of the projector. I asked him if he would be good enough to turn the sound down a bit. He did not make a move.

A little later I asked him again. This time Greaney just looked at me. He did not say a word.

The third time, I asked him if he would reduce the volume. This time he answered me that he could not hear the sound in the back of the room then.

As soon as I had told him the story, Dr. Smith excused himself for a moment, and returned from his room with a note Greaney had just given him, asking to be relieved of his duties as projectionist. His head had swelled so that he felt offended when I asked him to turn the volume down. It was unbelievable—but it had happened.

Dr. Smith and I had a long talk that evening on the need to get at the root of the disciplinary problems. We thought some of the men had grown far too fresh and careless of the rules of the camp. We had few enough implements: We could take away privileges, such as the movies and use of the Recreation hall. But that was all.

We would have to do something, before matters got thoroughly out of hand.

The U.S.S. *Staten Island* (GB 5) forges her way through the ice in the Weddell Sea, approaching the continent of Antarctica. Note Bell helicopter (upper left) returning from an ice reconnaissance mission.

Aboard the U.S.S. *Wyandot*, plans are completed for the landing at Ellsworth Base. Left to right, Capt. E. A. McDonald, Capt. F. M. Gambacorta, Capt. Finn Ronne.

A top view of the newly constructed tunnels and aurora airglow tower
before being covered by drifts.

Two men work inside one of the tunnels connecting the operational buildings.

A scene typical of the work left to be done at Ellsworth Base
after the Navy ships departed for home.

The men of Ellsworth Base receive their first meal in a makeshift messhall.

An aerial view of Ellsworth Base (upper center), showing supply
ships at the edge of ice in Gould Bay.

Almost completely covered with snow, Ellsworth Base is seen at sunset.

As the Antarctic
night descends, the
men occupy themselves
with . . .

radio contact with the
outside world . . .

model building and
leather work . . .

body-building
exercises . . .

and a variety of
games and recreations.

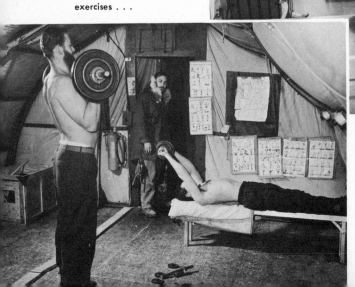

Station commander Capt. Finn Ronne is amused by "threatening" note pinned to his door.

Aircraft shown bearing the weight of the Antarctic snows.

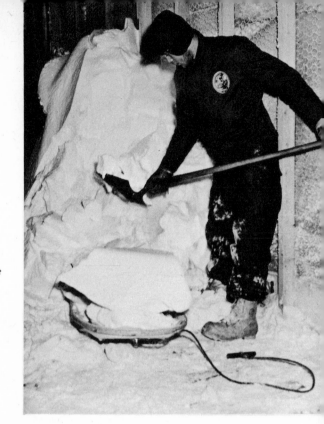

Right

Shoveling away snow that filtered through a small hole in one of the tunnel passages.

Below

Scientific work begins with a survey of the Filchner Ice Shelf.

Two men measure the density of the snow.

A balloon release for "upper air" meteorological observations.

The airglow tower with aurora australis overhead.
Streaks are moving stars in time exposure.

Left

The "Deep Pit" is dug 100 feet to collect samples of snow accumulation and compactness from past years.

Below

The arduous task of removing snow from the "Deep Pit" kept some IGY men busy for months.

Right

The OTTER aircraft
surveys a crevasse field
in preparation for
traverse trek.

Below

The Sno-Cat and sledge
are prepared for
exploration trips.
(Photo by Capt. Ronne)

Below

A close-up of a cargo sled caught hanging over a crevasse five feet wide and fifty feet deep.

Left

The traverse party to the interior of Antarctica, seen from the air. The front Sno-Cat was caught in a crevasse when the snow bridge covering it collapsed under the rear tracks.

The Sno-Cats stand in drifting snow in front of the 200-mile-long ice island discovered by Capt. Finn Ronne.

Left

Emperor penguin walks with a chick between its legs to keep the youngster warm.

Below

The rookery of Emperor penguins discovered on the sheltered sea ice at the western cape of Gould Bay, about ninety miles from Ellsworth Station.

A happy homecoming for Capt. Ronne as he is greeted by his wife and daughter on his return to Washington.

CHAPTER 10

GETTING TOUGH

D R. SMITH SUGGESTED THAT WE CRACK DOWN HARD AND QUICKLY, TO get the men in line so we would have no further disciplinary trouble. He decided on a logical candidate.

"If that man does not have a haircut by tomorrow morning we'll have mast on him and fine him two weeks' pay," Dr. Smith decided. "Further, the first man who disobeyed an order or showed disrespect toward an officer would be given exactly the same treatment."

Actually, I knew we had no authority to do any of these things, but, I figured it would do no harm to let some of the worst disciplinary offenders know that we had to have some order in camp.

I had to get out of the rather awkward position I was in, too, if we were to rebuild discipline. I had too much contact with the men. I had been trying, since we arrived, to be friendly. McCarthy thought I ought to mingle with the men—walk through the barracks and the camp from time to time, chatting with them.

I remember Admiral Byrd. On his second expedition I barely saw him ten times during the entire period we were on the ice, and then mostly in the main tunnel as he walked with a sheep-lined toilet seat under his arm.

After a few unfortunate incidents on his first expedition, Admiral Byrd became a master in keeping distant relationship with his men. He was on guard not to get too close with them—even his most dependent advisors. You always felt there was a gap which he maintained in conversations as well. He demanded respect and consideration from others; but he was gallant in his dealings, too. When he got into a conversation he could discuss a tremendous number of subjects with the keenest of interest based on a great variety of books he had read. I believe that he was a very lonely man—as all expedition leaders must surely be. While at Little America Byrd shared a small shack with another man, had all his meals brought over from the galley and he stayed away from the movies we had in the messhall.

I had tried to be companionable with the men on my own expedition with inconclusive results. Now, I had tried it again—and it had not worked.

Some of the men thought I was spying on them. Others just felt uncomfortable with a high-ranking officer around. The result had been the reverse of what I had hoped. Now was the time to change our entire approach.

McCarthy suggested that I let him and Dr. Smith sign the "ham-grams" the men were sending out from camp. There had been no censoring of messages until they began to include derogatory remarks about the Navy and base operations. I had been glancing through and signing the "ham-grams" myself, but now I authorized McCarthy to do it for the VX-6 detachment and Dr. Smith to sign them for the base personnel. Thereafter I would eliminate as much familiar contact with the men as possible and sit on top of the heap as commander.

McCarthy, Dr. Smith and I discussed the case of the recalcitrant movie projectionist. McCarthy said he had been trying to help the man for some time, without success. So he decided to set him straight for the incident of the night before, and called him in.

He stood at attention. I told him his request to quit as projectionist was accepted, as soon as we could train someone else to do the job. I told him a letter of admonition was being inserted in his official personnel jacket. Then I dismissed him sharply. He turned red in the face, then went out, followed by McCarthy and Dr. Smith.

I had a more friendly and informal meeting with Fierle that same day, to settle the question of his help to Chief May and the over-all IGY program. McCarthy had advised me to send a message straight to Mr. Humphrey his immediate IGY discipline leader at Little America without giving Fierle a copy, but I had decided to wait until I spoke to Fierle once more.

Fierle told me now that he was helping with the RAWINDSONDE balloon program, and Chief May confirmed it. Both said there would be no curtailment in the program whatsoever. So I told Fierle a message was ready to be sent and asked if he still wanted me to send it to Humphrey. He said it would not be necessary, since he was there to do anything possible to help the IGY program. I let it go at that.

Generally speaking, our crackdown was producing good results. Some of the men, for example, took a definite turn for the better. They appeared with fresh haircuts and cleanly shaven and looked very respectable for a change. It was the custom to allow men to grow beards and long hair in the Antarctic, but the carelessness they displayed in their personal appearance seemed almost immediately to reflect itself in their work, too. Most of the men who did not shave or cut their hair got slovenly in their personal hygiene by letting their faces go unwashed as well as unshaven. They wore filthy clothing, and kept their work and bunk spaces in sloppy condition. Inspection once a week, at least, rectified the slackening off of some of the men.

In the beginning of our stay, McCarthy had grown a beard along with the others, making it harder to crack down on the men for sloppiness. But without my saying a word just after we went on winter schedule he appeared one morning clean-shaven. I was very pleased.

Now, in an attempt to promote morale and enforce discipline we took a sharper line at our regular Saturday inspections. All the sleeping rooms had been tiled by now except the one occupied by Cox, Mathis, Ray; and the ones occupied by civilians Augenbaugh and Fierle, and Brown and Skidmore. It was understandable why the two last men had not been able to fix up their rooms. They had been working day and night to get the ionospheric recorder operating, and Brown indicated that he would get at it as soon as things slackened a bit. For the other men there was no excuse. In very certain terms McCarthy told them to tile their bunk rooms immediately.

The next few days were quiet inside the station, although outside the wind began to howl, and a sixty-one-mile-an-hour gale knocked down our radio antennas, putting us out of contact for two days.

Discipline seemed to be better, but we noted a growing amount of excess profanity, particularly at the movies. Perhaps this was the result of the resentment of some of the men against the crackdown. Dr. Smith and I discussed the matter, and he put a note on the bulletin board against profanity and excess noise in the movies. We had decided that the first violator would be punished.

After the movie that night, he discovered his note had been placed upside down on the bulletin board. A wag's gesture, one might think— but in the tense atmosphere that now existed it was obviously more than just a joke. Dr. Smith took a very serious view.

The next day, Ensign Sumrall came to confess to Dr. Smith that the men had gotten completely out of hand as far as he was concerned. Long after I had warned the officers about excess fraternization with the enlisted men they had continued to do so. Trying to be a good fellow, he finally burned his fingers. The men had begun making fun of him in the Recreation hall—because they saw they could get away with it, and their natural antagonism to officers came out. Someone had posted a lampooning sketch of Sumrall.

There was no real break in the tense situation for several days. Then, one morning I went to the messhall for breakfast as usual and found only a handful of the IGY men in the building. Fierle was there and apparently for my benefit, was extremely profane, larding his sentences liberally with scatological four-letter words.

It finally got to be too much for me. I asked him if he could not at least cut it out here for meals.

His answer was: "I don't give a damn what you think. I swear whenever and wherever I want to. If you don't like it, why don't you get the f--- out of here?"

I bridled. I told Fierle I wanted him to come and see me in my quarters at 10:00 o'clock. His reply was that he was too busy—and he interjected profanity in that remark as well.

I went over to the science building to see Dr. Thiel and tell him what had happened. As assistant scientific leader, he was my deputy in charge of the IGY civilians.

At about 11:45 he brought Fierle over to my quarters. Meanwhile, I had discussed the situation with McCarthy and Dr. Smith, and Dr. Thiel, all of whom found it urgent that Fierle be disciplined the sooner the better. I told him that he had shown disrespect and that for his discourteous manner he was banned from attending the movies for two weeks.

Fierle began to argue. He was a civilian, he said, and I had no jurisdiction over him. I told him that he was under the Uniform Code of Military Justice as long as he was in the Antarctic, just the same as all others at the station.

He wanted to argue, but I told Thiel to take him out. In the doorway, Fierle growled that no one at the station was going to bar him from seeing a movie.

After lunch I talked to Thiel about letting the civilians see the letter from the IGY headquarters which put me in charge of the civilians, and stated they were subject to military control. I copied off the pertinent points and gave a memo to Thiel. He passed it around among the IGY men for initialing. Fierle and Augenbaugh refused to initial the memo.

That same day I prepared a message describing the incident to the IGY headquarters. I showed it to Fierle. He had no comment. Then I ordered the message sent.

I spent the entire next day on the Fierle case. First, I explained to McCarthy that I must enforce the ban on the movie. It was that important an issue at this stage of our stay. If I didn't, it would be almost the same as abdicating my command of the station.

Then I spent several hours going through the court-martial manual, drawing out the pertinent portions to show Fierle the case against him. I wrote a rough draft of a letter to Fierle, and discussed it with Dr. Thiel, Dr. Smith and McCarthy. We decided to appoint Chief Spear as the station's Master at Arms.

Finally, Fierle was brought in again by Dr. Thiel. I read him the letter, concluding with the statement: "You will comply."

Fierle's attitude was slightly different now. He realized he had gone too far. He spoke up and said that when he signed a contract in Washington that he had been unaware that he would have to comply with the orders of the military. He would not have come, he said, if he had not believed this was a civilian expedition. He had had enough of the military during the war, he said, and did not want anything further to do with military men.

McCarthy reminded him that this base was run by the military, and that the Department of State's legal counsel had informed all the civilians they were subject to punishment under the uniform code of military justice. We handed Fierle the letter, listened to his arguments for a moment or two longer, and then he left. That same day Chief Spear told Fierle that if he showed up for the movies during the following two weeks he would be removed by force.

The effect on the entire camp was soon felt. The men apparently realized that we meant business. The next day I went to see Fierle to check his part of the monthly *Situation Report* I was to send off to the IGY. A report on the status of operations was sent IGY headquarters in Washington once a month. It included detailed information on progress of work in the various disciplines, problems encountered and recommendations for improvements that would benefit the group that would relieve us at the end of the first year. Fierle had toned down considerably. There was no swearing; he was co-operative in changing the report to include his latest work.

Yet in the camp, morale was far from improved. The next few days, it became apparent that the enlisted men were boycotting the movies. When we checked into it we found they regarded Fierle as a hero for talking up to a Navy captain and getting away with it, and this was a sympathy walk-out.

At this time, the morale of the Navy's enlisted men was at a new low —though due to a situation over which we had absolutely no control.

When the Navy's enlisted men had volunteered for service in the Antarctic, they were led to understand that, among other things, they could save money and would not lose anything in advancement. But they did lose. First, their selected examination papers for advance in rating did not come through as planned. The papers had not reached the ship when we pulled out of South America. In order to alleviate the situation somewhat, the men, without an opportunity to review the subject matter, took makeshift examinations, before the ships departed from the ice-shelf to return. Most of the men knew they had not done as well as if they had been given the examination under normal conditions.

Second, after we had been at the station for several weeks, the men learned that the Navy had decided to cut them off the *per diem* on which they had been placed on beginning the trip. This action came as an unpleasant shock to the enlisted men, for it cut their chance to save money.

Third, the examination results came back just after Fierle's punishment was announced. Most of the men had failed in their bid for advancement. Even those who had passed the examinations had no assurance that they would receive the advances in rating. All this occurred while the temperature at the station was hovering around −60°.

The Fierle incident had brought up again the need of reviewing mess duty of all IGY personnel. So far, although the IGY men were specifically told they could be required to perform mess duty, we had exempted them because they had all been so bitterly opposed.

McCarthy felt they ought to go on mess duty regularly, just like the enlisted men. Dr. Thiel had said repeatedly that the IGY men did not come to the Antarctic to do dishes and serve food.

Finally, I had to make a decision. Since I knew I would have to answer both to the Navy and to the IGY, I had decided to put the civilians on the mess duty. My problem, although I did not tell them, was that the civilians had created so much trouble and exhibited such deplorable behavior, we could not treat them as officers. They refused to act as officers should. The Navy was interested in morale and the welfare of Navy personnel. The IGY was concerned with the welfare of the IGY men and the scientific program. I was caught in the middle, to report to both.

I had a discussion with Brown, Thiel and Neuburg, and directed that Behrendt, Walker, or Augenbaugh would start their tour of mess duty on Monday morning, May 13. Brown argued that the entire IGY program would suffer from such action, but I could not agree, and told Brown and the others I would take the responsibility if it did suffer. For that matter, I reminded them that they had taken on a number of projects that were not within the framework of their orders under the IGY. I did not object to such projects certainly; we should accomplish as much scientific work as possible. But all of the civilians were not kept as occupied as they could have been, and those who weren't could carry their weight in the household chores.

Back in the 1920's Admiral Sims of the U.S. Navy stated that there were only two ways to get results out of a group of men: Instill the fear of punishment and the hope of reward, and during the war, Captain Ellsberg re-emphasized the advice. Having set forth the punishment, it was time to offer the reward.

Since the second Saturday of May was approaching, it was time to have a birthday party for the men who were born in May.

I told Dr. Smith to serve liquor, but not too much of it. This alcoholic beverage had been provided for use on special occasions, such as Christmas, New Year, Thanksgiving, Mid-winter night and for birthday and monthly parties. The men could always fill up on beer if they wanted, but I did not want them drunk if I could avoid it.

The Saturday night "sprees" undoubtedly gave some of the men an outlet for their pent-up emotions stemming from their isolation and the

150

absence of feminine companionship. Photographs of families and girl friends decorated the walls of their small rooms. But these formed only a part of the picture-gallery of pin-up girls with which many were surrounded. The aviation group was particularly ambitious with their "girlie" exhibitions. In each of the two aviation buildings one entire wall was devoted to a conglomeration of shapes, forms, and colors, both draped and undraped. Sex was always a legitimate subject of conversation, and as usual tended to conform to exaggerations of the normal male ego. Interestingly enough, I know of only one case of homosexuality in Antarctic history. Although the exploration field appeals largely to non-conformists —these eccentrics are invariably the distinctly masculine type.

I did not attend the party because I had lost much respect for many of the people at the station, and found it difficult to be congenial with the IGY people. To my way of thinking they would have to change their attitude if they were to be treated differently.

The party, I learned afterward, was a tame affair. It broke up about 10:30 P.M. when the liquor was gone. However, all the men seemed more subdued.

The next day, Hugo Neuburg went to McCarthy and asked for a letter stating that I had ordered the IGY men onto household duty. McCarthy came to me because he did not want to get caught in the middle. He agreed with the position I had taken. He did not believe any officer should take mess duty, since it would break down discipline completely. Furthermore, at that time the officers had their hands full in taking inventory of all equipment for replenishment the following year; and were kept busy with the never-ending radio dispatches that were coming in and required immediate answer. I never knew that so much paper work could be a part of a wintering expedition. McCarthy had the major burden of this work while Jaburg supervised the work of the VX-6 men. Sumrall, in addition to writing news stories for the Navy Information Office assisted generally where needed, and Dr. Smith had his medical work and the administration of the SeaBees.

That same day when I went to the messhall for my afternoon coffee, the men were showing movies—all those who had boycotted the movie the night before were seeing it at a "matinee." Then and there I let it be known that was the last matinee they would have. After that the men began showing up for the evening movie again.

It had not taken the men long to get over the good effects of the Fierle incident—or so I thought.

But unfortunately trouble with the IGY men was just beginning.

The very next morning after the "matinee" incident, Chief Spear reported to McCarthy and me that Behrendt and Walker had flatly refused to go on mess duty, as ordered. They would not have dared refuse if all the IGY civilians had not been behind them.

In the previous conversation with Brown, Neuberg and Thiel they all had complained about not having enough time during the day to do the work they were supposed to do under the IGY program. All three of them stated that they wished for more available working hours—and said not a minute a day could be spared by the civilians in taking their share of the household duties.

This, of course, seemed ridiculous. So Dr. Smith, McCarthy and I got together to find a way which would afford them a longer working day. McCarthy thought they should start work earlier in the morning; that would also cut down on their late evening bull-sessions. After all, we did not wish to be responsible for retarding their IGY work. As of that day, we issued an official memorandum, stating that the IGY civilians would have their meals with the enlisted men, at the general feeding a half-hour earlier than our officer's mess. They would mix with them, sit on the round stools, and in general be treated as enlisted men. They had complained from the beginning that they preferred to eat with the enlisted men; now they would have their wish.

As the memorandum was being typed up, I asked McCarthy to tell Dr. Thiel to come and see us. He showed up a few minutes later; I told him everything would be under military control from that point on, and handed him the note.

Thiel looked down, read the note, and then looked up.

"What about the officers?" he said.

"I will take care of the officers. Don't worry about them," I said, "they are kept busy. Furthermore, they did not request additional working hours during the day as you fellows did. They are able to perform their duties under the present set-up, so I see no reason to change that now."

He started to argue. I told him I had been on a number of expeditions but I had never been with a group that showed such poor spirit. When they go back to the United States, I added, they would be very sorry for the way they had acted, because they would realize, as others had before them, that they had been acting childishly.

I pointed out to him that the IGY men were now working only about four hours a day, five days a week, and that I proposed that they work eight hours a day. That way they would be sure to be on top of their work when the winter night ended. I also reminded him of the provisions in their IGY contracts which specified an additional payment of $818 a year for overtime whether they worked extra hours or not.

I also wrote him a memorandum on the overtime provision, and suggested, among other things, that the IGY civilians be allowed only a twenty-minute break for coffee twice a day, the same as the Navy personnel.

That same day I received a letter signed by Thiel, Neuburg, Brown, Fierle, and Malville, requesting clarification of a certain Navy regulation relating to Navy Technicians. Their status was not that of Navy tech-

152

nicians, and they had been so informed. While some of them were temporary employees of the Bureau of Standards and the Weather Bureau, others were temporarily hired and paid through Government Contract by the Arctic Institute of North America, a private organization which has no official status with the government.

I ignored the letter.

No IGY work was accomplished that day, but for several days the station was quiet. Whenever I entered the science building, I would find several of the men there. As soon as they saw me, just like a group of kids they jumped up and got busy.

As I looked at these highly paid individuals (all of whom, as I have detailed, made more money that I did) I reflected back to the fine spirit among most men on my previous expeditions. The question, it seemed to me, was whether expedition personnel should be unpaid volunteers or highly salaried men. The two methods of selecting the group attracts different types of men.

The first group would draw men who had an adventurous spirit, those who would not seek monetary or material gain. It would consist of men who would do anything to satisfy their thirst for doing something out of the ordinary and would gladly suffer hardship. They would do anything they were asked to do. They would also be appreciative of the opportunity given to them to participate in something unusual. They would feel amply rewarded by the results obtained by the group as a whole. Eighteen of the 21 men on my own expedition in 1946-48 had been in this category, and I am willing even today to have our final results compared with any previous private American Antarctic expedition.

The second group draws men seeking an easy way to make money and to be recognized. These men usually feel they are doing work that is so valuable they could not be replaced. They believe they are unique, and untouchable. They have no idea of what they are facing. Some of them, only a few months out of school, are wined and dined as great scientists. They are being sent out at great expense to further their own proficiency in their chosen field, but by departure time they seem to feel they have conquered the world.

On shipboard their idle time is spent in scheming how to get away from obligations and responsibilities they took on when they signed their contracts. They get their hands on books and regulations of the Navy and use them to protect themselves against any eventuality, as my IGY civilians were then attempting to do.

Our IGY men did their utmost to violate ordinary rules and regulations of good conduct and of the Navy by sitting on tables, loitering around the wardroom when they were not supposed to, coming to meals dressed like tramps, etc.

Aboard ship, the civilians had made themselves completely obnoxious.

They dug up Navy and IGY booklets—booklets that they tried to use to place themselves in categories other than those in which they had signed on.

One small booklet, which they now brought out, was one covering Navy Technicians. But here the civilians had forgotten they were not Navy technicians, for they had not been hired by nor were they being paid by the Navy.

The second type of expeditioner—the type of most of my IGY colleagues—when faced with the reality of moving onto the barrier ice and finding more strenuous conditions than those aboard ship—realized what they were in for only after reaching the Antarctic.

Most of them took the attitude that every order given to them, even before we moved into the camp, was an insult to their dignity as human beings. They banded themselves together—stronger than any fraternal order—and made Neuburg, Brown and Thiel their spokesmen.

Every day during the construction period it was the same: Some would complain about working on the tunnels, although it was written into their contract that they were to do camp work. They talked constantly about their own work, and the trouble I would be in if their discipline-chiefs knew what they were doing instead of their own scientific work.

As a group these IGY civilians were strong enough to make or break the camp's morale. Immediately, some had started to mix and drink with the enlisted men. Fraternization was fine but not to the degree that it undermined camp discipline and morale. These acted and wanted to act not as responsible, mature professional men—as some of them did, but others acted more like immature juveniles out from their protective environments. They were always unco-operative. These never volunteered to do any work, unless they had an ulterior motive. They were selfish. They never saw or yielded to the paramount need of the entire group.

All too frequent some in this element violated many rules: Breaking into boxes in the tunnel and helping themselves to many things that did not belong to them—an all too prevalent attitude toward abundant and expendable government equipment.

Even so, within fourteen days after the ship left on February 11, they were free to do their own scientific work, and had not been imposed on for any camp work until three months later.

They all had good traits as previously noted. Any one individual probably could have been assimilated into the group but collectively their attitude became like that of a family's self-centered, spoiled child.

At times, to be sure, all the civilians had worked hard but when they were released from close supervision I saw less and less work being accomplished. Only when the question of mess duty came up did they suddenly become very busy with their scientific work.

Now, in May, all the IGY men shut themselves off from the rest of us. They kept to the science building except during meals and movies. Some

154

of them—Brown and Skidmore—never went to the movies at all. In the Recreation hall, they began to keep away from the enlisted men, too, even when they did visit the area. Few of them visited this building except Fierle and Augenbaugh. They, the highly paid expeditioners, were the least co-operative and most troublesome.

In a radio message from my wife in late May I learned that Dr. Wilhelm Filchner, for whom this gigantic ice shelf was named, had died in his native Germany on May 7 at the age of 79. He had been intensely interested in our venture. In 1912 his small ship the *Deutschland* became trapped in the pack ice less than a hundred miles from here. The German scientist-explorer and his men drifted northward with the ocean current for ten months before their ship reached open water. How different from ours their problems had been.

Although the IGY civilians were trying to be self-sufficient, within a few days Brown came to me and asked that we return to the twenty-four-hour generator watch, because we had increased the hum that bothered the recording of the Whistlers, when we had changed the generators in order to cut down on the hours of manning them.

It was all right with me to increase the generator watch, *if* the civilians would supply a man to do the work eight hours out of the twenty-four. I told him that.

That day, Thiel came in with a memo while Brown was in my office. Thiel wanted a representative of the IGY civilians to handle their own radio contact with the United States. He said they had been promised this.

Promises made in Washington about affairs that will develop in Antarctica are very difficult to keep. But that was fine. They asked for a representative in the radio room. I asked for a representative in the generator room.

The civilians were now in trouble with everyone. Chief Spear wrote a memo to Neuburg asking him to keep out of the garage unless he had a signed request from the Executive Officer or the Captain for a job to be done in the garage. He was tired of the IGY civilians violating their status and calling on him for work he should not have been required to do in the first place.

I spent an entire day trying to straighten out this situation. I had Brown over to my quarters first to hear his side of it. Much came out in his torrent of words—mostly his intense dislike of Spear. Then Neuburg came over. He admitted that the IGY men were supposed to work at camp duties. His only question was how much they should do. Finally, Thiel showed up. His gripe was mainly against the change in status of the IGY men as compared to the officers.

The result was that we sent a dispatch to Albert Crary, who was spending his first Antarctic winter at Little America. He was the senior scientist for all Antarctic IGY programs. I wanted him to resolve the question of the IGY men's status with regard to station obligations.

We could not go on as we were with the IGY men refusing to help with the work, and claiming all housekeeping duties would interfere with their schedules.

That day I went outside to the tent where Neuburg was beginning his 100-foot–deep pit for glaciology and seismology studies. So far I found it about fifteen feet deep and ten feet square. It was tough going, and they had gotten to the point where they were using a block and tackle and a weasel to pull up the hard compressed snow. Right then three of the IGY men were on the job, but soon they said they would need five of the nine.

I still wanted one of the IGY men to man the generators on an eight-hour shift, or to go on mess duty in about three weeks' time.

While we waited to hear from Crary, I learned that at Wilkes Station (almost completely across the continent from us) the IGY men were preparing all food and washing all dishes two nights a week—Friday and Saturday. Otherwise, the enlisted men took care of all household duties. The IGY men there had even offered to take the job twice a week At Paul Siple's Pole station the IGY men kept the snow-melter filled, supplied fuel oil for the heating units and took regular turn in galley work as well. But here, our IGY men were doing their best to get out of everything possible—even shovelling snow in front of their own entrance.

When we finally got Little America on the radio-telephone, we talked the problem over for about an hour. Crary got all the facts on the problems as I saw them and I left it up to him to make a decision. Then I let Thiel come on the air and he made an erroneous presentation completely—which I then had to correct on the air. They had not taken their turn at household duties as he insisted. Such correction on the air was not good for any of us.

Crary settled the basic issue—not the way I wanted it settled, but at least it was settled. No discipline in one science would support another discipline, except on a voluntary basis. That meant that as far as Brown was concerned, if he wanted a twenty-four–hour generator watch to help in his ionospheric program, he had to provide a man for eight hours during which the regular housekeeping personnel would not normally man the generators. Crary advised that he should ask for volunteers among the IGY men.

With regard to galley and mess duty, Crary left it to me what to do, except I would have to explain upon my return if the planned IGY program suffered in any way. Crary seemed to take it for granted that everything the IGY civilians did in the way of housekeeping duties would be only in emergency—quite a different attitude than the written instructions provided me by Washington's IGY officials and the Navy.

Actually, Crary's viewpoint coincided with the one I had been following until the civilians had made so many infringements on law, order and some semblance of discipline that the threat of mess duty was the only means I had to bring them in line. Now, Crary's decision made a straw out of my weak stick.

Captain Dickey, wintering for the first time at Little America as the Navy's senior representative in charge of all military operations on the continent, mentioned over the radio that I had the full use of the VX-6 aviation personnel, and I could use them as I saw fit. In that, he meant I could use them for generator watch and other jobs if I felt this necessary.

In fact—I had been exercising very little control over the VX-6 people because of McCarthy's attitude and conflicting orders. While I did utilize the VX-6 personnel in assisting in the messhall and filling the fuel tanks in the buildings during the winter, I did not direct them to take over the generator watch—so as not to conflict with Crary's decision that the civilians had a responsibility with the generators. Furthermore, the VX-6 personnel was kept busy in the two aviation buildings with sorting spares for the planes and helicopter. Otherwise, they had very little to do during the winter.

Well, that was now settled. Navy personnel would do all the housekeeping duties at the station from that point on. Clearly, I could not be put in the position of forcing the IGY men to do household work, and then having them come back with the charge that I had sabotaged the IGY scientific program. It would be easy enough for them to do just that, too, and in their current mood, I was sure they would do all they could to retaliate for fancied wrongs.

From now on, the IGY men would not be requested to do a single thing about camp, except in absolute emergencies.

CHAPTER 11

THE CAVE DWELLERS

During this period when tensions were growing worse almost every day between the IGY civilians and the rest of us, Lieutenant Commander McCarthy was doing an excellent job as executive officer.

We had our differences nevertheless for he was of the opinion that he had been given orders to report to authority outside the station. McCarthy also felt himself his own boss as far as aviation activities were concerned at Ellsworth. He had refused to take my advice about storing the planes, and now the left wing of one of the OTTERs was completely buried in the snow—with a resulting heavy stress on the wing. But then we did not know each other well; a fault of the personnel selection system, not of any individual.

Our only other difference concerned the degree to which officers could go in relaxing with the enlisted men. Yet the men liked McCarthy and he mixed well with them. Further, he had done wonders for morale simply by spending most of his free hours working the "ham" radio and putting through messages for the men.

Sixteen-year-old Jules Madey of Clark, New Jersey, made many phone-patches possible for us. Any time you operated the "ham-radio," Jules Madey was on the air—helpful and willing to have the men speak directly with their families and friends throughout the U.S.A. He knew each IGY station operator and most of the men intimately, and probably knew more about what was going on in the entire IGY program than any other single person. Madey certainly brought a tremendous amount of pleasure to all our men at Ellsworth.

Equally helpful in another way was "ham" operator Paul Blum of North Syracuse, New York. Each night he came through by radio to receive and send messages of a more personal nature than could be sent via Navy communication. These messages were neatly rewritten and mailed to their destinations, which made us feel we had a mail system of a sort. At Christmas time Paul had special cards attractively printed especially for us. We only sent him the names and addresses of the recipients. There was never any charge for the hours of work and all the extras performed by these "ham" operators, and there was very little we could do to show our appreciation in return. We at Ellsworth were unanimous in our appreciation for the immense pleasure that Paul Blum and Jules Madey and the other "hams" gave us.

It was lucky that McCarthy was so effective at this time for matters were going from bad to worse with the IGY personnel. I had made a number of tape recordings from records in the Recreation hall. These I played in my room to pass the time away as I worked. When I looked for the entire lot shortly after I settled the responsibilities of the IGY men, I found they were gone from my room. McCarthy and I both scoured the station for them. The only conclusion I could reach—and I reached it reluctantly—was that someone had taken them from my room out of spite, to deprive me of the small enjoyment I was getting from this music. So I spent part of one day putting hasps and padlocks on my door. It was not pleasant to feel that I could not leave my room without locking it—with only thirty-nine of us in the entire area the size of a nation—but that was the way it had turned out. Dr. Smith had felt the need to put a hasp and padlock on his door long before.

Two days after our talk with Crary, Dr. Thiel came to tell me that he was sorry to have given incorrect information over the radio, and sorry about the entire incident. I told him I hated to have people fail to be accurate—but that I would forget about the whole thing. The important matter at hand was to carry out the scientific program of the IGY. That was what we were down here for.

Since we were in the depths of winter, scientific work was limited. We rarely ventured outside even in the bright moonlight. It was too cold, and there was no useful reason for most of us to go out. Malville was very busy in his dome on the nights we had aurora displays, and at other times with his study of meteors and his magnetograph. The seismologists were at the low point in their activity, having wound up much of the interpolation of the graph from their seismic shots in the fall. Behrendt and Walker were finishing up their two weeks of mess duty we had previously assigned them in late May—they were the first and only two of the civilians to perform such services during the winter. When the IGY men finished these two weeks of household chores we did not intend to use them again, outside their own area except for emergencies. About this time Thiel had begun to help Neuburg in the deep glaciology pit—in exchange for the help the glaciologists had given him in the fall and would again give him in the spring.

The meteorologists were having real trouble with the launching of balloons, now that winter had set in fully. The inflation building originally was designed in such a way that balloons could be released through an opening in the flat roof. Because the building had been placed in the wrong location in relation to the prevailing wind-direction, winds sweeping over the surface would carry a balloon sideways where it often struck the many antenna wires before it had gained sufficient height to clear the obstacles. By installing side doors to the inflation building the aerographer would be able to walk out through a wide door, onto an ascending ramp and carry the balloon a good distance away before releasing it, so that the balloon would not hit any obstacles. When they did hit something, the tiny fragile instruments attached would break to pieces. Each one of them cost something like $20 apiece.

On occasion they had broken three instruments in one day to make a launching. To rectify this we built the walk-out doors but then had to wait several days, during high winds that went to fifty-nine miles an hour, before we could put them in place. The meteorologists could then launch their balloons without hitting aerials and sides of our buildings—despite the poor planning in layout of the station.

We also had a great deal of trouble with our Whistler program. The generators interfered with the recordings and it became impossible for Hannah, the electrician, to keep both generators in phase. Until that time we had sporadically successful results, but at the end of May the program had to stop, it was so unsuccessful. We waited while we sought advice from Little America on the problems of electrical interference in the camp.

Personnel problems continued. Now that the IGY civilians had ended their round, Cox, the photographer, came back into the picture. Dr. Smith had given him a directive on operations of the photo-lab, and Cox resented it. Previously, he had intended to volunteer for a second year at the station. Now he came in to tell me that he was not going to ask for an extra year of duty in the Antarctic—just because of that.

It was nothing very important—just the nagging of a man who was unhappy and eating on himself, but it added to the general problem. In his photographic work, however, Cox continued to do a good job.

We faced a more serious problem for a few days. The snow level began to rise. The wind blew hard, and we were in danger of being snowed in. That created an immediate and serious threat, to our water supply. Davis, the mechanic, went out every day to dredge up snow for the snow-melters. He and Leonard Craus, one of the youngest men in camp, kept the tractor motor running continuously during the four-month–long winter night for fear of not getting it started again in the low temperatures when the oil would congeal like heavy syrup. Heavily dressed, Davis would go topside, crawl into the tractor cabin, drive fifty yards or so away from the camp area and scoop up a load of clean snow in the bucket. Back again to the snow-melter, he removed the trap door that covered the opening and dumped the snow load into the chute. It fell into a tank with heating coils snaking around the sides and soon the snow became some of the purest germ-free water on earth.

But in the blizzard conditions we faced now, we could not go out for several days, and the snow had reached the tops of the roofs of the buildings. Then heavy winds had deposited a blanket of snow on top of all the buildings and blocked all our passage ways to the outside. We began cutting down on our water use. In less than a week the water problem was under control again, as the weather took a mild turn.

I wish I could have said as much for personal relations within the camp. I found my three rolls of tape just outside my door but never did find out who had brought them back.

June rolled onto the calendar but it brought no summer warming of any kind among the men. The IGY men had almost completely given up fraternization with the enlisted men and with the officers. They stuck to their work, ate with the enlisted men in the messhall, and stayed in the science building. They always seemed to have a chip on their shoulders.

The IGY men had made a mistake in not offering to help occasionally with the household chores but it was too late at this point to do anything about it. They would have to suffer through the long months. Neuburg several times swept the floor of the messhall. But I told him not to bother. They had made the household duties issue a prolonged source of irritation to all hands. Now that the matter was settled, I was not going to give them any cause to complain that mundane chores had interfered with their IGY work.

Morale seemed better than it had been, after the IGY men separated themselves from the military—and after the news came through that a number of the enlisted men had received the promotions they were seeking. Brown decided to try to do something with his Whistler program again by moving the equipment for his observations to the Aviation Building. He hoped that would eliminate the humming sound in the recording equipment due to the proximity of the instruments to the generators of the station.

But while these were good signs, trouble arose from another quarter. The officers now began letting down. After the movies one night some of them stayed up half the night drinking martinis. Day after day I watched their work slacken off.

One Saturday night in June, a couple of the officers, enlisted men of VX-6, and some of the IGY civilians threw a wild party. It went on all night. At 9:30 the next morning three of the participants—two enlisted men and one of the IGY civilians, were still sleeping it off in chairs in the Recreation hall. They were a miserable sight when I found them there after 12:30 brunch.

I could do nothing locally to cope with the situation. After my discussions on the IGY men, their jurisdiction had been settled; and since the higher command had not provided me with the mechanism and legal authority to levy any punishment on personnel at the Ellsworth Station, I was hamstrung all along the way without any deterrent to maintain normal discipline.

Yet I still had the responsibility to be sure the IGY program was carried out and that the men stayed safe through a year in the Antarctic.

The problem of safety bothered me when I examined the dispensary. We had been at Ellsworth Station for four months, and yet the dispensary still looked like a junk-shop. We had no sick bay, and we were in no way prepared for an emergency operation, if one should become necessary.

I talked this problem over with McCarthy, who agreed with me that something was wrong with Dr. Smith. Recently he had been keeping to himself, locking himself in his room and barely speaking when spoken to.

Despite the fact that the Doctor found administrative duties distasteful, he had been performing many of these sticky functions satisfactorily. Our relations had been good and I had relied on him on many occasions.

I told McCarthy to tell the Doctor I wanted the dispensary fixed up immediately. The doctor should be up for breakfast every morning, the dispensary open for sick calls, and a notice posted on the bulletin board telling the men about the hours.

McCarthy must have done something, for the next day all officers showed up at breakfast for the first time in weeks. I relieved the Doctor of duties as recreation officer, and told McCarthy to sign "ham-grams" for *all* the military personnel from now on. The Doctor said nothing. He just continued to go into his room and lock the door.

In the middle of June it seemed to me that McCarthy, too, was showing signs of strain. He began telling me what a mistake he had made in coming to the Antarctic—how he would regret it all his life. He was not the only one. Washington had sent us a message a few days before asking for volunteers to stay over another winter. Not one man wanted to be listed. But I was beginning to worry if some of the men, and now some of the officers, would make it through this one year without cracking-up.

Now we were in for some pulling and hauling. One night, after the movies, I asked McCarthy to go to the Recreation hall to play our usual game of pool. He demurred, because he had to go to a meeting. A bit later, wandering into the science building, I found him huddled around a map of Antarctica on a table with Thiel, Neuburg and several of the other IGY men. Apparently they were planning a flight without my knowledge.

Later I asked McCarthy about it, and had to remind him that no plans were to be made without my knowledge since the sole responsibility for all operations fell on my shoulders. Those were my written instructions, and no one here would change it.

Dr. Smith and Cox, the photographer, were having difficulties. Cox was an excellent man in many ways, and after our difficulties of the past, he had begun to come in to chat with me from time to time. One morning, at this time Cox came in to tell me of an incident involving himself and the Doctor.

Cox had been sitting in the Recreation hall listening to some records when Dr. Smith and Lieutenant Sumrall (he had just been made Lieutenant, Junior Grade) came in and began playing pool.

Dr. Smith began to whistle. He kept it up for some time.

The whistling began to get on Cox' nerves—it really made it impossible to listen to the music, he said.

Finally, Cox spoke up:

"Excuse me, sir, but in the Navy only fools like Bo'sun's mates and guys like myself whistle."

Dr. Smith took offense and threatened to report Cox.

By June 21, the darkest day of the year, the Doctor had made himself the most disliked man in camp. It was an honor that changed regularly, so it was not as serious as it sounds; nevertheless, this was quite a change in status for the Doctor.

The inactivity and the depression that Antarctic winter brings in some men seemed to have taken their toll especially hard on the Doctor. At the movies one night he sat on top of a table during the showing. Since he had raised the roof with the galley personnel not long before for sitting on top of the meat block in the back of the room, it was understandable that the men should complain about his reversal of position.

The next day he did not get up at all. I had about decided to take a tight grip on him to be certain that he would not fall into a kind of laziness that makes a person lose interest in even his most pressing problems. The Doctor already had given up his duties as ship's store officer and recreation officer. What remained of his responsibilities were the SeaBees records, requisitions for replacement of personnel and his medical duties. He was obviously depressed by the tensions under which we all were living; but I could not seem to get at the root of his problem. Lately, he had not even attended the regular evening movies where a chair was usually provided for him, McCarthy and myself. Chief Spear who arranged those reserved spaces for us had long since eliminated a chair for Dr. Smith, reasoning that, if he came back to the movies, he could find a seat along with the rest as did Jaburg and Sumrall. The whole movie showing was a subject of contention anyway and as the winter crept on the problem got worse. The next night Dr. Smith appeared and not finding his accustomed chair, he took a chair belonging to Chief Spear.

A minor incident? Of course, it was minor, but in the grating of the winter night minor incidents loom large. The next day Spear came to me, and finally he took the matter up with Dr. Smith, as a spokesman for all the enlisted men. They wanted their own movie! They did not want to be around the officers, he said. They resented having to sit through the movie with me, too!

Early one morning in mid-June I climbed topside through the narrow trapdoor next to the generator building. There in the bracing out-of-doors I scanned the frigid, silent, desolate scene as long as the −58° temperature would allow. Moisture exhaled from my breath froze immediately. The tiny ice crystals ground together as they left the mouth and nostrils breaking the silence with a hissing reverberation. The level, lifeless ice-barrier extended in all directions as far as the eye could see in the semi-darkness. Even in the bleakest time of winter, outlines of far distant objects can be seen clearly in the uncluttered, smokeless, and dust-free atmosphere. In a few days the sun's path would reach its northernmost point. A somber full moon now looms overhead, casting pale shadows of red, green and blue over the hard-packed snow. A week before the moon had moved above the horizon—there to rise and set twice a day. It would continue to repeat this high latitude phenomenon daily for another week until it disappeared for the remainder of the monthly cycle. Its golden disk, haloed by concentric rings of its corona, seemed cold, and lonely and tired of its eternal heavenly traverse. Its own terrain and secrets, perhaps, were not too different from this monotonous landscape where time and distance fade beyond human grasp. In the hushed surroundings of the barren isolation you can almost hear your own thoughts. Such a forsaken panorama—native only to the polar regions—can cause a deep depression to some, while to the restless soul it is one of the Antarctic's mystic drawing powers.

Nowhere else on earth can man observe such stark forbidding magnificance—nights when whole oceans of constellations and stars flicker and streak through the sky. The "Southern Cross," a four-star cluster—beacon for navigators in the southern hemisphere—stands out above all the others. You are particularly blessed on nights when the Heavens suddenly seem to awake. Then the shifting mood of the Aurora Australis throws out red, yellowish-green and blue arcs of light spanning the sky from its zenith to the horizon. The symphony of shimmering lights mold into patterns of wavy curtains and streaked illuminated columns. The incomparable setting reaffirm's man's infinitesimal place in our universe.

I was relieved to be alone—momentarily away from the many troubled situations which prevailed within the camp. Soon the dwellers of our ice-entombed city would be ready to roll out of their bunks and start the day. Meanwhile, the awe-inspiring beauty of the over-powering bleakness reacted on me as it has done many times before—it renewed my faith and gave me strength to meet the challenge.

164

On Mid-winter Day, June 22, we celebrated with a monster feast, and I broke out a few bottles of champagne in my quaters for Brown, Thiel, Skidmore, Jaburg and McCarthy. I still had some hope that we could break the tense atmosphere in camp, and get all hands to pull together. The time for us to end our voluntary stay in this "ice-box" was still many months away.

We were to have two and a half months more of darkness, and they would be difficult months, from the attitude that was sweeping the camp.

I had a talk with Dr. Smith finally, and learned what was eating him. *He thought I had implied he was a thief!*

His misinterpretation arose over some of the records in the Recreation hall. I had unpacked those records originally to make my own tape recordings from them. Later on some of them disappeared. Still later, some records turned up in the Doctor's possession; and while I expressed my satisfaction that the records had been found, I could not understand how he had gotten them into his personal collection since they belonged in the Recreation hall.

I spoke to him on the subject of men's minds—how they change in determining the true facts, and how small things assume huge proportions in the Antarctic. I urged him to assist in creating a harmonious feeling in camp, and to attend the evening movies. There would be a chair for him, I said.

The winter days dragged on, filled with a sameness that got tiresome for all hands—a sameness and tension well-illustrated by entries from my diary of two days, June 26 and 27:

26 June (Wednesday)

First thing this morning was the aerologist (Chief May) who is now upset over the many hours the rest of them must work when one of them (Butler) is on mess duty. McCarthy spoke to me about it, and asked to delay Ackerman (aerologist) from going on for a few two-week periods. Fierle, he said, has much additional work to attend to—the automatic equipment. I told McCarthy to work it out with Chief May. At least I've done my utmost to get no enlisted men exempt. Next, McCarthy showed me some notes from the "Public Works Department" (Chief Spear). Spear outlined difficulties in his department of theft, pilfering, and how the IGY civilians help themselves to general supplies, etc. I have lectured the IGY men against broaching cargo many times—and caught them at it, too. They were told always to see Dr. Smith or myself.

Movie arrangement (seating) now seems to work out well. The sketch on the messhall board is a good one.

Hugo Neuburg saw me last night about sending a Class E message (personal) but we found out from the radio men that it will take many days to get it out due to too much official traffic. Since the "ham-radio" is more or less out for time being, nothing can be done. It was a message of sympathy to his mother for a brother killed in the war. I sure wish there was something we could do to get that message out for him. I told Chief Kent to try to get it out on the "ham" radio by the 29th if possible. The "ham" was dead tonight again when I listened.

27 June (Thursday)

Kent got "ham-grams" in today (this A.M.) but none went out. About thirty of them are stacked up. I received one from Admiral Miles, McCarthy got one and so did Jaburg. He was told one of his girl friends got married. He had thought she would wait for him. Said he was relieved.

Temperature now is —38° (10:00 A.M.). At 8:30 A.M. it was down to —48°. Great changes occur often.

Watched the meteorology people at work. Three men are steady at it during a balloon run. Chief May and his men, Camp, Butler and Ackerman are all doing an excellent job. They deserve all the praise I can give them.

Neuburg and his gang are spending the day in the deep pit. For the last few days they have done ice-studies. Thiel and Behrendt are taking gravity readings every two hours and plotting recordings on a graph. During the night Malville is taking the readings for them since he is awake and spends the time in the Aurora tower anyway. That means there are continuous readings without a break.

An English movie tonight. Rather good. Most men came to it. It is better to spend one and a half hours here at night. It breaks up the day some. From the messages the men are sending to family and friends now it appears they are all longing to get back home. The ships cannot get in here soon enough. In evenings a large group of men go to Recreation hall and sit around, drinking beer. Very little talk among them. No more to talk about appears to be the case with most of them. I still keep busy in my own cozy corner where I always have plenty to do. Writing takes up much of my time, then painting and working on other handicraft. Then, of course, there is my daily ping-pong and pool games with one or another of the men. I managed to win as many games in ping-pong as I lose in pool and probably spend as much time in the Rec. hall as anyone. Radio is very poor tonight again, so probably not much hope of getting anything out.

Those were typical days, dull days, in which the men struggled to keep control, and in which the slightest misstep by a neighbor might result in frayed tempers and harsh words.

A day after those entrees were made, several of the officers and a few IGY men, and some enlisted men had another hilarious party in the Recreation hall. The next day, Skidmore turned up with a black eye and a bruise on one side of his face. He had gotten into a fight with Haskill the radio operator. Haskill had a big cut on his nose, but he had obviously gotten the best of it. He usually did.

Parties were held almost every night at this point. The men began to disappear to various rooms to drink beer and very little sociability was established around the camp as a whole. The IGY men, except Brown and Skidmore, seemed to have nothing at all to say: Neither to me nor to anyone else. Thiel had not said a word when he came to the champagne party I had held in my quarters on June 22.

166

Without speaking to me about it, Malville put a notice on the bulletin board that he was giving a lecture in the science building for all those interested in the aurora. All of the IGY men knew of my desire to have them give talks to the men on subjects of their specialty as they had done on the ship sailing south. I was waiting for the word from Thiel as to when we should commence the organized lecture series. I knew from earlier winterings that it always helps the morale for the men to know what was going on in the various sciences we were investigating.

Malville came over to see me the next day with a message on the aurora program, and did not say a word about his self-appointed lecture series. I mentioned it, and pointed out that the lectures should be correlated so that our evening's movies would not compete with him. He didn't think, he said. He had the time now and just wanted to give the lecture. I told him I was all for it and would speak to Thiel about setting up the full program.

A few nights later the series began. They were constructive and informative talks but unfortunately less popular than the evening movies. Other than Chief May, who attended every lecture, the audience consisted mostly of the IGY group and a few sporadic visitors.

On July 4 very few of the men showed up for breakfast since it was a holiday, and since most of them had stayed up late partying the night before.

We had a special turkey dinner in the evening. It was lonely for a holiday—the five officers were eating together, alone. We ate family style, but it was miserable these days, for none at the table seemed to have an ounce of sociability left in them. It wasn't just the officers—the IGY men were eating with the enlisted men now—but only Brown and Skidmore were friendly. The rest had nothing to say.

It was too bad that in their effort to evade their fair share of camp responsibilities the IGY men had ended up eating with the enlisted men. I would have liked to have them continue to have their meals with us, but it didn't work that way. Malville, in particular was a problem. When he finished his Aurora work, I planned to have him spend a few weeks on mess duty. Here was a young man, just out of college, who had worked conscientiously when his scientific program had called for it. Now, when his responsibilities were tapering off, he began to invent all kinds of excuses to prevent being called to pitch in with the more routine chores.

We had ended our monthly birthday parties and holiday parties, because none of the men wanted to continue them. They did not want to have any meetings or over-all group activity, and the doctor got nowhere with the men when he suggested it. It was just cliques and party, day and night.

Activity had somehow shifted to the Science Building. It turned out to be a regular workshop for all hands, with handicraft work and everything else going on about the shoulders of the scientists, whether they were asleep or awake. Lieutenant Jaburg practically lived there—in fact I could never enter the door without seeing him. He was even doing his handicraft there. I could not see how Thiel and Walker, who had to be out on the job early in the morning, stood for the racket. But they did not seem to mind.

Communication continued to be bad. Apparently we were in the worst spot in the continent for radio interference. At best, communication in the Antarctic leaves much to be desired, but I knew that the Palmer Peninsula—Weddell Sea area always has more disturbances that affect radio signals than at other places I have been. Malville was to participate in an "All-Antarctic" radio round-table discussion of Aurora findings, but it turned out to be fizzle from our standpoint. We could barely hear even the South Pole station.

Our "ham-radio" seemed to be out of commission more often than not. But, one bright spot, however, occurred when Brown moved the Whistler equipment into the Aviation Building, and the hum that had bedevilled them practically disappeared.

I had been willing to bet that the IGY men would not complete their deep pit by the end of the winter, but on July 9 they had reached sixty-five of the 100 feet they planned to excavate. It was tough going, pick and shovel all the way.

I had walked out several times in the dark to watch them work. Even at noon the wind-blown ridges and dark made it difficult to tramp over the snow. The weasel stood there in the dark, too, running as a "donkey-engine" to pull up the frozen snow.

The men worked in a tent, covering the pit itself, to give them protection from the wind and drifting snow. The weasel pulled the box up and two of the men lifted it clear each time and swung it onto a wooden platform, where the lifting gear was changed so the box could be lifted flat. Then the box was snaked out into the middle of the snow field, and three men emptied it. It came back and down into the snow hole where two men worked in the lightest clothing.

They felt they must finish the job by the middle of August, because the five men were the same who would go on the traverse party. Already they were making their plans.

Those plans did not coincide exactly with mine. Neuburg thought he would be the leader of the party, although I had already informed him it would be Dr. Thiel. He thought he was going to take three weasels and the single working Sno-Cat on the trail. The IGY had been assigned only one weasel, but since the other Sno-Cat had broken down, I would let them have another weasel. But not a third. We would need that for transportation to the ships when they came in—and while the traverse party was still out in the field.

The men knew so little about the Antarctic that it was hard for me to understand how they would survive away from base. Dr. Smith began to give them instructions in first aid and trail practices, just in case someone was hurt on the trip. The worst thing was their absolute uncooperative spirit—if it continued on the trail, a man could freeze apparently, and the others would not lift a finger to help him.

They seemed to be growing more distant every day, as the monotonous winter wore along. I got into several scraps with Neuburg, whose temper was growing short, and finally told Thiel that I wanted to discuss the traverse plans only with him, and not with Neuburg.

This spirit showed itself again and again. Chief Davis complained that when the deep-pit men came in for meals and coffee breaks they always placed their heavy, dirty clothes on the mess tables. Coat hangers were fastened to the walls inside the door some time ago, but they ignored them. McCarthy spoke to Neuburg about it, asking if he would be good enough to hang up his clothes instead of leaving them on the tables as the cooks liked to have a nice, neat and clean messhall. I was present at the time. Instead of being fair about it, Neuburg started to give me hell, saying that he and the other IGY men were here for science, and that was the main reason for the existence of the station, and that the rest of the people better take it and like it regardless of how he and his cohorts acted.

I told Neuburg that he must conform to standard procedure of the station for good morale and friendly co-operation. Those back home would find this kind of occurrence hard to believe, as would I if I had not seen it happen.

On July 17 the wind started to blow some forty to fifty miles an hour, causing heavy drifts. As a result the snow backed up against our buildings. Someone had left the tunnel door behind the science building open, and the tunnel was filled with snow in the morning when I came around to look. I went to the science building, got Thiel out of his bunk, and told him to get the gang out and shovel snow before it got into the main tunnel.

He started an argument, and so did Skidmore—because no IGY man had left the door open. I could have argued back with them on that point, because they are the only ones who ever used that door. But instead I just ordered them to get the work done. Otherwise, Malville would not be able to get up into his tower.

Half an hour later I went back and they were all out shoveling. The temperature was −28°—a little chilly.

Later I came back to see that they had shovelled the tunnel clear of snow. Still Skidmore told me then that it should not have been their responsibility, since others used that entrance, too. In other words, they would not willingly do anything that would benefit anyone else.

Even McCarthy was letting down. He was socializing more and more with the enlisted men, and calling them by their first names. I spent much of my free time in the Recreation hall now, playing pool and ping-pong with the enlisted men, but the officers (except Sumrall) and IGY men seemed to avoid the place. They spent their free hours talking and drinking beer in little groups.

Matters rocked along until Saturday, July 17, with no more than the expected increase in complaint and strain. That was the day several of the men went on a real spree. One officer did not show up for supper; he was finally found in one of the aviation buildings with three of the aviation unit enlisted men. The enlisted men had smuggled liquor into camp before the ships left us. They had been drinking since early afternoon. When the movie started after supper, they all showed up and made a great deal of noise in the back of the messhall. One of them even squirted beer on my head.

They made a terrible noise. Meanwhile, several of the other enlisted men were making just as much noise up front. It was disgusting for those who were trying to watch a movie with all this distraction.

After the movie the carousers disappeared, not to show up again that night.

CHAPTER 12

SHOVELING OUT

THE DRINKING AND GENERAL DISCONTENT CONTINUED ALL WINTER. I had been on three previous wintering expeditions and all had their share of personnel difficulties, but I had never seen a crew of men so near the breaking point as this one. It was not that conditions were worse—quite the contrary, conditions were the most luxurious I had ever experienced. The problem was caused by the very nature of our triple-headed group with no clear definition of areas of responsibility and all reticient to relinquish prerogatives to a single over-all commander.

At the end of July, McCarthy told me about the complaint going on among the men about my spending an hour and fifty minutes on a phonepatch—and tying up the "ham" radio for that long. In the first place it was only forty minutes. In the second place I had gotten to the point where I did not care what any of them thought. My nerves were getting ragged, too. Others were on the radio two and three hours at a stretch without anyone complaining about it. But, with me it was supposed to be different, of course.

Expedition leaders are as human as the next guy, it is only the public who makes heroes out of them, for, to my knowledge, while still alive few have been so considered by their men. More often the reverse is true. On an earlier expedition when I returned to base after spending almost three months out in the field, I found that not one man in camp was speaking to the leader. He was eating his meals alone at one of the two large messhall tables while the rest of the men jammed themselves around the remaining table. He had made some mistakes, like we all do, and the group had voted to ignore him. A mild form of mutiny—perhaps, but one time or other, just about every expedition in history has suffered from the same malady.

Dr. Smith and Skidmore were the loudest in complaint about my phone-patch. I spoke to Skidmore and told him it was none of his business. He said it was his business—that he had been keeping track of everyone's phone-patches. I put a stop to his self-appointed assignment. I told McCarthy, and he agreed, that no one but authorized personnel was to have access to the log-book, and that all others were to keep out of the radio room except on business.

McCarthy made one last effort to get the IGY men to help in camp duties to alleviate the pressure on the enlisted men who now had started a huge overhaul job of all the heavy tractors and sledges. McCarthy had asked if any IGY man wanted to volunteer to help. None did.

It was a strange situation. The IGY men at the South Pole station were taking their turns at mess duty, along with everyone else at camp. With a total complement of only eighteen men they were a tight-knit group—without either an aviation unit or traverse plans. Some days the IGY men there were working eighteen hours a day, Paul Siple had told me in a radio conversation one winter night. But our IGY men would volunteer to do nothing whatsoever. Their *esprit de corps* was lacking from the very beginning, and no matter what efforts McCarthy and I made to instill a fair balance in their mental approach, it met with failure.

Even at Little America, the largest station with more than 100 men, the civilians pitched in to assist the enlisted men in household chores when regular duties allowed. Nor did the IGY men there insist that officers also take their turn. In that respect the officers there took the same attitude as we did so as not to break down the officer-enlisted men relationship.

The one thing we had to look forward to now was the return of the sun, and on July 31 we saw the first sign of it. That day the northern horizon glowed fiery red around noon time. It looked as though the sun would break through any minute, although, of course, it would be two weeks before the upper portion would be above the horizon. Yet the reflection reminded us that the long night was ending.

The weather was very cold at the beginning of August. One day we walked over to the area where the airplanes were stored to see how they had taken the winter. The temperature was $-45°$, hardly the time to begin a shoveling-out party, but McCarthy and I could see that we had plenty of work cut out for us. The airplanes were completely buried in the snow and the snow was packed tightly around them, as I had feared it would.

We were almost ready to go on the summer work schedule, which would give the men many more hours of productive time than they had in the winter. It would mean reveille at 7:00 o'clock, breakfast until 7:30, lunch from 11:30 to 12:00 and supper from 5:30 to 6:00 for the enlisted men and the civilians. The officers would have their meals a half-hour later. I made myself the lone exception. At breakfast I would eat alone, I hoped that would help me preserve the slender thread of authority I had managed to hold through a most trying period.

We had not been helped by a series of mechanical failures in the past few weeks. The snow-melter in the men's head had broken down completely and the men had been rationed on water for washing and for showers. Brown's ionospheric recorder seemed to be broken down almost as much as it was operative. He and Skidmore spent a great deal of time tinkering with the machine. Even Cox' photographic equipment was sorely tried by the cold. On the first of August, when he went outside to try to take pictures of a balloon launching, his batteries refused to work in the cold. Our photographic equipment was just not properly adapted for −50° weather, and through the entire year he had a great deal of trouble with it.

The "ham" radio was as skittish as a horse full of oats all winter long; that was probably the worst morale factor of all, for after many months away from their families the men felt completely cut off. They took it out on one another.

So at the first of August our little camp of thirty-nine men was split into four factions: The VX-6 enlisted men, the SeaBees enlisted men, the IGY civilians, and the officers. It was like fighting on four flanks as we continued to press forward.

Yet through all the strife, we had managed to keep the scientific work on schedule, and we would be able to complete all the work that the IGY plan called for, perhaps even more.

Everyone was itching to get back to active work. McCarthy proposed to begin shoveling out the airplanes. I told him we had some bad weather coming, for one can expect anything in the Antarctic until the end of October, but he wanted to go ahead. One of the first things he and his men discovered was that a wing of one of the OTTER planes had been damaged by snow pressure. Luckily we had spare wings so this did not permanently ground the airplane. After a few weeks of shovelling, only to see the snow blowing and drifting right back almost as soon as they could get it out, McCarthy decided to wait. The temperature was in the minus forties, and the wind blew about twenty miles an hour. It was just too early in the year for that kind of outside work.

The glaciologists, whom by now we called the "icemen," had dug their pit to a depth of 100 feet. The seismologists then took over. Thiel brought out a four-inch auger drill, with which they would go down another fifty feet. At that depth the hole would be about ten feet below the water-line of the ocean at the edge of the barrier. It would be interesting to see what they brought up in the drill cores.

I believed that the ice shelf had been formed hundreds, perhaps thousands of years ago by sea-ice attaching itself to the shores, which would eventually be land-fast ice. As such, snowfalls and drifting snow would build up and form a shelf that gradually would be pushed seaward by the weight of glaciers flowing from the interior. But analysis of the cores would tell.

As we started back to work outside, I was relieved to find that the spirit was rising. We planned a series of parties—one every two weeks— at which the men would have drinks, but also some planned entertainment. At Davisville before embarkation, Mathis, the medical corpsman had packed ninety-six bottles of whisky and 4,500 small bottles of brandy. In addition, some of the men had smuggled in their own supplies, which, of course, was against all rules and regulations.

At the first party, Cox, the photographer, was master of ceremonies, a job of cracking jokes and razzing the men which he did very well. Everyone seemed to enjoy himself in the Recreation hall, playing games, ukuleles, singing and letting off steam in a good-natured instead of a tempered way. Cox razzed the IGY men unmercifully, but they took it well.

At one point in the evening, Cox, on the speaker's stand, asked Augenbaugh, the geologist what he had come down to the Antarctic for and what he was doing.

"I am a geologist," Augenbaugh answered.

Cox pretended surprise.

"A geologist? What do we need a geologist here for? We are 200 miles from the nearest rock, so what are you being paid for?"

Augenbaugh wasn't quick to answer. There was a second of silence.

"That's what I thought," said Cox—and the men roared.

The next morning the men liked the tape-recording so well that they played it over several times. It raised their spirit, as did the ever-rising and ever-brightening rays of the sun.

In our eagerness to get back outside, we began laying our plans for spring and summer work. None of us would stay over. Fierle, the Weather Bureau man, had applied for permission to winter the second year, but the IGY had replied that it wanted all civilians to return home for consultation and report on their work. The second-year crews to replace us had already been appointed—second year because while the International Geophysical Year was called a "year," it actually was to last for eighteen months.

The outside work the men could accomplish between August and January when our ships were scheduled to arrive would be all the work they would do in the Antarctic on this trip.

Thiel and Behrendt had been doing some gravity measurements all year. We had word now from IGY headquarters that they would like to have us compare notes with Dr. Fuchs' team at Shackleton, so we made plans to fly over there at the first opportunity to do that job. At the same time we would give the British a hand in fixing one of their Sno-Cats which had broken down. Davis, our mechanic was a real expert, and since the British had the necessary spare parts, we had no doubt that he could do the job for them.

We planned other flights, too. Ed Thiel, who would lead the traverse party, and Hugo Neuburg wanted to get a good look at the area they would enter, to warn themselves against crevasses and find a free area for passage. There would be some problems, I knew, because we did not have an unlimited supply of aviation gasoline to make the number of survey flights the IGY men would want. But we could cross that bridge later.

On August 6, McCarthy and Jaburg and I walked down to the ships' landing for the first time since winter had set in, to see how the landing site had taken the weather. We left at 11:00 in the morning, to catch the full brightness of the rising sun, even though the sun had not yet peeked above the horizon. But it was overcast that day, and even at noon it was so dark we could hardly see the uneven surface beneath our feet. The winds had been at work for months. They had piled ridges several feet high along our beaten tractor trail, but we could still see the tracks as a solid line, all the way. Where the snow had blown across the packed trail, the tracks had stayed impressed, with loose snow on either side.

Going down was comfortable enough, even though the thermometer stood at −35°. Our heavy parkas and boots protected us against the fifteen-mile-an–hour wind, and, anyhow, it was at our backs. We could see the bamboo snow marker poles along the trail, some with shreds of flags still whipping in the wind.

At the edge of the ridge we could look down into the landing area at the barrier edge—there was enough daylight at noon for that. A lead of open water stretched along the barrier edge, about a quarter of a mile wide. We looked for the killer whales that must have been playing in that open lead all winter long, but did not see them. Northward, as far as we could see, the sea was frozen over. The recent northerly winds had jammed the ice against the barrier edge.

In our area the barrier had broken off in several places but was still relatively intact. The line was straight enough that we need not change the landing place. The dead-men and hausers were still in place. We need not make any new preparation for the landing of the ships, if all remained as it was at that point.

We stood on the edge of the cliff for about ten minutes, hoping to catch a glimpse of the "killers," but we had no luck. Then as the cold began to bother us, we started home. When we climbed back over the ridge, the wind began to bite into our faces. Fortunately, I had my fur parka to shield my face, and by rubbing my fur gloves across my eyes and nose from time to time I did not get frostbitten.

The cold in the Antarctic is dangerous if you don't take proper precautions. Jaburg, for example, did not protect his neck that day, and when we got back to the camp he was suffering from frostbite on his neck. Luckily, it was nothing permanent. But even when mild frostbite does not leave damage, it is a painful affair.

There is always a tendency on the part of some to exaggerate the discomfort of the cold. Lieutenant Sumrall, our public information officer, prepared one human interest article at that time that made me smile a bit. It was a press release to be published in the men's home town. He reported, with a straight face, that when the men of the aviation unit were digging out the airplanes they had to quit digging in the open because of the cold.

"When breathing the cold, raw air into the mouth," he said, "the tongue froze to the teeth."

That, I must say, is stretching it a bit. If it happened, it was the first time anything like that happened in all the years I had spent in the Antarctic, and the fellow who suffered the discomfort certainly must have had his mouth open for a long time.

However, one must not underestimate the dangers of cold and frostbite. On my expedition of 1946 one of my men had been badly frostbitten on his toes. The skin and flesh sloughed off—the cells had actually been killed—and it was a long time before his foot was comfortable. Others have lost toes and fingers, and even parts of noses and ears due to frostbite.

The weather was nasty those first few days of August, with heavy winds and frequent overcast. But toward the middle of the month the men began to make real progress in digging out the airplanes. They had to dig through the hard-packed snow we call névé—snow so hard that a jab with a shovel or a pick breaks off only a small piece that is like ice. But little by little, sweating in their heavy clothes, the men began to clear the planes. Later the big tractor would be out to help clear a runway, too.

At this time we received a message from the senior man in charge at Little America suggesting that the best way to store aircraft in the Antarctic was to store them in the open, secured to the ground by lines fastened to "dead-men." Then the planes could move enough to allow the blowing snow to escape. I had to laugh. We had been doing that in the Antarctic for twenty-five years or more.

Jaburg showed me that message. He thought it was quite a joke that he had sent the message *after* the winter was over. When I told him that I had tried, without success, to persuade McCarthy to do just that months before, Jaburg didn't think it was so funny. Now it was dig and dig in the cold to get the planes out of their snow-mounds. Experience is a great teacher. Next time, I hope the persons responsible will do it the right way.

Experience does not always give the correct answers, however. Take the question of colds. For years all the books on the Antarctic, including my own "Antarctic Conquest" (pub. 1949) have said no one gets colds in the sub-zero weather. Our experience was belying this assumption. I had a throat cold that had been hanging on, nagging, since we first came ashore in the fall. Several of the enlisted men had developed colds, too. I don't know whether it was the more civilized accommodations available for this expedition, or what was the cause, but the theory that the Antarctic ice box killed whatever causes colds seems to be in need of drastic revision.

One possible explanation is that when we opened boxes and crates during the winter, germs, which had been dormant inside the boxes were activated by the warmth inside the buildings. Men who packed the boxes for shipment originally, probably had colds and germs were deposited months earlier.

Yet our health was excellent—better I would say than that of thirty-nine men quartered together in any spot in the United States. There was little work for Dr. Smith to do except administer to some injuries, and to give physical examinations to the Naval personnel when their annual check-up time came around.

The IGY civilians seemed to be in good physical condition, too. They were preparing now for their traverse. It was not too soon. The amount of preparation it takes for a trip across the frozen interior of the continent is phenomenal.

One of the first jobs was to prepare the supply of rations for the trip, and be sure that exactly the proper items and amount were taken. This demanded packing and repacking, to achieve the loads that would stand the trip, yet make the supplies available when needed.

The IGY personnel began to take over some of their own housekeeping chores, too. Since they would not co-operate in the messhall and galley work, we requested them to fill at least their own tanks for the jet heaters in their work areas and quarters.

I had my first view of the returning sun August 16, a full day before it was to be visible. I had gone out to help Skidmore and Neuburg repair the "ham-radio" antenna, which had slipped in the winter winds. It was a difficult job, for the temperature was −48° and a five-mile wind was enough to cut through anything. The job required climbing up to the top of the forty-foot mast and hoisting new cables up with block and tackle. Since I was wearing my warm caribou fur parka I was snug, although my nose and chin were occasionally bitten by frost. I helped a little to hoist the heavy block to the top.

From the top of the pole, at twenty-three minutes before 12:00, the time the sun was at its zenith, by looking north I saw the first view of the sun disk as it slipped above the horizon. I never saw a brighter or more welcome yellow picture.

Two days later, on August the 18th—most of the men abandoned the comfort of their snug living quarters to climb the vertical ladder and crawl to the snowy surface above. It was −56° and a ten-mile wind lashed their faces while they waited to view the sun for the first time in nearly four months. Northward over the treacherous Weddell Sea pack, scattered clouds reflected the colors of the spectrum; most prominent were the crimson red and yellow arches rising about ninety degrees along the surface. At exactly 11:36, local time, the sun's upper rim appeared while blazing orange stringers of light outlined the shadowy silhouettes of ice bergs frozen into the pack. Streaking rays from the sun's narrow rim lasted for only three minutes, but the glorious sight was well worth the chilly effort to those who saw it. The sun's return after an extended absence invariably produces quite a psychological impact, both mentally and physically—you can almost feel its warmth flowing back into your veins.

Every day the brighter sky cheered the men's spirit. Almost all of us were working outside now. The tractors and weasels were dug out of the snow. The big thirty-five–ton Caterpillar tractor, which had been deeply buried, was released by application of a heating unit where the tread met the surface. The men at Little America had a bad experience getting their Sno-Cat out, and tore loose part of one tread because they moved it when frozen in. They had relayed the information, and we were glad to have that piece of advice.

One work party was tearing down the tunnel that ran between the garage and the generator building. The tunnel had collapsed because of the heavy weight of snow. Now it was to be rebuilt.

All the exercise had a remarkable effect on the men's appetite. A few days after we had begun outdoor work, I came to lunch and the cook told me the men were eating as much as sixty men would eat under normal conditions. That day it was macaroni and meatballs. By the time I arrived it was all gone and we had to improvise. It made little difference to me, for my appetite stayed the same. By this time, I was numb to vegetables, in particular. All of them had the same taste, watery and flat, no matter how much spice I added.

On August 18 we were disappointed to see that the second plane, which had been stored in one of the U-shaped revetments, was quite seriously damaged. I walked over to the aviation area to take a look. I found it badly twisted. The wings were not parallel with the tail section. Deep bumps scarred the fuselage on the right side and the tail landing ski was pushed up into the after part beyond repair. The plane looked as though it had been in a wreck. That was an example of the power of wind and drifting snow.

That plane had less than twenty hours of flying time on it, but now it was a total loss. The first one had a damaged wing that needed repair. The aviation unit had a third plane that had never been uncrated. But now we were down to two planes, with relatively few spare parts, and our flying was just beginning.

The aviation unit had its hands full to put together the new plane and repair the one that could be repaired. That meant the base personnel had to take on more responsibility about housekeeping duties, since the IGY men were so unco-operative. But we received a blow here, too, when our hard-working, dependable James Hannah, the electrician, came down with an injured leg. Dr. Smith said he had cut the shin bone and had hurt his ankle. He thought Hannah would be laid up for about six weeks. With two men on mess duty that meant Chief Spear would have only one man to work for him on outside projects of camp repair. All the rest of the men had specific duties of their own, and could help only in spare time.

That created problems, but there was nothing to be done at the moment. Most of the IGY men were truly busy now. Neuburg, the glaciologist, reported that he had bored a four-inch hole at the bottom of his deep-pit down the additional fifty feet he had planned. At that depth, he said, the snow that came up in the core was as hard as glass. He was having a difficult time, too, because the boring rod kept breaking. The rod was more than fifty feet long, with a cross-pipe at the end so it could be twisted and operate the auger. But the rod had a good deal of spring to it, and the constant twisting set up a torque action that broke the rod from time to time.

The physical labor was difficult. Every time they wanted to pull up the core, they had to hoist the whole rig by block and tackle, carefully so they could save the core for further study.

Neuburg had believed that the temperature of the snow would be higher, the deeper they dug. The reverse proved to be true, as I had suspected. Originally, the glacier ice had been formed a long way further inland at higher elevations — perhaps hundreds or thousands of years ago. At that time, temperatures dropped to $-80°$, $-90°$ or even $-100°$. Some of the cold was preserved in this frozen snow. At 100 feet down—at the bottom of the big pit—the temperature of the snow was $-12°$. At 150 feet down, the temperature had dropped to $-14°$, and dropped, I believe, until the temperature of the water beneath the ice shelf began to affect the snow layer. That was another 300 or 400 feet down, however, to the point where the sea water would make a change, for sea water with the salinity of that fronting our shelf froze at $28.6°$ above zero.

The other scientists were busy with their work as well. Thiel was getting his seismic equipment ready, hoping that the Air Force would use fifty pounds of their precious cargo space to send a new clutch for the Sno-Cat. Several of the enlisted men were rounding up materials for the traverse party and helping pack them. The meteorologists had their work neatly laid out for them and it did not vary too much according to season. Malville, the aurora man, was nearly through with the intensive phase of his work. When the aurora ceased altogether in a few weeks, McCarthy intended to put him on mess duty for at least one period, per-haps longer. With Hannah laid up and our increased outside activities we were short-handed in the messhall now, and this move was essential.

Skidmore, Brown's assistant, seemed to have less to do than any other civilian at this point. He had been spending a great deal of time operating the "ham" radio, after I had granted him permission to help with that work and lifted his restriction of entering the radio room. But he was not very helpful as far as the station personnel was concerned. He liked running the radio and talking with other "hams" from Taipei to Portland, Oregon and Washington, but he preferred to talk to them about things that interested him, instead of putting out "ham-grams" and arranging the phone-patches that we all wanted so badly. I began to think that perhaps he ought to be the next to go on mess duty, since he was so little help in any other way.

It was important that we keep our camp operations in good shape because we could expect a rash of VIP visitors during the summer, when high-ranking officers and important civilians would come down to say they had been in the Antarctic. Headquarters at McMurdo had already warned us of this.

By Labor Day, the days had grown much longer. We had daylight from about 6:00 in the morning until 5:00 in the evening, and the weather, while still fitful, was beginning to grow more placid and warm. In another seven weeks we should have the sun above the horizon twenty-four hours a day. And yet, September 3 was one of the most miserable days the Antarctic could offer. It was $-43°$, the wind was blowing at thirty miles an hour, and the men who ventured outside said it was im-possible to see or walk because of the drifting snow. Communications were blacked out, too, and stayed that way for three days. No weather report, no official messages of any kind came in or went out.

The evil weather had several repercussions. Skidmore, the irrepressible IGY man, began to get into trouble because he had nothing to do. First, he got into an argument with Chief Spear about the restacking of some boxes of supplies. Then he was in trouble with Chief Kent, who was in charge of the radio room, in a difference over radio communication. Fin-ally, someone complained because he was fooling with the hot water sys-tem when he had no business doing so.

Hannah fell ill with influenza and was totally laid up. And finally, the wind blew snow all through the camp, nullifying most of the digging efforts of the past few weeks. The airplanes and tractors had to be dug out all over again. We had to use heaters to melt the snow out of the wings and fuselage of the planes, so that the control cables would not freeze. The IGY men spent one entire day digging out the Sno-Cat sledges, which had been buried in snowdrifts six feet deep.

On September 8, after days of faulty communication, I finally talked to Major James Lassiter in Washington on the "ham" radio, and learned the Air Force plans. They would come in with enough gasoline to do their own geodetic work of survey, he said, and asked us to supply the rest they would need.

I knew well that he could not carry more gasoline in his two planes than just enough to reach our station, let alone to carry out his survey work without a resupply. But first we would have to wait until he got to Antarctica before trying to work out the gasoline problems he would have before our ships arrived carrying additional supplies.

I finally got in contact with Dr. Fuchs at the Shackleton base. I learned that he had the parts to fix our Sno-Cat clutch, and that he thought they could manage it if we brought the parts there. We made plans to go over there as soon as the flying weather cleared to do just that, and to help them with some of the problems they had with their Sno-Cats.

Dr. Fuchs was then getting ready for the overland trip to the South Pole. A party would leave Shackleton in a few days to scout a route through the crevasses thirty miles south of their station. They knew dog teams could make the trek, but they were worried about the heavy Sno-Cats. He planned to leave on the long traverse on November 14, hoping to arrive at the Pole on Christmas Eve.

After my talk with Fuchs, I went over to the science building to meet with the IGY men ostensibly to discuss our own traverse party. But the IGY men had something else on their minds—namely the availability of gasoline for a number of flights they wished to make. I explained once again that my interests were solely attuned to obtaining maximum results for the entire IGY program. An adequate number of reconnaissance flights would be made, I said, to assure the traverse party a safe passage through the crevasses south of us. Neuburg wanted me to tell Lassiter and the Air Force to leave one of his men at home so he could bring the new clutch for the broken-down Sno-Cat.

Neuburg continued to hammer on the use of the airplanes as he, Thiel and Augenbaugh were planning on making flights. I pointed out I was willing to listen to and consider any suggestions they might have for the good of the party.

Neuburg was not satisfied. He then stated it was their aviation gasoline, everything and everybody at the station existed solely for their support and all should be subservient to them.

I was so angry at the end of the meeting that I went back to my quarters and looked up the directives relating to the IGY traverse. Three points were mentioned: (1)—to make aerial reconnaissance for the party, (2)—to make aerial pictorial coverage of the route, and (3)—to support the party while it was in the field within 250 miles of the station. That, and that alone, was what they would get, unless I considered something else more important, and I would make the aerial search for the route to their objectives.

The attrition to machinery, and particularly the way it was used by the civilians, made me wonder if they would ever come back from their traverse. I learned from the garage men that all seven of our weasels were broken down. In July, they had all been operating, but since that time the IGY men had been using them to work the deep-pit, inspect the stake system, and for various jobs around the camp.

Consequently, we did not have a single working bit of transportation for the IGY men to use to get to their Sno-Cat which was now a mile and a half away, rigged for the seismic recording which Dr. Thiel had started again. The weasels could be repaired, but it would take time, and Davis, our mechanic, had to get the big tractors in for overhaul, too, before the ships arrived. They were needed to haul supplies from the edge of barrier to the station. Five of the weasels were buried deep in the snow where they had been abandoned after they broke down. It would not only take time to repair them, but a great deal of effort to dig them out. I estimated that it would be another month or more before they would be in running condition.

I had learned, through some tidbits dropped in conversation, that the IGY civilians had gotten together and determined that they would be as unco-operative with me as possible. They all were *prima donnas* now, despising supervision. Dr. Thiel, who was my assistant, refused to serve actually as deputy, and that was probably as much the cause as anything. The result was real chaos in our relationship—chaos which had resulted in such truly disgraceful incidents as that first radio conversation with Crary at Little America.

We had another occasion to consult the higher authorities at Little America on the problem of the traverse party. On September 15 our "ham" operators contacted Crary. Neuburg got on the line and began to talk about his work, and various items of information. Suddenly, he asked that the question of airplane flights be clarified. Specifically, he wanted the right to go along on all flights we would make in search of a traverse route. The way he put it, he sounded as though he just wanted "someone" to go, but the fact was that both he and Thiel wanted to be sure they had their way on everything.

Crary properly told them that the Navy was to make the flights, but hoped that an IGY man be taken along as observer if at all possible. I had already considered that and still intended to include them even though I knew they were totally unco-operative in all of my endeavors, and furthermore, had proved on the flights in the fall that they were so untrained in aerial observation that they could not translate what they saw into topographical terms anyhow.

As the end of this conversation, I asked Neuburg to come to my room and showed him the orders relative to observation flights. He claimed never to have seen them before. During the conversation he said flatly that he saw no reason for the IGY civilians to clear things with me or to take up any problems with me. I was only there as an advisor, he said, not as their boss. He accused me of sabotaging the entire IGY effort at the station.

The next day I had a talk with Thiel on the same subject. He was much more amenable, and before we were through he understood my authority over the flights, and over the IGY men, as station scientific leader. I told him then that I would not let any IGY men set foot in a plane until he acknowledged this fact. Then, and only then, would they go on flights which I considered would benefit the program.

Two days later a poster went up on the bulletin board in the mess-hall—one that showed the stupidity to which some of the IGY men had sunk. The poster showed an octopus (supposed to be me) with an IGY man on each of the nine arms. Fierle was sitting like a king on top of a throne. The arm that held him was broken with a lot of blood on it. That was supposed to show that he had come out victorious in the struggle I had with him in the fall.

I wanted that poster to show the kind of warfare the civilians were making, but when I went to get it, the poster had been taken down. Later, I saw Dr. Thiel and spoke of the poster. He apologized, said he, Neuburg and Brown had all been upset by the appearance of the lampoon. One of the younger IGY men had had the idea, he said. He would not identify the man; but all the men made reference to Malville as the brain in the plot.

It made little difference who the man might be, for all of them had shown such disregard for my status that there was little choice among them.

An incident occurred on September 20 that brought the entire matter of the IGY men and discipline to a head. Skidmore, to whom I had granted permission to work the "ham" radio, had been asked to get me a phone-patch of an official nature with Washington (relating to the Air Force flight). He completely ignored the request.

I called him in to my quarters to find out why. He and McCarthy came together. I asked Skidmore to explain. He said he didn't think it mattered when the patch came through. Instead of my patch, I had noticed, he had arranged one for himself, one for Brown, and one for another man.

I told Skidmore that I saw no reason why we should stand for such insubordination, since I had told him it was very urgent that I get that radio contact with Washington. After I consulted with McCarthy, Skidmore was told to stay away from the radio shack until further notice.

Then he blew up.

"We had an agreement for me to be on the radio, for the pictures I let you and Cox take of me operating the "whistler" equipment. I want the pictures returned."

He continued to rant, and I paid no attention to him. He went on.

"You are the most inconsiderate individual here. You are a thief. You stole a lamp from Behrendt. You went into his room and took a lamp from his table."

I told him that the lamp I had borrowed and already brought back had come from the science library, not from Behrendt's room. I emphasized that it belonged to no one but that I was the custodian and responsible for all the IGY equipment.

He paid no attention but ranted on. Finally, he went out of the room, slamming the door hard, and did the same to all the doors in the building, as he passed through them, one by one.

Ten seconds later he came rushing through the building again, once again slamming the doors until the entire building shook. He came to my door, opened it, stuck his head inside and shouted:

"I will have no more contact with you for the rest of the expedition." Then he slammed the door again, and was gone.

CHAPTER 13

FLIGHT OF DISCOVERY

TOWARD THE END OF SEPTEMBER WE LEARNED THROUGH DR. FUCHS that one of the men at the Halley Bay base had fallen and ruptured his liver. Halley Bay was the British Royal Society IGY base about 250 miles north of Shackleton. Halley Bay had called Shackleton for medical assistance, but when the Auster plane tried to fly their doctor there, the plane was forced down on the way.

There was only three days' food aboard, and no one knew where it had landed. The weather was alternating between fair and foul. At the end of five days the Fuchs party still had not located their missing flyers.

On September 24, Dr. Fuchs asked if we could bring some medicine over for the injured man at Halley Bay, and also bring our Harman-Nelson heater, to help them melt the snow inside the wings and tail section of their OTTER plane. We warmed up one of our OTTERs, and McCarthy took off for a series of test flights, landings and take-offs. Then we took off with our load for the British. But ten minutes out of Ellsworth we ran into solid overcast. We could hardly see the barrier edge—our main point of visual navigation. There was no open water in sight, since northerly winds kept the pack close in to the edge, and there were no recognizable features to be seen. Reluctantly I asked McCarthy to turn back, for it semed too risky to continue. He agreed and in a few minutes we were on our way back to Ellsworth. Twenty minutes after we landed, our own field was socked in with solid overcast. Had we not turned back when we did, we might not have made the base at all.

The next day was too foul to fly. The missing men had been out for a week now, with three days' ration. We spoke to Dr. Fuchs by radio, but there was no way anyone could get off the ground that day.

September 26 the weather was completely closed in, with a twelve-mile wind and no horizon.

185

September 27 was the same. In addition, there were heavy magnetic storms and we had even lost radio contact with McMurdo Sound.

September 28 seemed clearer locally, but as we warmed up the plane, our radio contact with the British revealed solid overcast at both their bases. They had their OTTER at Shackleton ready now without our heater, and as soon as the overcast cleared, they would try to rescue the downed men themselves. But they still needed our medicine for the sick man at Halley Bay.

We waited, watching the sky.

On September 29 I woke up early. The weather was as thick as soup, and worse—three inches of snow had fallen. Yet we had one good bit of news. Dr. Fuchs told us by radio that they had spoken to the men in the downed plane. They had a special homing beacon in the Auster, which was adjusted to their OTTER. If they could once get in the air, they could have no trouble locating the Auster on the ground.

We offered to help search if they could wait, but they said they thought they could handle it alone.

On September 30 our field was still closed in. We were prohibited by directives to fly unless we had horizon, so we could not go over to Shackleton, although Shackleton was clear. By 10:00 o'clock, however, the weather had cleared, and we took off. Flying toward Shackleton, the overcast became worse as we continued east. Jaburg thought we were crazy to go on, but McCarthy could see the open water leads on the edge of the ice, and they gave him a reference point.

We did not know it, but when Ellsworth had radioed that we were on our way, Dr. Fuchs had told our base that Shackleton was completely enshrouded in a "white-out," and it would be impossible for us to land. By the time Ellsworth informed us we were practically there.

As we flew over Shackleton, the men came out, and set off flares, which we could see, although we could not see the surface of the snow, because of the glare of the "white-out." McCarthy made a bumpy, but under the circumstances, masterful landing.

We delivered our medicine and material to the British. Dr. Fuchs was short of anti-freeze for his tractors and Sno-Cats that would soon be crossing the continent. Since we had a good supply, I took him thirty gallons of Prestone Anti-freeze. We had a friendly time with them before we turned around and came back to Ellsworth that afternoon. Our flight back was easy. We circled the Argentine base that lay between Shackleton and Ellsworth, and dipped our wings in greeting. Below the whole camp seemed to turn out to wave at us.

Back at Ellsworth, I delivered copies of the Shackleton group's aurora records to Malville. Immediately he wanted to go over to Shackleton to confer with them. But I let him know this would not be done until a later date because too frequent visits by us would retard the preparations

186

the Britishers had to make for their forthcoming crossing of the continent. On all our visits to Shackleton, our British friends stopped their own work in order to entertain us, and it was unfair of us to hamper their activities. They had their programs they wanted to complete, too.

By October 3 it was apparent that summer had come to the Antarctic. A bright twilight extended throughout the night. At midnight I could read a book without artificial light.

The morning sun was very bright now, and we were making ready for our big push of work for the summer. The VX-6 unit began work on the helicopter to get it ready for the air. The newly installed motor was tried out and functioned perfectly. It was now a matter of getting the whole unit out of the snowdrifts, attaching new rotors, and then practicing flights under Antarctic conditions. Jaburg, the helicopter pilot had finished helicopter flight training just before we sailed so he wanted to take advantage of every break in the weather to sharpen his proficiency in this unique aircraft. Before long he would have to concentrate on getting the traverse party through the crevasses to the clear area south of the fifty-mile rift.

We had wanted to visit the Argentines at Belgrano Station before we got too far immersed in our own work. Luckily, at this time we were handed an official reason for a visit. We learned that they had an ionospheric sounder like ours, and received a request that both stations make simultaneous soundings for comparison. The best way to establish that was to fly Brown over there to talk to them.

On the morning of October 3 we made an observation flight for an hour and a half, and then decided to go over to Belgrano Station in the afternoon. At lunch, I told Brown to be ready to make the trip by 12:30.

At 12:30 I went to his room and asked if he was ready to go.

"Yes," he said, "I will be ready provided Neuburg comes along. He speaks some Spanish and I want to have him come."

I told him that I had already made plans for interpretation. Chief May spoke very good Spanish. We had decided to take him with us also because he needed some time in the air to earn his additional flight pay. McCarthy had decided to let all the enlisted men who were short of flight time this month come along, so not a seat was available. It was important for the men to get time in the air for their pay. They were getting little enough out of this as it was and it helped a bit to boost their morale. If anyone deserved a break in a strenuous routine, it was Chief May.

In matters of this nature, I always followed McCarthy's decisions. No one better than he knew how many men could be carried in the plane on a certain flight. So if Neuburg should have replaced one of the enlisted men, it would only lower the morale and provide another source of contention between the military and civilians. Furthermore, McCarthy could not see why Neuburg more than anyone else should suddenly make such a big issue of trying to force his will through to be included, and neither did I.

Brown kept insisting that he wanted Neuburg. I finally told him that I was taking *him* over there, and that was final. After some argument Brown agreed.

But the battle was not yet over. In the passage way from the science building, I passed Neuburg. He stopped to ask if we were going to Belgrano. I said that we were going, and walked back to my quarters.

Five minutes later came a knock on my door. It was Neuburg. He had a memorandum in his hand, which he said dealt with Belgrano.

I told him I did not want to read any memos on Belgrano, and when he flung it at me, I calmly tore it up, and threw it in the wastebasket.

Neuburg blew up and started to call me names.

I did not reply except to tell him that the sooner the IGY men realized they were not running the station the better it would be for all concerned.

He slammed his way out, rip-snorting mad.

Even before the ships left us I had learned through those who had spent the summer with him in Alaska, that Neuburg was very hard to handle. This behavior was no news to me.

At about ten minutes to 1:00 we finally took off for Belgrano, with Jaburg piloting. When we landed Jaburg and his crewman, Jackson, remained with the plane since they did not want to shut off the engine. It might have been difficult to start the motor again since the temperature was $-30°$. Chief May, Brown and I went into the new buildings the Argentines had put up since fire had destroyed part of their camp the previous year. We got along pretty well, even with the language barrier. *Chief May's Spanish was excellent.* The Argentine scientist, Navy Lieutenant Barroli who handled the ionospheric work spoke good English, and he and Brown were able to work out their approach to the problem of achieving simultaneous readings. I talked with one of the men in German. Brown was able to finish his business in an hour, and we walked over to the plane for the return trip.

On the return flight we detoured to the southern shores of Gould Bay, only to find crevasses everywhere in the area. We followed the extension of Bahia Chica, the inlet two miles west of us which pierces like a dagger into the ice shelf in the direction of Gould Bay. Before long, this gigantic chunk of ice between the bays will break away and form a huge 'berg. The peninsula on which the Ellsworth Station is located will probably follow it since another dagger-like slit penetrates far into the ice shelf about twenty miles east. There are numerous inter-connected crevasses which cover the entire area for eighty miles or more south of Bahia Chica and Gould Bay. Perhaps twenty to thirty years from now, if not sooner, Ellsworth Station will become a free-floating 'berg of ice caught in the west-flowing current and later carried northward to open water and ultimate disintegration.

188

When we got back to our base, McCarthy took Augenbaugh on a flight to get an aerial view of the station and the depression in the ice shelf where the glaciologists had completed their snow pit. Without knowing it, they had dug the pit near the center of a shallow trough. The trough ran from the edge of the barrier cliff to a point about four or five miles inland. This location of the pit is probably a factor in accounting for the abnormally high density of the icy layer which had been dug up. During their stratigraphic studies, the glaciologists recorded snow layers within the pit dipping at angles up to forty-eight degrees. These facts indicate that the Ellsworth pit is located in a disturbed area.

That evening Brown came over to my quarters to discuss the entire situation of the civilians. I found him to be just as radical as the others, and just as unwilling to obey orders. I let him know that I was as interested in a full scientific program as anyone, but that it was going to be done in an orderly fashion and co-ordinated with consideration for the base personnel who were giving them the support. Once again I spoke of the responsibilities of the Navy and the Navy's relationship to the IGY. We just could not have the civilians dictating to us what to do, deciding when and where they would go with no consideration of safety, and ordering Navy personnel and equipment about to suit their every whim.

We discussed Hugo Neuburg's stand on the Belgrano trip. Brown did his best to convince me that Neuburg needed to speak to the Argentine scientists because it would advance the IGY program. But Neuburg had told me earlier that the only reason he wanted to talk to the Argentine glaciologist, Dr. Cecar Lissignoli was that he had met him in Greenland the summer before, that the Argentine was a nice fellow, and that Neuburg had promised to fly over one day and visit him. I didn't object to the noble idea. I did object to the finagling. In view of the fact that his visit would have no official standing and the plane was loaded to capacity, I saw no reason to take him at this time.

The next day I had a radio conversation with Dr. Fuchs at Shackleton. He suggested that our mechanic, Walter Davis get together with his own mechanic; and he thought that something could be worked out to make our "burned-out" Sno-Cat clutch operatable. Walter Davis and another plane load of enlisted men—short of flight time—went with us to Shackleton after we first investigated the crevasses around the huge rift due south of us.

We had hoped to take Cox along to cover the entire area in photographs for the use of the traverse party, but the weather, although clear at the horizon, was cloudy for photography. Unless the sun is striking the surface, none of the white surface features, such as sastrugies or snow-covered crevasses will show up in a photograph.

At Shackleton we learned that the British had found their downed "Auster" airplane, with the crew safe and sound. In the overcast they had overshot their destination by about 75 miles. The medicine had been delivered to the doctor who was making great strides toward recovery. A more cheerful atmosphere hung over this base now than on our earlier visit. Their planes were expected back within an hour, so we did not stay long, but did make arrangements to get some help in repairing our broken Sno-Cat springs. Walter Davis and the British mechanic devised a method to repair our clutch. We were given a new disk for the clutch, a sample spring, and specifications on how to make use of the "burned-out" springs which we had considered useless. These springs would first be annealed, then tempered to carry a specific load.

After Davis showed him how to do it, Neuburg set to work to try to temper the springs for the clutch. He had to do it himself. Davis, our mechanic, came to me to tell me how much work he had to do to get the camp garage and equipment ready for spring. There was too much work to do the IGY men's work, too. So we told Thiel, as head of the traverse party, that they would have to pitch in. If we could repair the Sno-Cat, fine. If not, they would have to take two weasels, improvise cabins on them, and build shelter on sledges, to make the trip possible. Neuburg had great difficulty in securing enough even heat to anneal and temper the steel sufficiently. Finally he succeeded in doing an improvised job by using the galley range. Although the cooks objected, I did not stop him from using the range, even though I had suggested he substitute three blow-firing simultaneously.

We made several more trips over to Belgrano, to work out scientific problems with the Argentines. On one trip, Colonel Jorge Leal, the commanding officer, put a wolf-grey puppy dog in the plane as a friendly gesture toward me. This, of course, I appreciated. But, in thinking it over I recalled the problems we had had with dogs running loose around camp on some of my earlier expeditions. Food, for example, could not be stored outside the galley or in the food tunnels, and the cleanliness in the buildings would also suffer. Since we were not depending upon dogs for our program, I felt one would be just a nuisance. Some men would take more interest and attachment for the dog than others, and the dog would become another item of contention, I thought. After all, this type of dog is not the house-variety kind; it is big, clumsy, rough out-door husky with lots of wolf-interbreeding. I therefore asked the Colonel to take the puppy back for the time being.

We had not been back at Ellsworth more than a few minutes before I heard of some of the men's desire to have the dog. Later, therefore, I relented and said that we would go back for the puppy, if the men would agree to keep her tied up. If I found her running loose in the tunnels or the buildings, I promised them I would return the dog to the Argentines.

On our next flight we stopped at the Argentine base to pick up the puppy-dog. Their leader, Colonel Leal was very pleased that I accepted the puppy for our station, and my own enlisted men were elated having a pet around. The aviation men made a fenced-in space between the two aviation buildings and she was fed all the left-over meat scraps from the galley. Undoubtedly, it helped somewhat on the morale of the men, at least in the beginning. David Greaney immediately took charge of the dog and he did a good job in looking after her welfare.

We kept on flying, both to ascertain the lay of the terrain for the traverse party and to understand that area of the Antarctic in which we were located—for it still had some undetermined features. I foresaw that a major geographical discovery was shaping up. On a flight south of the rift on October 18, McCarthy and I sighted and determined the location of an inlet that stretched westward, and further to the northwest I saw the two capes of what appeared to be a second inlet. I had an inkling that the land I saw on that flight was an island and decided then to return for better inspection of the area as soon as time and weather permitted.

On October 23, I asked McCarthy to prepare the plane for a reconnaissance flight. We had been discussing the best route inland for the traverse party for weeks. I was certain that the route directly to the south, from the station was far too dangerous for the civilians to tackle. Thiel and Neuburg argued endlessly that they must be taken up again to see for themselves. They would not trust my judgment. They still believed they could somehow travel directly west from the station, and that there must be a safe route through the crevasses. Admittedly, the rear window of an OTTER plane is not the best vantage point for viewing of terrain but I had now had enough experience with Thiel and Neuburg to know that they were untrained in the techniques of aerial observation, even under the best of conditions. Truly, it would be a waste of time to cart the civilians back and forth, and I was tired of the endless discussions of their impractical ideas. They could not be expected to gain a clear picture of the land even if they went on every flight. I would take one or two of them along as often as possible, but the quickest and safest procedure would be to find the trail for them. We would map as much of the area by photographs as possible, present them with a map, and then have them led as far as possible by helicopter.

To that end, the VX-6 men began preparing the second OTTER, which had been damaged by winter snow packing, and put together the helicopter for flight service. McCarthy and I continued the search for the safe route from Ellsworth either through or around the crevassed areas in a southeasterly direction.

We took off on October 23, with Lieutenant Sumrall as co-pilot and myself serving as observer. Because we were carrying extra gasoline to give us longer range, there was room for only one more man. I chose to take Dr. Thiel, whom I had appointed leader of the traverse party, to satisfy the IGY men's complaints that they would not believe the western route was impossible until they had seen for themselves.

This was the situation I had been awaiting since I first flew close to this area in 1947 and first established the fact that higher land existed to the south and west of Gould Bay. To understand this fully, I quote from my book *Antarctic Conquest*:

This was as far as we could go, then, in this direction, and we turned to starboard and headed off on a course of 218 degrees true, along the edge of the overcast. I scanned the horizon with the glasses for signs of break in this flat white surface—but nothing was visible but this vast plain of snow-covered ice masking the land beneath. We could see 200 miles ahead to the horizon to the left between clouds, but no sign of any mountains or outcrops.

At eight-fifty, Lassiter said we'd have to return, and the engine missed as he switched to a full tank. Latady again dropped an American flag and an Explorers Club flag, and I designated this territory as the eastern-most extremity of Edith Ronne Land, named after Jackie.

Then we swung again to the right and headed north toward the edge of the barrier and home. While I took a sight with the bubble-sextant to determine our approximate position, Latady got a reading from the radio-altimeter that showed the surface beneath us was 700 feet above sea level. A while later, another reading gave 300 feet, and a final reading at the edge, 100. The upward slope of the ice sheet to the south—or inland—plus other indications like the position of the lines of crevasses, finally eliminated the possibility of a bay or strait extending far inland at this point.

Now I hope to see what was beyond the range of our flight in 1947. Most of the time I sat in the co-pilots seat and took notes, to provide proof of my observations. I measured the drift and kept track of the ground speed, while Lieutenant Sumrall took sunsights in the center of the plane. I also took constant readings of the radio altimeter to determine the elevations of the land under our flight track.

We flew south on a course of 190 degrees true to the steep escarpment. South of Gould Bay this elevated land which I had first seen in 1947 showed up on the radio altimeter. The height of the land gradually rose to 1,900 feet above sea level. This later increased to 2,300 feet above sea level, and we continued measuring for about 150 miles, when the elevation dropped to 1,000 feet.

At eighty-one degrees, thirty minutes South, I saw mountains to the left of the plane track, about fifty miles away. They were the same mountains I had seen on our last flight the previous fall. This time, we found a cloud cover straight ahead of us and McCarthy decided to climb above it. We made a steep climb right into the soupy clouds. We could not even see ten feet ahead of us. Finally, when we reached 10,000 feet we were on top of the cloud mass. Just as we came into the open, we had a clear view directly south. And what a view! Mountains brilliantly bathed in the sun lay ahead and on all sides as far as we could see, stretching to the horizon. From east to west, the range must stretch 150 miles, and the same distance, perhaps more, from north to south.

From the 600- to 700-foot height of the ice shelf, the elevation rose sharply to an escarpment of 5,200 feet. This later dropped further south when we came across a kind of a basin with mountains surrounding it. At eighty-two degrees, thirty-five minutes South and a longitude of fifty-one degrees West, we made a circle and then flew around the nearest range to the west of us. This mountain was about thirty-five miles long, lying in a northeast, southwest direction. It stood no less than 9,000 feet above sea level—a massive piece of rock, with no crevasses showing.

When the mountains first came in view, I called then to Dr. Thiel's attention, since he wanted to photograph them and since he had already demonstrated on our earlier flights that he could not pick out distant features readily.

I hoped we had discovered a new mountain range. We obtained several "lines of position" by shooting the sun and thus established the approximate location of the mountains. And I took many photographs. Later we were to learn that what we thought was a new mountain range actually was the range which included Dufek Massif sighted and named by a U.S. Navy flight crew of a long-range Neptune plane from McMurdo Sound in January, 1956. I had not thought it possible that the U.S. Navy crew had discovered new mountains in this area because their declared positioning of the range was about 140 miles in error—undoubtedly due to navigational difficulties on their lengthy flight. Although Dr. Fuchs at Shackleton had been supplied with copies of our Navy's photographic coverage of the mountains, we at Ellsworth had not been. However, I also learned later that what is now referred to as Dufek Massif and the surrounding range was actually those mountains first seen by the leader of the Argentine Belgrano base, General Hernan Pujato, as early as October, 1955. The Argentines, therefore, should have the credit for the original discovery of these mountains. For example, the Argentines have named Dufek Massif "Santa Teresila Range."

Eighty to ninety miles south-southwest of this Massif, I discovered an impressive cluster of mountains stretching for 100 miles or so toward the South Pole. The highest summit I estimated to be about 11,000 feet with other peaks almost the same elevation. *These mountains had never been seen before.* Before us lay the explorer's incentive. That tantalizing question of what lays beyond the horizon certainly is one of the things that has driven me back to the Antarctic time and again. Those distant mountains were challenging, but the allowable distance of 250 miles from Ellsworth already exceeded made us retreat to home base. These new distant mountains had neither been seen nor photographed by the Navy's flight slightly south of this area, because of heavy cloud cover.

Both before and after this flight, we made reconnaissance flights for the traverse party. Early in October, the IGY men had insisted that they would travel directly west from Ellsworth to get inland. It was only after I had taken Thiel along repeatedly, and shown him time and again the unending series of crevasses to the west that they agreed among themselves to travel east along a path I had long since laid out for them. Cox was sent out with the pilots to take pictures over the eastern route I had described to him and to McCarthy. It was obvious that this was the only safe route for the men to travel on land. As leader of the expedition, both for the Navy and the IGY, I was not only responsible for the safety of the men, but the success of this surface trip into the untrod land to the south of us.

Just to prove our case to the IGY men, I took one flight with Cox aboard, in which we photographed the western area. First we climbed to 10,000 feet and levelled off. Then we went southward along the Bahia Chica inlet that lay next to our camp. We followed that inlet to Gould Bay, and then headed for the huge rift area, where the crevasses abounded. This flight along with the photographic evidence finally convinced Dr. Thiel that the overland party would have to go southeast toward Shackleton.

Yet Neuburg was not convinced even by that. He insisted on seeing for himself. So finally we again took several of the IGY men out to see for themselves. It took that much convincing to get them to follow my orders. By this time I was pretty thoroughly disgusted.

With the summer weather, morale in our camp improved remarkably, but there seemed to be nothing we could do to get the civilians on the right track.

Brown, for example, flatly refused to go over to the Argentine camp again to help them get their ionospheric recorder going. He said he had too many things to do at Ellsworth. Even on the day that we had that conversation, both Brown and Skidmore were still in their bunks at 11:00 in the morning.

The result of that conference was that Lieutenant Sumrall and I delivered the parts for the ionospheric recorder to the Argentines.

Skidmore continued to be on the warpath. He sent "ham-grams" to friends that hardly veiled the animosity he felt for me. He was entirely unco-operative in every way. From time to time he asked to operate the "ham-radio" again, but I kept delaying that. Chief Kent could not abide Skidmore's present in the radio room, and I found Kent more important there than Skidmore. Skidmore also had his scaling job to do. On this he was far behind.

We used the process of "scaling" for transforming the images on a film negative into a useable form. This negative was obtained while making soundings into the ionosphere with the Ionospheric Recorder. The observer would project the negative onto a frosted glass which contained grid-lines. The vertical lines would give the frequency values while the

194

horizontal lines would give the height of the layers in the ionosphere above the surface of the earth. The values thus obtained were converted into a coded message for radio transmission to an evaluation center in the United States.

At about this time, two "ham-grams" that I had written and given to the radio operators to get out for me disappeared completely. Hannah was on the radio that night. He had my "ham-grams" on top, ready to send them, when he stopped to drop over to the messhall for a cup of coffee. When he returned, my "ham-grams" were missing, and he could not find them anywhere. Someone obviously had it in for me—and I was told it was one of the civilians.

Now that the beginning of the traverse route was pretty well established I finally took Neuburg and Paul Walker, the other glaciologist, on a flight to the Argentine base. The two spent all their time at Belgrano talking to Dr. Lissignoli, the glaciologist from the Argentine Antarctic Institute whom Neuburg had met the summer before on Greenland.

I spent my time with the physicist, who speaks English and the commander of the base with whom I could converse in the most broken Spanish. It was a pleasant change from the lack of companionship I had at Ellsworth these days.

I couldn't blame our fellows for looking forward to these visits. Other nationalities have the knack of making their bases far more cozy and homelike than Americans normally do. I noticed this first in 1947 at a British base close to mine on the Palmer Peninsula. Other Americans who visited the various bases of countries participating in the IGY, including the Russian base at Mirny, have made similar observations about the friendly warmth a bit of chintz, a wall hanging, or a flower pot can create. Like a home, I have often wondered if our barren interiors don't influence or reflect the personalities of their occupants.

At this time, the five officers were messing together, and the enlisted men and civilians ate together. But of the five officers, Lt. Jaburg and Lt. Smith were both sulking. Smith had been sulking for months. He never spoke unless it was absolutely necessary. No comments, no remarks; only answers delivered curtly when addressed were his contributions to social life. When he finished his meal, he rolled up his napkin and left the table, meal after meal. McCarthy and I were really the only ones of the five who spoke and carried on conversation, for Jaburg was sulking because he was not allowed to operate the "ham" radio—a request I had turned down a few weeks earlier at the urging of McCarthy who was then trying to have him take on some of the responsibilities in the aviation unit. In addition, we did not want to give the impression that the "ham radio" was being monopolized by the officers since it was one of the enlisted men's greatest recreational diversions. Lieutenant Sumrall, while good humored and a pleasant person, just naturally had little to say to make lively table conversation.

Lieutenant Sumrall, nevertheless, was my "teacher" in ping-pong and the sharpest player in camp. He continued giving me the fine points of the game right up to the last. Both with him, and Chiefs Spear and May, and the electrician Hannah, aerologist Camp, and utility-man Ray and very often with Thiel, I had many pleasant associations in the recreation hall, all during my stay at Ellsworth. McCarthy and I also had pool games after lunch and the evening movies.

After our Sunday "brunch" during the darkest period, I had played bridge for a while with Walker, Behrendt and Skidmore. Even during the most controversial sessions we continued the bridge playing and passed the time away rather pleasantly. I was also busy with my own projects: administrations and writing occupied much of my time. It was relaxing to mix with the other men on these occasions.

The flight to Belgrano had created some unusual problems. The Argentines were most hospitable, too hospitable to our plane crews in fact for they fed them more liquor than they should have had. On the October 13 flight we nearly had an accident on the return trip. McCarthy had let one of the enlisted men take the controls, at the time of landing. The man, an aviation mechanic, may have been a competent pilot, but at least he did not know his plane. As the plane was coming in to land, the main tank ran out of gas. McCarthy saw what was happening, and switched to a full tank just in time. But it was too close a call for Dr. Thiel's liking, and he complained about the "near-accident" in the flight.

Further, after we returned from Belgrano and I left the plane, McCarthy let another enlisted man take the controls to practice landings. One of them was so rough Dr. Thiel, who was watching, thought the undercarriage of the plane would break off.

Yet we had no accidents, luckily enough. Our record for both health and safety for the stay was proceeding remarkably well. Dr. Smith had very little to do in the medical line, except to patch up cuts, or give heat treatment to men — like John Brown who strained his back lifting some heavy boxes in preparation for assembling his ionospheric recorder. We would have been a happy camp had it not been for low morale. This factor, of course, was largely attributable to the interpretation of the entire command, both by the civilians and the military, yet that was not the only aspect.

On October 15, for example, the men in the radio shack made contact with the Navy Station at Davisville, Rhode Island, and learned what their duty stations would be when they came out of the Antarctic. Almost to a man, the enlisted men were unhappy about their new assignments. Rather than being honored and receiving some recognition for their year of service in the Antarctic, it seemed that they received worse billets because of it. Men who had been on sea-duty before they came to Ellsworth were re-assigned to sea-duty—perhaps in someones' mistaken opinion that Ant-arctic duty was comparable to a pleasant shore assignment.

As one man put it: "If the Navy fails to get a ship in here on time to take us out, they will have a 100 percent record of not carrying out any promises they made when I volunteered."

The men had been taken off per diem. They had lost their chances for promotion when they did not get the examination papers in time. They were to get no bonus, few advancements and only a few of the men got the assignments they requested.

The officers were equally disheartened for various reasons. At about this time we learned that instead of being charged $1.00 a day for our food during the time we were in the Antarctic, we were to be charged $2.25 per day, plus extra charges for mid-morning coffee and late evening snack. Some of the officers had volunteered in the hope that they could save a considerable amount of money. But with the cutoff in per diem, which had not been expected, they would not save very much. The fact that the civilians, in addition to their tremendous salaries, got their meals free, did not set too well with the rest of them.

We finally heard from Major Lassiter of the Air Force again, in a radio talk with Punta Arenas, from which he would fly down to us around the middle of November. Even Lassiter had made his plans in accord with the changed regulations. He let me know that he would supply all his own food while he was down in the Antarctic. His men would be dependent on us for nothing, and thus not subject to the high charges that the Navy had in-augurated.

Yet in spite of the bad feeling inevitable when individual desires and ambitions are frustrated for various reasons, the work had to continue. Thiel and Neuburg finally admitted that they could not possibly travel by the western and southern route to get inland, off the barrier and onto the land. It was a big day for me when they finally admitted they had been wrong about something. Had they shown such good sense before, the whole feeling in the camp would have been better.

I had no power to order the way in which they would conduct their traverse, even though I was responsible, but I could give them plenty of advice, and I did. First, I suggested that they work out a regular system in operations, so that each man on the trip knew exactly what to do and when to do it. That pertained to driving, stopping, taking equipment off the sledges, starting a heater for water, preparing the food, arranging the sleeping bags, putting up tents, operating the radio. I suggested that they work out a procedure for taking seismic shots, so that each man's duties were clearly defined, and he would do them without loss of time or breath in argument.

I also urged them strongly to live outside the station area here for at least twenty-four hours, to simulate exactly the conditions they would experience in the field. They would then be able to discover what equipment or plan was not functioning properly. They would quickly find what items they had forgotten in the cooking, sleeping, in the instrumentation of their scientific projects, or traveling departments, and they would be able to correct errors before they became important to the success of the trip. But they never did.

Another important item to be watched was the procedure of resupply for food and gasoline. Even when not travelling, according to Thiel, the party would use fifty gallons of gasoline a day, just to keep the Sno-Cat that contained the seismic equipment warm. I recommended that they always keep enough gasoline on the sledges to supply them for six days in case of bad weather. They must also carry enough food for at least twenty days.

While the scientists were prepared to take some of my advice about the traverse, I continued to have trouble with them about their daily work.

On October 19, John Brown turned up in the radio room with a whole stack of recordings to be transmitted to the Bureau of Standards. These recordings were the finished product of our ionospheric work for eventual use by physicists to aid their prediction of frequencies and time of best long distance radio transmitions with least static interference. It would take a radio operator at least five hours to get them out. I wanted him to stagger his work so that he would give the operators smaller amounts of material every day. Still, they were 19 days behind in one phase of their work, the scaling of their observations.

I called Brown in to discuss these matters with him. First, I directed him to bring the scaling up to date, and to put Skidmore on day work, rather than night, and see to it that he was kept busy.

The second thing was to carry out McCarthy's recommendation and put Skidmore on mess duty. For Skidmore to keep abreast of the scaling procedure would require only a couple of hours' work a day. Mess duty would occupy him no more than three to four hours a day. He could handle both assignments and still have time to indulge in his own personal interests. Malville had served a two-week tour of mess duty and although he was not very happy about it he was needed there at the time, and otherwise, with his aurora program completed, had very little to do. His attitude had improved remarkably following the assignment.

But Brown objected violently to putting Skidmore on mess duty. Brown said Skidmore was a Bureau of Standards employee, and his boss was in the Bureau at Boulder, Colorado. If someone there wanted him to do mess duty, let them order him to do it.

Brown said he had nothing to do with the National Academy of Sciences, the IGY, with Dr. Gould, Chairman of the U.S. Antarctic Committee, Mr. Odishaw, the Secretary of the IGY, nor did he take orders from any of them or from me or from any man in uniform.

He also added that as station scientific leader I had no authority to direct any activities of any of the IGY scientists. The military men, he said, were supposed to be down in the Antarctic to assist the civilians, to provide them with food, housing and other things they needed, while the scientists did their job. Assisting in any household duties was not their job.

If I wanted to have Skidmore do anything but his own work, I would have to get an order from the Bureau of Standards, as far as Brown was concerned.

One interesting fact came out of the conversation: Brown charged that I had done my best to have him and Skidmore ousted from the IGY personnel roster. In view of the true facts this was rather amusing. Soon after we had settled down for the winter, Skidmore told me how he had been selected. He had read in the newspapers about the upcoming IGY program. Based on his knowledge of radio and some electronics with a commercial background, he wrote a letter of application to his Senator. The Senator, in turn sent the letter with his recommendations on to the IGY officials in Washington who felt obliged to find a place for him. According to Brown, when he and Skidmore were being briefed at the National Bureau of Standards at Boulder, Colorado, there was strong pressure from some of the officials there to have Skidmore dismissed. Through Brown's intervention, however, he was allowed to go anyway.

Then they both had a run-in with an IGY official at Davisville, R.I., where all the IGY civilians received indoctrination before starting for the Antarctic. This IGY official thought that both Brown and Skidmore were trouble-makers. So Brown was partly right. What Brown did not know was that talks went on in Washington to replace them. When I heard of it I spoke up in Brown's and Skidmore's behalf and thought they would work out in the long run and since they had gotten this far, should be allowed to continue. Any further talk of replacement was then dropped. As it turned out, they had obviously influenced Thiel, Malville, and the others against working in cooperation with me the way I had hoped the IGY men would.

McCarthy told me one evening when he was pretty low in spirit that he had become unpopular with the civilians, as well as with the enlisted men, because he always went along with my orders and wishes. He was growing quite depressed because he had no one to talk to. And since no one would become chatty with him, he had no way of keeping up with the gossip of what was going on around camp.

I had to tell him that no officer could hope to be popular with the men. McCarthy said he realized that officers would always be subjected to bitching by the enlisted men, but he felt our troubles at Ellsworth went much deeper.

Ninety-eight percent of the trouble, McCarthy said, had been caused by the civilians. He vowed that he would never again volunteer for service where the military had to mix with civilians. The civilians egged the enlisted men on to disobey orders. The civilians disobeyed orders themselves. They caused the enlisted men to lose respect for the officers, and that caused the civilians to lose the respect of the men, too.

I tried to raise McCarthy's spirit, but I must admit that he mirrored my own exact feelings about the civilians. Perhaps nowhere was the conflict better exhibited than at the movies, when in one scene of a Navy picture, a lieutenant in uniform made the remark: "We in uniform should not meddle in civilian affairs." At that point in the movie Skidmore spoke up and said, "I wish someone here would do the same thing."

It was a slap at me.

CHAPTER 14

THE CRISIS

M cCARTHY BADLY NEEDED A MAN TO REPLACE ONE OF THE ENLISTED men who had an important repair job to do, so I decided to put Skidmore on mess duty, in full knowledge of the unpleasantness it would create in camp. He certainly had the time for the job, the hours he spent in the recreation hall alone were enough to carry on the job of mess attendant. So, McCarthy and Chief May put Skidmore's name down for the two weeks beginning Monday, October 28.

When Brown heard of it, he prepared two dispatches to the Bureau of Standards, protesting my action. I flatly refused to allow them to go out. I believed Skidmore's services could be lent to the messhall for two weeks without injuring the IGY program, and that was that.

There was not as much complaint as there might have been because five of the nine civilians were making ready for their cross-country traverse. Several of the rest of us were busy investigating a penguin rookery we had discovered on the coast to the west of Gould Bay. The first time we flew over it, then came down to land to take pictures and look at the birds. We centered our interest on a group of some 8,000 Emperors, many of the young chicks still tagged after their mothers.

We spent only forty-five minutes at the rookery that first day but decided to come back the next, not only to gather more information, and some eggs, but to give some of the men a break from the routine of camp. McCarthy loaded the plane with seven altogether. I thought that was too many, but he was the pilot and the aviation chief.

At any rate, we went over there—about 95 miles from our camp. The rookery was actually located directly at the end of the iceberg, thirty-four miles long that was broken off from the shelf. We flew low over the birds, and frightened them, I am afraid, but landed, to observe them more carefully. All told, we made a number of trips to the rookery, and on October

30 we flew Kim Malville over to make observations and take a census of the most southern of the group of birds.

This was important, because while there is a great deal of talk about penguins, this rookery was the ninth discovered of only fourteen Emperor penguin rookeries known to exist on the Antarctic continent's shores.* This one covered an area of several square miles, bordering on the south by iceberg cliffs, and the rather smooth sea ice area offering access to the sea northward.

Although the majority of the birds was concentrated in three groups, individuals and groups of from three to ten birds were scattered throughout the entire region. Many of the birds, we found, were travelling, perhaps to the feeding grounds northward or back from them. North of the groups of birds, a track, or rather many tracks were seen leading to a once-open, but presently closed lead of water in the ice, about a mile from the most northern of the three groups. At this point it seemed that the birds must make a trip of several miles to reach water.

Besides the moving birds, many individual birds guarding chicks were visible. One such parent, several hundred feet from her nearest neighbor, was feeding her chick. In this area between groups, one saw frozen eggs and dead chicks in all stages of development, but inside the big groups, no dead chicks or eggs were found.

Some of the station's personnel noted that near the northwestern group, a clearly defined area was found where there were a number of eggs and dead chicks—a sort of infant cemetery. Near the southern group, we saw eggs both to the east and west of the live birds.

Malville discovered that the southern group of Emperors was divided into four sub-units, and he counted the adults and chicks of each group using a hand counter. It appeared that the group contained 1,200 adults and about 1,000 chicks. One significant characteristic was the concentration of chicks in the middle of the group. These inner groups of chicks, some of them numbering more than thirty, under the eyes of four or five adult birds, pointed to the establishment of a nursery system, where unemployed birds watch over the young while the parents are afield collecting food.

The high proportion of chicks to adults suggested to Malville that the mortality rate of 77 per cent observed by others in 1911 at Cape Crozier rookery was too high for this colony. Scott's man had found it difficult to collect frozen chicks in good condition. The maternal instinct of the chickless birds was so strong that they carried lifeless chicks around for days, until their down was worn away. But by contrast, this rookery showed very little evidence of the fondling of dead chicks. It was also

---

*As of Dec. 1, 1960—total of fourteen.

significant that in only one instance were two birds seen fighting over a chick. At Cape Crozier there were so many chickless adults that fighting was common—frequently resulting in the death of the chick.

Certainly there was no lack of live chicks at this rookery, in comparison to Cape Crozier. It was probable that the climatic conditions were less severe and that was the major reason. At any rate, this rookery represented a significant departure from the subject of Edward Wilson's classical study of the Emperor penguin.*

From his observations, Malville noted three stages of relationship between the chicks and the adults. First, there were the nursery groups in the center of the milling birds, guarded by unemployed adult birds. These adults usually ignored the individual chicks, and appeared to have no parental interest in any of them.

Second, a large number of parents remained close to their single chicks. When an adult with a chick moved about, it kept the chick going in the proper direction in front of it, by prodding with the bill. These adults always tried to keep the chicks directly in front of them. If the chick changed direction, the adults revolved behind them. Occasionally, when the parent wanted to move quickly, it would hurry off, leaving the chick to scurry along behind. Although Malville never saw more than one chick standing against, or between the legs of an adult, he frequently observed pairs of chicks following one adult with the adult aware of their presence.

Sometimes parents of one chick would peck at another chick if it came too close to their baby. Malville also saw one penguin come walking in from outside the circle to the area where the chicks were thickest. She was carrying a chick on her feet. Suddenly, in the middle of the youngsters circle, she pushed the baby off her feet, and waddled away to disappear in a large crowd of penguins standing a bit away. Malville watched the chick she had put down, one of the smallest in the group. It walked around in a circle for a time, then headed into the thickest part of the group of chicks, and disappeared, too. The mother penguin did not ever come back for the chick. It seemed to Malville almost as if she had the chick out on a loan basis, and then brought it back to deposit in the communal nursery.

There seemed considerable evidence of communalism in the raising of the young. Yet some parents kept their chicks resting on their own legs, or on the feet, with the chicks' head facing either forward or between the parent's legs. These chicks, so protected, seemed to be smaller than those in the big nursery groups, and perhaps the parent-chick association at this

*Wilson, Edward A. 1907, Aves. British National Antarctic Exped. 1901-4. 2. Zoology, Pt. 2, 1-31.

stage was still in the guardian category because of the slow development of the chick.

When these adults with chicks moved, they did so very cautiously, always keeping the chicks resting on their feet.

On one occasion, Malville saw a chick try to climb between the legs of a chickless adult, but get pecked away instead. One other thing became particularly noticeable: Whether they carried chicks on their feet or not, the adult penguins stood on the backs of their feet, always keeping the front parts of their feet off the surface of the snow.

Thus, at the rookery, we noted both communalistic and individual behavior. Before we could draw any conclusions as to which behavior pattern is basic, it would be necessary to mark chicks that were fed in the nursery groups and others that were kept by individuals, to see what happened to them.

Six feet seemed to be as close as one could approach without frightening the birds. The Emperors seemed to be more easily frightened by a squatting form than by a standing figure. Perhaps a squatting body looks too much like their only land enemy, the leopard seal.

One sub-group that Malville watched particularly seemed to be a clan of birds, numbering some thirty adults and twenty chicks in the center. When this group was approached most of the birds grew nervous and the entire group moved. However, one adult advanced toward Malville and stopped directly between him and the group. When Malville advanced a foot, the bird backed off, but still maintained his position between Malville and the group. At no time did the penguin make any attacking motions. Perhaps he was moved only by curiosity but in contrast to the Adelies, curiosity does not seem to be an Emperor trait. Perhaps the bird was showing acceptance of responsibility for the safety of the group.

Some forty feet away from the group there were three depressions in the snow, two or three inches deep, roughly circular, and eight feet in diameter. The depressions were solidly covered by ice and purple penguin excreta. No such hollows were seen in the middle of the group, and these three had not been used for some time, gathering from the collection of hoar frost in the center. In one of the hollows were ten pebbles, up to three-quarters of an inch in length. Similar pebbles were also found in a chick we dissected at the base. Although pebbles are to be found in the stomachs of most Emperors, they are particularly interesting in this area of the Antarctic, for the shallowest water along the Filchner Ice Shelf, just a few miles west of the rookery, is 400 feet deep. The nearest exposed seaward rock lies at Moltke Nunataks, about 160 miles east. Another rock exposure lies northwest, about 300 miles, at Bowman Peninsula. Otherwise, to man's knowledge, there was no possible source for the rock. Where did it come from?

Neither this question nor many like it could be answered in the brief time we had to study penguins. The study was not a part of our IGY discipline. Malville undertook his observations solely from his own interest.

The rest of us were interested in the big birds, too, of course. On our first flight to the rookery, McCarthy and I herded a pair of penguins into the plane. At first, when they were lifted into the OTTER, the birds raised a terrible rumpus. But when we had taken off, soon they were sitting up, and looking out the windows of the plane, quite like any other passenger.

I had collected several eggs at the rookery. I proposed to drill a small hole through the shell and take the inside out, as the egg warmed. If I did not, they would explode, and spatter the area with an alarmingly bad odor.

I had known of the smell of penguin eggs for years, but in case I might have forgotten, coming in for a landing at Ellsworth on our way back from the rookery, the penguins made such a rumpus that they broke one of the eggs on the floor. The smell was so strong that when we landed the men came out the door at the front of the plane instead of the easier doors at the center.

One of the VX-6 men braved the stink, and rescued the two penguins. He put them in a large box, and left them standing outside in the snow.

The next day McCarthy and I disposed of the two penguins, cleaned them, and packed them in burlap bags. Before the weather warmed up we would put them in our deep freeze unit below ground—just a dugout where the temperature never rose above $-20°$. They would keep all right until the ships came in. Spoilage was one problem we did not have in the Antarctic.

We had a difficult time killing the penguins. We tried to get a little chloroform from the doctor, but he was quite unfriendly about it and said he had none to spare. Then, when we were disposing of the birds, he wanted to photograph the whole unpleasant procedure. I had no use for that kind of turnabout, and told him there would be no pictures.

The next day we flew over to Shackleton to visit the British again. When we returned, I found the penguins gone. I had a feeling that I knew the civilian who was responsible. This man had become quite open in his antagonism to me. A few nights before, he had made a loud remark about me in the movie. And when I had walked out of the terrible film they were showing that night—he had clapped his hands in applause.

So that evening, after supper, I asked the man to come to my quarters. He would not, he said. He was much too busy. If I wanted to see him, I could come and see him at his room.

I discussed the affair with McCarthy. He thought I had to take some action. As a result, I wrote up a dispatch to be sent to Captain Dickey, preferring charges against the IGY man for disrespect and disobedience. I intended to have him reported to higher authority.

The next morning, coming out of my quarters, I spotted our penguins, standing against a supporting post in one of the side tunnels off the main tunnel. Someone had cut their heads off and left the bodies standing there. Now the entire job had to be done all over again, and two more penguins needlessly killed. When I went out to my weasel, I found the head of one of them on the driver's seat. I had my own opinion as to who had done the job and McCarthy and Chief Spear agreed with me.

I decided against sending the wire to Captain Dickey. I would handle the matter myself at Ellsworth. It would only be a few weeks more until the ships arrived. Because of his insulting remarks at the movies, I would ban him from the movies for an undetermined time. I would also write a letter to his superiors in the government telling them of his conduct.

Also I would harass him a bit as he had harassed me.

That morning, when the man showed up to take mess duty, dressed in his usual filthy clothes, and looking quite dirty and shaggy, I called Dr. Smith and asked him to check the fellow for cleanliness—since he was handling food.

Then I wrote him a letter on National Academy of Science stationery, detailing his violations of the rules, and setting down his restrictions. I also prepared a memo for Clyde McCauley, a third-class seaman, who was serving now as master at arms, and another memo for Chief Kent and Spear. McCauley was to present the offender with the notice that he could no longer attend movies. Spear was to give him the letter outlining his reprimand. Kent was to notify the radio operators at our station that he was not to be allowed to work the "ham" radio or hang about in the radio room—although his privilege of carrying on phone-patches with his family back home would continue, as there was quite a specific ruling on that.

I had expected some reaction from the other civilians regarding the incident, but they were much too busy preparing for the traverse. It is amazing how total interest in the job at hand will minimize the complaints. This day, October 28, they were ready to leave, finally. They loaded their sledges, and took my advice and reduced the load by about 300 pounds of non-essential items. In addition to scientific instruments, they took a thirty-day food supply. Periodic plane flights would resupply them with fuel and food as they requested by radio and there would be essential items which they had forgotten entirely. Before Thiel crawled into his seat in the Sno-Cat, I slipped him a small bag with some bottles of wine I told him to open for special occasions. After much picture-taking and some last-minute delays to recover forgotten items, the party got off at 11:30.

206

By the end of the day, when Jaburg flew the helicopter out to check on them, the party had covered only twelve miles. The rear of one of their sleds had fallen into a four-foot–wide crevasse, but after a great deal of effort they had pulled the sled out. They told us they needed some extra supplies, which we planned to take out the following day, and I planned to visit them when they reached an agreed stopping point on the east side of the Belgrano crevasse, a deep rift in the barrier that runs about due south for sixteen miles.

In the course of working out the penguin affair I learned that five other penguins had been brought up to camp and killed without my knowledge. It was a direct violation of orders for any person at the station to kill penguins without first receiving permission from the commanding officer. Admiral Dufek had given specific written orders on that. And I agreed with him completely. Otherwise, there would be a mass-slaughter of penguins and other wild-life, and that is one thing every expedition leader has enforced most rigidly, to preserve animal life along Antarctic's shores unless needed for maintenance of man's life. We knew that some men would want to take them home as souvenirs, but to keep the matter under control had demanded that each man who wanted to kill a penguin must deposit $50 with me. The $50 deposit would be returned to the individual provided he presented a certificate from a taxidermist that the bird had been stuffed and mounted within six months after return.

None of the men who had taken the five penguins had deposited the money. One of the five was Skidmore. I had the four enlisted men in and read them off for taking penguins in violation of orders. I also informed them that I wanted their deposits, and that this time I would not go any further with disciplinary action. I told them, too, that Skidmore's penguin was totally unauthorized and asked that the specimen be returned to me.

Within twenty-four hours all four had made their deposits. Skidmore had done nothing, neither had he spoken to me nor had he made any move to return the penguin. As far as I was concerned now, he would not be allowed to take a penguin out, even if he did want to deposit the $50.

The traverse party, it seemed, was in trouble from the very beginning of its operations. In the beginning, they asked that we send one of the radio men out to show them how to operate their sending and receiving sets. They had set out from camp without even learning how to run the Sno-Cat radio! We flew Forlidas, one of the operators, out in the helicopter. We had to make resupply flights nearly every day, to bring along items the men had forgotten. Luckily, they had excellent weather, or there is some doubt in my mind that they would have survived.

The sun, by this time of the year, was shining brightly above the horizon—and around the clock. At midnight on October 31, it was bright and glorious daylight. Due south lay the sun, yellowish orange and slightly tinted with gray. I could see the cold air vibrating, much like heat waves over a hot pavement in summer. All the men, myself included, were thinking in terms of the day we would go home. On this day I heard the figure seventy more days—the men were keeping track of each day as it passed, one less day they would spend in the sameness of the cold and snow, one less day until they were home again.

No one used the Recreation hall very much at this time. Where before the men had competed for the best hobby kits, not one of them wanted a kit. Neither the pool table nor the ping-pong table were in use more than a few times a day. I know I did not play ping-pong myself for several weeks, and I played pool with McCarthy at about this time, for the first time in a month.

McCarthy was feeling the tension, too. He had grown very moody, and something else had come over him, a kind of lassitude that made him seem sullen. Perhaps he was concerned with his loss of "status" with the VX-6 personnel, or with the OTTER plane which was ruined by heavy snow accumulation as a result of not following my advice. I asked him one day to talk to Air Force Major Lassiter if he came up on the radio to discuss last-minute plans before he flew in with his crew to begin setting up radio schedules and fix frequencies. McCarthy refused. "I have nothing to talk to him about," he said. As a pilot and a Navy man McCarthy probably was not looking forward to the coming of the larger Air Force planes and personnel.

McCarthy was not the only dispirited one. Hannah, our hard-working electrician, had been working the "ham" gear along with Camp, the aerologist. These two men usually took turns working the radio by dividing the night into two watches. But while they were supposed to be handling it, not a "ham-message" had gone out in two weeks. I had Hannah over to talk about it, and he said he was tired—he was on mess duty at this time, which took about three to four hours a day, and he still had to do such electrical work as came up. That was understandable, but Gary Camp's story was quite different. He would just not do anything because he did not like the way the whole radio set-up was being handled.

In the interest of keeping our airways open and on an equal basis to all, I would have preferred the use of the radio limited solely to our professionally assigned operators—as is standard procedure the world over. The honor carries considerable power and prestige—particularly in isolation—and requires individual trustworthiness. Our regular operators had about all they could handle with official traffic. Also the "ham" facilities were regarded in a slightly different category; they were included at U.S. bases mainly to help the morale of the men. Unfortunately, at times the opposite effect was produced and in trying to work out equitable solutions, the issue frequently became involved in our local politics, as was true in this instance.

And although McCarthy was working the "ham" radio almost every night, he now seemed to slacken off. The men had expressed some resentment against the Executive Officer's presence in the radio shack over extended periods. They felt it cramped their style. Perhaps that got McCarthy down, too.

At any rate, on November 3, McCarthy came to me and asked to be relieved as executive officer. I was shocked, and I showed it. On the defense, he began to complain about the way the station was being run. Since he could not go along with that, he said, he thought he ought to resign as executive officer. Of course, I made the final decisions. But the funny thing was that most of the points about which he complained were points he had brought up—and policies that had been laid down on his advice or with his concurrence.

Nevertheless, I could not budge him from his determination.

His excuse was that with the flying season on, he had more than enough work with the running of the Aviation Unit. But the fact was that he was quitting when the going got rough. It *was* getting rough. The men were all on edge. Even the respite from tension that the appearance of the sun had brought with it had now passed. The camp was a sullen, cold place.

I went to bed that night with a heavy heart. The next morning I had another talk with McCarthy and again tried to persuade him to stay on. He stood firm, and when I pressed him, he began arguing about many events of the past in which he had not agreed with my actions. I wanted no part of that, I wanted only constructive comments that could be put into effect in the future. So I wrote McCarthy off as executive officer that day.

With McCarthy temporarily out of the picture the burden rested squarely on Dr. Smith, who had been sent out to command the SeaBee unit in the first place. I called him in and told him about McCarthy. He would have to take responsibility for station operations now, I said. He seemed quite amenable and amazed to learn of McCarthy's action, so we discussed some changes in the routine. To alleviate the pressure on the men's "head," the three Chiefs (Spear, May, and Kent) would use the same washing facilities as the civilians and the officers. This would divide the men into two more even groups. We would check out a number of men on the "ham" radio (Dr. Smith included, and Skidmore given another chance in the last desperate attempt to have him change his attitude).

These changes seemed to help ease tension at the station, but they did not solve the problems McCarthy had raised by quitting. Most important of those was the attitude of McCarthy himself.

We ran into considerable difficulty in resupplying the traverse party. Within the first few days the civilians got lost several times. Lieutenant Sumrall spent an hour one day flying in a circle around their given location but could not find them. He had to return to base with three drums of gas and a number of items the party had forgotten.

The next day, we did get in touch with the party by radio. They were fifty-one miles from the station, in an area entirely surrounded by crevasses, and were waiting air help before moving on. I told McCarthy to load the party with more gas on their sledges so they could go without resupply for at least two weeks. We were going out every other day at this point, and could not continue to keep such a schedule.

The written instructions were that we were not to fly beyond the 250-mile radius with the OTTER planes, although the gasoline carried with a load would allow over three times that distance; but these were Admiral Dufek's orders, and I could not change them. Dufek confirmed this restriction again after he had seen one of my press releases in which I described the discovery of new mountains on our first flight. We had then flown beyond the 250-mile limit. In his message, Dufek emphasized that the gasoline left should be used exclusively for support of the traverse party, and not used even for the pilots in proficiency flights around the station. The message was a direct slap at me, and McCarthy confirmed my views of the message. With such a detailed directive, it seemed to mean we could not even visit Shackleton or Belgrano again, nor fly as far as the Gould Bay area for observations, even though we had 9,000 gallons of gas left and the traverse support should take only 4,000 gallons.

Dufek's message also revealed the point of the whole move, when he noted in it that the mountains we had found were already discovered. They were called the "Dufek Massif." He noted that the peaks had been seen by his air-squadron during Operation Deepfreeze I, the year before, and pointed out they had been covered by aerial photography, so there could be no question about them. The point, of course, was that the new crop of explorers, the Navy's summer experts, did not want me, or any of the members of the older Antarctic generations flying about and discovering lands that would redound to our credit.

I might disagree, as I did, but those were orders. We would comply.

That first range of mountains did prove to contain the misplaced Dufek Massif, but the mountains I found beyond them were new ones. In January, 1956, on a flight from McMurdo the Navy crew saw "Dufek Massif" on the extreme left on their return flight track; but the new group beyond they could not have seen, nor are they visible on their photographs. But, because of the 250-mile flight limitations imposed on our planes, I was afraid I would not be able to investigate these distant mountains further. The more important issue as to how we would supply the traverse team should they succeed in going beyond the 250-mile flight radius does not seem to have been taken into consideration.

I was prepared to do all that superior commands dictated but I was not prepared to encounter new interpretations of orders by McCarthy. Yet that is exactly what happened.

The day after we received Dufek's message, I told McCarthy that I wanted to go out on the next flight to the traverse party. He said he did not know if there would be room for me if they had to take three drums of gas along.

The issue came to a head the following day when the flight was actually scheduled. I reminded Sumrall that I wanted to go along on the trip. He said McCarthy thought the plane was already overloaded, so I asked him to tell McCarthy to come and see me.

About two hours later, McCarthy showed up.

"What's up?" he asked.

I started by asking for his opinion with regard to the aircraft and my participation in flights.

He said: "You have nothing to do with the aircraft. They are under my direct control. *I* say who is or is not going on a flight, and it is up to me to say whether or not you go inside a plane, captain."

That was really an eye-opener for me. I said: "If I want to go out into the field to see my own men on the traverse, which, by the way, is included in my instructions, I will have to beg you for permission to do so?"

He said yes, that was the way it was.

I then told McCarthy that he was an officer of a small detachment under my command and that the attitude he had adopted was unsound. How could he report here for duty, when I had orders that specifically put me in command, and still not recognize me as commanding officer. I reminded him, too, that I was to make a fitness report on him, and he still maintained his position.

He answered: "I would rather have a poor fitness report than recognize your claim to have anything to do with the VX-6's activities here."

McCarthy told me frankly that he had been told by his Air Staff officer of VX-6 at Quonset Point, Rhode Island, when a copy of my flight orders had come to their office that McCarthy did not need to take me inside a plane unless he wanted to. Further, he mentioned the name of a captain who had laughed when he saw my orders, and had told McCarthy just to forget I ever had any orders to direct any activities of the aviation unit.

That was not the end of it. I told him I had flight orders, and intended to fly in order to carry out my mission. He declared that *he* would decide when I could fly. And it was left that way, after considerable recrimination, with McCarthy seeming to carry a large chip on his shoulder for some reason.

It was too bad—we had worked so well together until the question of who had jurisdiction over flight operations finally erupted. Less than two months before when McCarthy had overheard Skidmore's rantings, he immediately volunteered his support. He would back me up, he said, in everything I had done at this station.

I was worried about our traverse party getting through the crevasses I had surveyed and mapped for them. That same day we had word from Little America that a glaciologist in Crary's traverse group suffered severe body injuries when he fell more than sixty feet into a crevasse on the Ross Ice Shelf. He was flown out and later evacuated to New Zealand and home.

I thought of Peterson who had fallen 110 feet into a crevasse on my own expedition in 1947. He and Dodson had been skiing back to base from our 6,000-foot–high Palmer Peninsula plateau weather station. Deep, hard, and wind-blown sastrugi persuaded them that better time could be made by removing their skis. Dodson soon found himself walking alone. Peterson's concentrated weight had been sufficient to break through the snow-bridge of a hidden crevasse. There he remained face down with his arms pinned behind his back for nearly twelve hours until we finally rescued him unharmed—but well chilled.

Normally, our men did not use skis—there were only about eight pair in camp.

Luckily, our traverse party got through that very same day, driving until 3:00 o'clock the following morning. They stopped at a point 78 degrees and 50 minutes South by 38 degrees and 40 minutes West, to set up a full field station.

A few days later, I did have the opportunity to fly out to the traverse party, although I did not ask. Lieutenant Jaburg asked me if I wanted to come along. I did, with four others, but we did not find them in the overcast, and returned to base.

Several days later I finally did get out to see the traverse party. I spent most of the time there talking to Thiel. It was pretty rough, he said. They spent most of their time driving or taking their measurements, and the rest sleeping to conserve their strength. Four of the men slept on the floors of the two Sno-Cats, while one had to pitch a tent each time they stopped. They cooked out in the open. From what I could see, they were living more like gypsies than the efficient Antarctic cross-country travelers I had known.

On this trip I discussed the problem of resupply outside the 250-mile limit imposed by Dufek. Despite that order, they would need supplies when they got beyond that radius. Without informing me they had already changed their plans to include a geological stop at the western end of Dufek Massif, 350 miles from base before they would head westward toward Mount Hassage. They could use supply caches at both spots, if I would have the Air Force group to fly them out in their C-47 transport planes. Providing the Air Force planes arrived at Ellsworth I thought this could be arranged as the Task Force had not placed any flight-limitations on the C-47 Air Force planes.

These two caches would be enough because from Mount Hassage they would head toward Gould Bay where the Sno-Cats would be laid up in a temporary cache for the next year's traverse group to take over. The plan was that the Thiel group would be flown out from Gould Bay to Ellsworth, in time to catch the ship.

After this talk, I flew back to Ellsworth and for the next few days occupied myself with getting the Jamesway huts ready for the Air Force crew. They had complete facilities there, once we had turned on the space-heaters. They had a messhall, cooking ranges, and everything they would need for their stay. Only one problem arose: During the winter some of the men had broken into the huts where Lassiter's extra equipment had been stored, and a number of miscellaneous items were missing. We did not even know what was gone, and would not know until the Air Force group arrived and needed it. Then, perhaps we could recover some of it.

Since I decided to wait a few days for developments before pressing the McCarthy plane episode further, I spent a great deal of time in my quarters. Skidmore never had turned in his penguin, so I issued a final warning that I was going to file charges against him and deny him all recreational facilities. He came to me that same night, and promised to put up the $50 deposit as soon as his checkbook was flown in. I said nothing, but felt that because of his actions, Skidmore did not deserve to have the penguin at all.

Perhaps a week had gone by after my run-in with McCarthy when Jaburg came to see me, all excited, after having returned from spending seven hours with the traverse party. They were about 100 miles due south of Ellsworth and stuck a mile or so from the escarpment of the island I now was certain lay beyond. Their journey so far had progressed as planned, but an area of hidden crevasses was now causing trouble.

Jaburg started off by saying: "They are in a hell of a fix, surrounded by crevasses."

He went on to tell me how one of the Sno-Cats had fallen in a crevasse, and the rear end was still stuck. One of the aviation mechanics, Atles Lewis, had fallen into a crevasse that day. Luckily it was narrow, and he had stuck in the rift some twenty feet down, so they were able to get him out. Had he gone in a bit further down, where the split was wider, they would not have rescued him, for the chasm was hundreds of feet deep, and a fall almost always meant death.

There was hardly a place to land that was free of crevasses, Jaburg said. The traverse party needed my help.

I told Jaburg I would be glad to help, but that I had been denied the use of the airplane.

McCarthy, who must have been listening from his own room in the building, came charging in at this point.

In indignation he said: "Captain, that is not true. You are twisting the words to suit yourself. I never denied you the right to fly."

I smiled, perhaps a bit crookedly. "Mac, you certainly did," I said. "You told me in no small terms that you were running aviation, you were to say who went in the plane, and that if you didn't want to, you would not take me on any plane flight. You also told me you would not deny me the chance to get my flight time in. I wanted to go to the trail party when they said they were in crevasses at the end of the rift to help them out, but you said then you couldn't take me."

McCarthy was embarrassed. "I was overloaded then," he said.

"Overloaded!" I said scornfully, "overloaded with three drums of fuel and two men to fly sixty miles? Overloaded my eye."

McCarthy then changed his tune. He said he would take me whenever and wherever I would like to go, except not on a flight over 250 miles since that was forbidden by Dufek's constraining delineation.

I said that was fine. The discussion was over, and we settled down to finding a route out of the mess.

We hoped to fly out the next morning, but could not. Overcast and snow bothered us. The snow was hard, and irregular—as rough as it had been a few days before when one of the men, driving the tractor had gotten lost just outside the edge of camp, and had driven into a ten-foot hole where one of the sleds had been buried during the winter. He was not hurt, but he was badly shaken and scratched in the fall.

It was nearly two days before we got off the ground, then late in the afternoon (which was not important because of the ever-present sun), the weather cleared for a take-off.

We flew southwest until we reached the first high land south of Gould Bay, then followed the escarpment until we reached the traverse party. Instead of ascending the closest cape of high land where they would be safe they had attempted to save a few miles by making a diagonal short-cut to the eastern escarpment. From the air we could easily see the crevasses with the shadow of the sun cast along their ridges. Numerous others had opened up by the evaporation of the snow-bridges that spanned the openings since we last flew over this area a number of weeks earlier.

There in the middle of them sat the traverse party, immobilized. McCarthy circled for a while, then made an excellent landing in their Sno-Cat tracks. We staked the area as safe for the plane take-off then picked up Thiel and Augenbaugh and set out to find a way through the crevasses for the Sno-Cats. We retraced their tracks for four miles, then headed southeast for about seventy miles, through scattered crevasses. We traveled due west for a few miles, then paralleled our course to return to the Sno-Cats. If they would follow that line, which had few crevasses, they would be safe enough and be able to reach the high escarpment where there would be no obstacles to hamper their progress.

On our return flight to Ellsworth we evacuated Dr. Thiel. He had lost a great deal of weight and did not look well. He was troubled by intestinal bleeding, and naturally felt terrible. The trail-food was not suited for his digestion.

I had urged strongly that proven trail-foods be provided for all whose duties would take them away from the station. But the decision to eliminate pemmican rations from both emergency plane survival equipment and traverse use was made long before we departed from the U.S.

Internal disorders caused by improper trail diet are unnecessary. Good health and efficiency can be maintained in Antarctic travel. In 1940 my companion, Carl Eklund, and I lived exclusively on the highly developed and nourishing pemmican for eighty-four days on the trail. Our health and digestion were excellent at all times. We had to be in proper physical condition because we sledged on skis with dogteams for 1,264 miles.

But for modern Antarctic travel, pemmican's chief advantages—compactness, and well-balanced, high-caloric content—are deemed unnecessary considerations. Weight, bulk and long periods of strenuous exercise in the cold are no longer the determining factors for the selection of food-stuffs. Obviously, the transition still presents some unsolved problems. Long-term subsistence on food consisting mainly of items from a tin can—the type which can be picked up on the shelf of a super-market undoubtedly constitutes the major cause of traverse party ailments. This, coupled with the lack of exercise of the modern trailman (who spends much of his time riding and working in the heated cabin of the Sno-Cat), may build strong minds, but not strong muscular bodies.

Dr. Smith's care and a few days' change of diet at Ellsworth should help Thiel, we decided.

When we returned to base, we found that Skidmore had had the gall to move into Thiel's room, even though he knew that I had scheduled a visiting Argentine Naval officer in this room for a few days during Thiel's absence. I told him he would have to be out by noon of the following day. But the next day he had not done so. I went over to speak to him. He walked by and ignored me completely. I touched his arm, whereupon he flew into an uncontrolable rage. Luckily Dr. Thiel was there and saw the entire affair, or I am sure Skidmore would have accused me of striking him.

215

That whole day was then lost in trying to deal with Skidmore again. I directed the master at arms to remove Skidmore's material from Thiel's room. I wrote an official letter, explaining the restrictive measures: Skidmore was restricted to the science building, the messhall and the bathroom facilities. I wrote a dispatch for Crary at IGY headquarters in Little America. And finally, I asked Brown to keep Skidmore's working hours confined to the normal daytime schedule. We could not have him wandering around at night getting into any situation he felt obliged to cast himself.

The lack of a minimum amount of self-discipline under tension had continued like a plague to which few were immune. But, luckily, the time we spent on this floating ice shelf was not solely devoted to controversies. We continued to obtain good results in the IGY disciplines, and for this I was gratified.

Despite a small disagreement here and there, I had great admiration for the well-trained Navy enlisted men who carried on their work efficiently under trying conditions. They had served their apprenticeship to life and stood up well among us.

Chiefs Spear and May, particularly were solid men who showed their stability throughout the winter. They had experience in handling men. While McCarthy had done an over-all good job for me until recently, I realized that Spear or May should have done all of the supervision of the enlisted men rather than either McCarthy or Dr. Smith.

My diary for 28 November illustrates Chief Spear's attitude on our low morale problem. In a conversation after the evening movie he stated: "Captain, I have seen the calibre of your officers here and the problems you have here on account of them. If anything should come up about this station when we return, you can be assured that I can back you up 100 per cent that the actions you have taken here have been correct. I have not always agreed 100 per cent of what actions have been taken; but you are the head here, and I am a military man and just comply."

The Chiefs expertly managed to be friendly and still keep a greater distance of respect between themselves and the enlisted men than did any of the three VX-6 officers.

However, the two military units at Ellsworth did not get along any better with each other than either one of them did with the civilians. They had many disagreements when they came into close contact, which was seldom as the aviation group stayed mostly to themselves. There too more than intra-service rivalry that kept them hostile. The VX-6 men formed a small clique and considered themselves the cream of the bottle. But, when their three mechanics stepped out of line, they were invariably targets for a hoe-down with the SeaBee boys.

Our aviation crew was busy now. The planes were flying nearly every day.

216

Before the traverse party could extricate themselves to follow the new trail, we made no less than thirteen flights out to them in the eighteen days they were stuck there. Many mechanical faults had developed on the Sno-Cats. SeaBee mechanic Davis was flown out to make major repairs to the traction unit. Behrendt was evacuated to Ellsworth for an ailment which Dr. Smith treated for a week while he enjoyed more pleasant surroundings and more wholesome and regular meals. Numerous items that the party had overlooked in their requirements were now filled. The "daily express," as the enlisted men called the routine flights to the "sand-crabs" also supplied them with fresh bake products and complete dinners to brighten their life on the trail. On the last resupply flight we returned Thiel and Behrendt to the group. From their heavenly pinnacle, Amundsen, Scott and Shackleton must have gained a revolutionary insight into the luxurious workings of modern-day exploration.

CHAPTER 15

THE AIR FORCE UNIT

MAJOR LASSITER'S AIR FORCE UNIT WAS SCHEDULED TO ARRIVE ON November 22. We had been in almost constant radio contact with them since they had left the United States and moved down the coast of South America, preparing for the last hop across the Drake Passage to Antarctica. We had prepared the quarters they would occupy, and had made every effort to make them comfortable during their stay.

Originally, they were supposed to arrive on the day before, but they ran into bad weather near Mt. Tricorn, and had to turn back to Dolleman Island.

On the twenty-second, we were in contact with them by radio. On the twenty-third, they finally arrived. How they arrived was quite a story.

Lassiter's two planes and eleven men had flown from Punta Arenas, Chile, to Roberts Island in the South Shetland Island group, where the Chilean Navy had left a cache of gasoline for them. They had hoped to fly non-stop into Ellsworth from there. But on the twenty-first, near Butler Island off the coast of Palmer Peninsula, they ran into heavy weather. In an attempt to fly over the thick black clouds, the planes climbed to 13,000 feet, both using fuel for the climb, and using more fuel in the thinner air. Finally, the planes landed on Dolleman Island. That much we knew because we had been in touch with them and had asked them to wait out the bad weather until they received word from our end, telling them of weather conditions.

Meanwhile, there was nothing else for them to do than to sit the weather out in their tents, as I had done so many times during my surface sledging. Once, a companion and I had spent eleven days in our tents. The monotonous routine was broken only by going outside in the drifts to look after the dogs; in the morning and in the evening.

With ten men in their group, they should have no difficulty in waiting out the storm. Since my radio operators, who kept a continuous watch for radio signals from the group, could not hear a sign, we all assumed that they still were waiting for flying weather.

In the later afternoon on the twenty-second, contact was made with the plane. They informed us that they had taken off in one plane only, without obtaining a weather report from us. This appeared strange to me, since the chief pilot of the Group, Major Lassiter had all the knowledge of the changeable weather in this area; and his experience in polar flying when with me in 1947 had been well tested.

Suddenly, in the late afternoon Radioman Forlidas came rushing into my quarters to tell me that he had just had a radio contact with the chief pilot of the group. They had made an emergency landing somewhere in solid overcast and thought they were about 100 miles south of Gould Bay, about five miles from an escarpment, and they were completely out of gasoline. The other plane had been left behind with four men up north. By their description of the scenery, I knew pretty well the general area where the group was located. I called McCarthy over to my quarters and confronted him with the difficult situation in which the group now was situated. I asked his opinion about trying to reach the party before the weather closed in completely. The sky overhead was covered with heavy clouds, but in the general direction of our contemplated flight, I could see a clear horizon with a "white-out" in the background. McCarthy said he would like to make a try at it and ordered the aviation group to load two drums of gasoline for the downed plane, and also load emergency rations for the three of us, including Lieutenant Sumrall, who would make the rescue flight.

In the small OTTER plane we headed south of Gould Bay. After searching through rifts in the generally solid overcast for about ninety minutes, we sighted the plane on a bank in the middle of a heavily crevassed area about eighty miles southwest of Ellsworth. Judging from the huge potholes and hidden crevasses all around, I realized that luck had been with this group landing here. We came down for a bumpy landing under "white-out" conditions and taxied close to the downed plane. The smiles on the faces of the six men, even visible through the heavy beards they wore, transmitted to us their pleasure and thrill at seeing us.

Lassiter informed me that he was out of gasoline, not only in this plane, but also the one left behind on Dolleman Island. He told me that with the exception of about forty gallons, he had taken all the remaining gasoline from the other plane stranded up north, leaving only enough for them to run a small generator to operate their radio and for cooking purposes. Unfortunately, he told me, he had taken along too many sleeping bags in his own plane, leaving one of the four marooned men on Dolleman Island short of such an essential item. In the plane here I saw only a few boxes of Ten-in-One Army food rations and a few other items of gear; the rest had all been left on Dolleman Island.

In meeting these men, all of them new to me except Lassiter, I learned that Captain Roderick, the pilot of the other plane, also was included in this group. It made me wonder. What if anything had happened to this plane while cruising in the overcast, who knows? In that case, with both pilots here there would not have been a qualified pilot to fly the four marooned men out, even though there was not a drop of gasoline left in the plane to get it in the air. The men in the group had very low morale at this point, as they huddled together to keep warm in the lee of the cold fuselage of the plane. One of the men, an Air Force officer, expressed the sentiment of the group. He said they were extremely hungry and thoroughly disgusted at having allowed themselves to be placed in such a precarious situation. By this time the two drums of gasoline had been pumped into their plane and McCarthy and I took off, circling overhead while watching their plane taxi for a take-off. Lightly loaded as they were, it took only a short run for them to get into the air.

The clouds were still hanging low as the two planes headed back to the Ellsworth station. We were in constant radio contact with the base, and I requested our cook, Davis, to have a meal ready for the stranded men, a meal like they had not had for the past two weeks.

When our two planes landed, the entire complement was out on the runway to meet the new men. Their spirits soon fell, however, because the thing they most wanted was mail from home which Lassiter so graciously had offered to bring along. Now, he had forgotten to transfer the mail sacks from the other plane, which was 550 miles away.

It was a gala dinner that greeted the hungry and worn men upon entering the messhall. These men were the first new ones we had seen for many months, and conversations continued until late at night, or until the newly arrived men got so tired they could no longer keep their eyelids open.

During the many weeks they were our guests, the Jamesway huts were their homes and the entire station was placed at their disposal. Shower baths and washing facilities were shared with the permanent group and food stored in the Jamesway hut messhall was used by them. Fresh baked products, such as bread, cakes, pies, were brought over to the visitors every day by the station cooks. In addition, the medical department was continuously used by the visitors. In other words they were made a part of my station set-up since the group reported to me for operational control. We had our problems with the newly arrived personnel. The permanent group soon began to grumble about the new men—but there was nothing they could do about it. Specifically, my men were disappointed that their mail was not brought in on the first plane. The next day after arrival, Lassiter asked me where I had stored his gasoline. While we would certainly provide sufficient gasoline to rescue his stranded men, I had been ordered to tell him that no gasoline was available for his project's use until after the fifteenth of December, and only then by consent

220

of the Task Force Commander. Those were my instructions—not to touch the gasoline that was available in case of an emergency. Lassiter, the leader of the Air Force unit, was not pleased to learn of the true situation. As a result, I sent a message to Admiral Dufek for instructions on what action to take with regard to the gasoline. The next day I received the answer to the effect that no gasoline was there for the Air Force testing group until after December 15. On that day, however, the responsibility for aviation gasoline below the 15,000-gallon level was assigned to me. Since I realized fully the precarious situation in which Lassiter now found himself, I was most anxious to help him. He actually had no gasoline to carry out his program of testing the new method of aerial mapping. Right now he needed about 2,000 gallons of gasoline very badly to get the other half of his "unit" to the safety of my station. Luckily, I had a sufficient amount of gasoline on hand from my IGY stock and I was thus able to let him draw fuel from that stock, with the understanding that he would repay my pool later with his gasoline which would be brought down on the ship. I then had about 9,000 gallons left. The project men began immediately, with the help of my enlisted men, to fuel and load the C-47 plane and ready it to bring the second group in—the four men still living in the snow drifts 550 miles north on Dolleman Island.

While they were fueling the plane that afternoon, a fire broke out from the spilled gasoline running down from the spout on top of the right wing-tank. The metal was melting very rapidly on the cowling and trailing edge, as well as on the flap. Two of my enlisted men, Ronald Brown and Clyde McCauley came to their aid with fire extinguishers from the station, as the project's mechanic was unable to make the plane's own fire extinguisher work. At the risk of their lives, the two men went close in on the fire and put it out in a few minutes. The gas cap was off. Fumes and gasoline were everywhere and flames licked close to the filling cap. There was danger that the tank would explode any second. Had that happened, the two men would not only have been killed, but two of the Ellsworth station's planes and a helicopter standing close by would have been destroyed, too.

After the fire was out an inspection was made by my aviation group along with the project mechanic. It showed that the strength members of the wing had not been affected and that repairs would place the plane in a flyable condition again. The Air Force test group, of course, had no means to make any repairs to the plane as was required here, so Lieutenant Sumrall and mechanic Dyrdal went to work. They worked for forty-eight hours straight through on the job before they dropped from exhaustion. It was important to get the plane in the air as soon as possible to fetch the men still marooned on Dolleman Island. Lassiter expressed great concern for their safety and comfort, fully realizing that one man up there was without the essential sleeping bag, and their food consisted only of Ten-in-One rations. Since radio communication with the group now took place only every second day, we also assumed that fuel for running the generator was low. As the situation looked to me at this point, I felt like declaring an emergency unless the plane was readied in another week.

About ten days after arrival, the plane was once again ready for flight to Dolleman Island. After a number of abortive attempts in overcast weather, Lassiter and Roderick reached Dolleman Island to lead the second plane the remaining 550 miles to our station.

Upon my request, Lassiter wrote a statement commending my two enlisted men (Ronald Brown and Clyde McCauley) for their heroic deed. This report formed the basis of my recommendation to the proper authorities within the Navy that these men be given a special commendation for action beyond the call of duty. I am happy to report now that they eventually received commendation medals with ribbons; it was highly deserved.

A few days after the second plane had been brought in to my station, Admiral Dufek directed that the Air Force Testing Unit come directly under my operational control. Even though the group had been informed, prior to leaving Washington, that the unit would be Navy controlled while in the Antarctic, they did not take it well.

It was not my intention, nor did I ever interfere with any of the project's operations, personnel or logistics, but I was ordered to keep track of what Lassiter was doing with regard to the gasoline that I had advanced from my cache, as well as to report his activities. At one point in Lassiter's activities I had to turn thumbs down on his plan:

> "Captain," he said one day, "I want about 25 drums of gasoline to lay a cache about 300 miles south of here. By doing so, I know I can make the South Pole and return back to the cache again. You can come along with me, if you wish."

I protested this proposal vigorously and informed him that no gasoline would be available for such a venture. I knew that Navy officials would not have looked upon a South Pole flight by Lassiter with favor; not only because they disliked the project being in the Antarctic, but because of the serious situation that would develop had the project airplanes been forced down in the interior of the continent. There not only would have been a gasoline shortage for air-sea rescue operations, but many branches of science under the IGY program would have suffered. Actually, from my meager information of the project's activities, the unit came down to experiment with a previously tested method for aerial mapping and not to make a spectacular flight to the South Pole which was exclusively Navy territory. The principal purpose of the project conducted by the Air Force was to evaluate certain electronic devices for obtaining precise geodetic positions for ground-control points established in connection with aerial mapping operations. Because of the severe climatic conditions, Antarctica had been selected as a field for testing the instrumentation and method.

On 5 December, McCarthy and I flew a cache of gasoline to the traverse party before they reached the section of the Pensacola mountain range containing Dufek Massif which I had seen on my 23 October flight.

From co-pilot's seat, as usual, I scanned the surrounding terrain. Suddenly, about an hour after take-off, I heard a familiar voice. It was Rear Admiral George Dufek, commander of all of our Navy's activities in the Antarctic. He was talking on the radio from a C-47 plane flying over the South Polar plateau on its way to McMurdo in the Ross Sea.

McCarthy immediately cut in on his frequency and established contact. He was as surprised as we were. First he told me the results of Father Linehan's seismic soundings of the ice thickness at the South Pole and then he congratulated us on the accomplishments of our work at Ellsworth. But, before I had the chance to thank him, the signals faded and I learned later the plane had begun its descent for a landing at the emergency base at the foot of Beardmore Glacier.

We had been flying over the Antarctic about 2,000 miles apart, swapping yarns by radio—it was as good an example as any of the modern communication miracle.

On our return flight, I was able to see the southern and western ends of the escarpment of the island. The western end went in a northwesterly direction. I was just about positive now that the high land which I had sighted back in 1947 actually was a huge new island. The smooth and crevasse-free surface was found by the radio altimeter to increase in height gradually until the 3,200-foot elevation was reached in latitude of about 80 degrees South, longitude about 48 degrees West. This is the highest area of the island. Only a few remaining stretches including the western cape needed to be discerned. I assumed that the thickness of the ice sheet was about half the height, or about 1,600 feet. The land underneath thus would be about the same height above sea level.

On the eighth of December, our traverse team reported by radio that they were nearing Dufek Massif and that resupply of gasoline and other items was necessary.

I wanted to use Lassiter and the flight crew to fly the supply mission for our traverse party, now about 350 miles south, past Dufek's 250-mile restricted zone. They were most willing to do this—in fact, had volunteered, as their only determent was lack of gasoline. At the same time it would enable the Test Group to set up one or more control stations on the surface as part of their mission.

On December 8 I allowed IGY gasoline for use in the C-47 plane, loaded her up, stacked 13 drums of fuel for the Sno-Cats in the large fuselage, cases of food for the field party, and on the ninth we took off. There were five of us in the plane at the time. In brilliant weather with not a cloud anywhere and with prospect of continued high pressure in the entire Weddell Sea area we headed south. The huge mountain range we had seen in October soon loomed ahead and stood out as a huge monument in the otherwise pure white landscape. Heading for the eastern end of the range, we came down lower in order to get a better searching view for the traverse party. They should, according to calculations, be close by at this time. About half-way distance along the 9,000-foot–high range, we sighted the two Sno-Cats on the surface. Their orange color stood out well. We came down and landed and taxied over to the 'Cats. It took a long time before we saw any life in this camp. We had arrived shortly after the men had turned in for a much-needed sleep as they had been up the whole night. Only three men were here, the other two had skied in to the mountain with a small man-hauling sled, tents and food for a couple of days. There they would be joined by the men in the Sno-Cats.

Augenbaugh's curiosity to learn something about the rock type in these virgin mountains and also be the first to set foot where no man had previously trod, was too great for him to wait until the party moved in as one unit. While I admire his enthusiasm, it was a careless act—if a blizzard had sprung up they could have gotten into lots of trouble without a radio and only scanty trail equipment. Luckily, the good weather held.

There was no further sleep for the men now. Instead they all pitched in to unload their cargo from our plane and load it onto the sledges of the Sno-Cats.

Since the Test Unit had some work of their own to do here, I decided to join Dr. Thiel and Behrendt on an observation trip over to the mountains in their Sno-Cat. On the way Thiel told me that the seismic soundings he made along the eastern edge of the higher escarpment, which I suspected to be a part of a huge island, had measured the land underneath to be at or slightly above sea level. This corresponded to the radio altimeter readings of about 1,600 feet of the surface of the snow I had taken from the plane at this particular spot and was added proof that land above or close to sea level existed here. The thickness of the snow and ice then was almost 1,600 feet thick.

I spent some time observing their gravity and magnetic readings which they took every two and a half miles on this seven-mile journey. The rock samples I collected were all igneous. Augenbaugh and Walker came down from geologizing in the foothills to join us for a tasty supper combination of Irish stew and Hungarian goulash. I also delivered them the mail which the Air Force unit had brought from the States. Walker received a "Dear John" letter from his girl friend who had married his roommate in college.

But we were mystified as to why Neuburg in the other Sno-Cat had not followed us as planned. With a final good-luck hand shake, I skied the seven miles back to the plane, pulling a small man-hauling sled behind. On it, I had emergency equipment and cameras, and the up-hill pull over the long slopes for the last half of the less than two-hour trip was a bit tiring. In all, I had been gone about eight hours.

Neuburg with the other Sno-Cat was still there. He had been busy negotiating with Lassiter for future support flights. In view of Lassiter's own obligations to the Air Force, I found that this was getting complicated. Individually, and as a group the traverse team persisted in acting like a free-wheeling unit—steadfastly refusing to recognize anyone's control either over them or their co-ordination with other components. In order to avoid any future confusion, I took a Hydrographic Office map and laid out a course for the traverse party to follow toward Mt. Hassage. Their next rendezvous point for aerial support would be at latitude 79 degrees, 30 minutes South, longitude 65 degrees West, on a straight line from our present position toward Mt. Hassage in Edith Ronne Land. Neuburg, acting on behalf of Thiel, agreed that this was within the range of the fuel load now carried on their sledges, so I outlined the details on paper and had Neuburg sign it before he left to join the others at the mountain.

After a few hours' sleep, we took off in the Air Force plane and skirted the two Sno-Cats sitting close to the rock outcrops of the mountain range. Due west of Dufek Massif I found a narrow belt of crevasses which extended across the future route of the traverse party and later I told Thiel by radio how best to avoid them. Then we flew southwesterly to get a better view of the new group of mountains which I had seen for the first time on October 23. Before heading back to Ellsworth I was able to photograph them with my K-20 camera.

This traverse party supply mission had also given the Test Group its first opportunity to get their work underway. As soon as we had landed alongside the Sno-Cats, William Chapman, a Cadastrial Engineer with the U.S. Land Office set up his theodolite and started shooting the sun. He needed to obtain the height of the sun and the azimuth. With the correct time down to a fraction of a second and by using certain mathematical formulas, he would thus obtain a "line of position." By repeating this procedure three or four hours later to obtain a second "line of position," Chapman would then be able to "get a fix." That meant that by plotting these lines on a chart, he could accurately determine where the party was located now in latitude and longitude. Instead of taking only a few sun-line shots, Chapman took no less than a series of sun-sights every hour over a period of twenty-four hours; thereby most accurately determining the location of this observation spot.

In planning this operation, a total of ten points, laid out in a certain pattern, had been decided upon. To obtain these accurately established control points on the surface involved a landing at each of them; a stay there for a minimum of twenty-four hours to observe all the sun lines and then cover each one of the ground fixes with an orange-colored parachute stretched over empty gasoline drums. This was of greatest importance, because in order to use these accurately established control points on the surface the colored parachutes would have to show up in the aerial photographs that would be taken over the entire area later. It must be remembered that an aerial photograph, no matter how beautiful it is, is worthless for mapping purposes unless it is tied-in with accurately established control points on the surface. That was the first thing that the Testing Unit would have to do before they could commence taking aerial photographs of the area.

As it turned out, because of poor weather that stretched out for weeks at a time, only six points were set up on the surface; and when time came to fly the photographic missions, difficulties with the instruments coupled with poor weather made only one photographic flight possible.

By now I had made a considerable number of flights over this area. Already I had gradually come to the conclusion that an undiscovered island existed to the west and south of Gould Bay, a huge island, so large it was hard to guess its true configuration from a single flight.

It reminded me of the snow-covered Roosevelt Island which I had sledged over many times south of Little America on the Ross Sea side of the continent. After each flight I was able to fill in more of the details. On all flights, radio altimeter readings were taken. While the elevation on the ice shelf generally varied between 250 and 700 feet above sea level, the height of the escarpment at the edge of the island was generally about 800 feet higher. From there the height of the land increased gradually. Based on my knowledge of Roosevelt Island to the south of Little America, it became evident to me that if the escarpment continued all around the higher elevation, an island of land above sea level also existed here.

On December 15 with Lieutenant Sumrall as pilot, and two enlisted men along for their flight time, we flew slightly south of west on a course of 238° True. I was in the co-pilot's seat doing the navigation. With the driftmeter and ground-speed indicator, I was able to keep a careful check on the flight. We followed the northernmost of the three inlets of the island, determined its length and also found the important western escarpment of the island. The coastline was visible in all directions. I was able to delineate the western escarpment fairly accurately and tie it in with the rise in elevation which I had seen on my 5 December flight. At our furthermost western point, we changed course directly for the Dufek Massif until we found the southwesternmost cape of the island. We then flew southeast until the entire southern escarpment of the island was delineated. From here we laid a course directly for Ellsworth. We hit the northern inlet exactly on the nose, so the distance and dimensions of the island are correctly determined. The flight lasted for five hours and ten minutes.

While this was going on, the traverse party was still at the Dufek Massif, which they left either the fourteenth or fifteenth of December to head for their rendezvous point at 79-30 South and 65 degrees West. Thus, their future route from the mountain to the rendezvous point had been covered by our air flight. I called their attention to certain crevassed areas found to the west and northwest of Dufek Massif.

On Christmas Day, 1957, Lassiter and I took off in the C-47 to take the second load of gas to the traverse party. We had been without radio contact with them for more than a week, but estimated that by this time they should have reached the rendezvous point for resupply. We intended to fly to Dufek Massif and then follow the surface tracks of the party until we reached the previously determined rendezvous point. When we were within about fifty miles of the mountain, a solid curtain covered the area south and west, which forced us to return to Ellsworth. The following day Captain Roderick in the second C-47 plane took off and tried the route again. He also was forced to return because of heavy overcast. On December 27, Roderick took off again and headed directly for the rendezvous point over the same flight track I had covered on 15 December flight. He soon found their track, followed it and overtook the party a few miles west of the point where they were supposed to be. He landed, unloaded the gasoline and turned over to Neuburg a very important map which I had just made.

The information on this map was based on my latest flights. It contained all the geographical data I had obtained in determining the outline of the island. On it I had sketched a route which I recommended that they follow in order to reach the west cape of Gould Bay where they would be picked up by airplane and flown back to Ellsworth in time to make the tentative departure date. Later, when they returned to the U.S., members of the traverse party included my original geographical discoveries in published accounts of their accomplishments without any qualifying explanation. At the time I never dreamed my sincere concern for their success and safety would lead them to such an unworthy act.

Thiel reported that since leaving Dufek Massif they had relatively smooth going, and took the assigned scientific stations about every thirty miles or so.

During the half hour that the plane was on the ground, Neuberg managed to make a tentative agreement to have Roderick fly them an additional cache of fuel and food to Mount Hassage. He confided to Roderick their intention of not making the west cape of Gould Bay in time to return aboard the ships. Instead, they asked Roderick to use his influence with Lassiter to pick them up in the Air Force planes on their way north back to South America.

When Roderick told me about their plans, I thought they really had flipped. They had shown little enough common sense at the base but this last impractical dream was little less than suicide. I got on the radio immediately, but they would not answer. In spite of my messages to have them turn around at their northwesternmost destination, they remained silent. Finally, after referring to Admiral Dufek's most recent directive that all hands must return to base—as the ships would not wait for anyone, and that no additional flights would be made to them, I received word of their compliance.

This was indeed fortunate for them, for as it turned out, the Air Force Unit remained after our ships departed. But their planes never did fly back to South America. All their unit personnel were picked up by the Argentine icebreaker "General San Martin" ten days after we left, and the two C-47 planes remained grounded at Ellsworth until the following year when the same ship also took them back to Argentina.

But while I was occupied with the Air Force work and that of the traverse party a good deal of the time, I still had problems at the base to worry about.

While we were occupied with the fire in the C-47 on Sunday, and with the activities of the traverse group as reported by radio, Malville and Skidmore had gone down to ski on the edge of the ice, without telling anyone where they were going.

Skidmore managed to fall down a crevasse, where he lay with one arm wedged behind his back unable to move. Malville had to run back to the base for help to get Skidmore out of danger.

The men told the story around camp, but not to me. However, it is impossible to keep secrets in any polar camp. I knew about it in a few hours, mainly because of the apparent lack of gratitude he had shown to his rescuers. For his own safety, I restricted Skidmore to 500 feet from the nearest building, unless he had my personal permission to go farther. In his frame of mind, he was looking for loopholes in my restrictions, and I would have to keep a tight rein on him, lest he hurt himself.

Skidmore was now restricted from using the "ham" radio, until I received a message from Admiral Dufek noting that *all* personnel were to have the right to use the radio. But what Dufek meant was that all were to have the right to send messages and talk to home, by phone-patch. Skidmore had been restricted from hanging around the radio room, and using the radio to talk to "hams" all over the world. There was no comparison between the two matters, but obviously Brown who was very close to Skidmore had gotten in touch with "higher authority" through his nightly radio-contacts to embarrass me.

Time hung heavy now on the hands of the four remaining civilians at the station. Since the IGY operations had started on July 1, the scientific recordings at Ellsworth had provided a steady flow of data to the various collection centers at Little America and in the States. The observers in meteorology, ionospheric soundings, and aurora and airglow had done a good job. Only a few recordings had been lost. Those not obtained were mainly the result of natural obstacles or a breakdown in the equipment. But with the return of the sun, the programs dependent on darkness were over and idleness sought its own nuisance value.

In general, the work at the station took on a busier feeling with the new aviation unit operating out of Ellsworth. The Air Force men stuck to themselves pretty well—in fact, Lassiter declared the station off-limits to them and ordered them to stay in the Jamesway Hut area or the air operation center which was in our old galley-messhall. This included staying away from our nightly movies, a restriction which his men deeply resented. This did not disturb my men particularly because his lack of restraint in making nasty remarks about the Navy had already placed him high on their "blast list."

Our helicopter pilot, Jaburg, was one of the first of our men who let off steam about the camp personnel problem to the new group. McCarthy told him in strong terms to keep his mouth shut. I knew Jaburg had been critical of me with the men during the year, and on one occasion I reminded him that a commanding officer is only as successful as the officers he has to support him.

Lassiter, however, was having plenty of personnel troubles with his own small group. Apparently some of it had already started before they departed from South America as a result of impulsive changes of plans and instructions to personnel. It was evident the men were quarreling among themselves. A big gripe was being ordered on a flight just as they were sitting down to Christmas dinner, which consequently they never ate. But one of their more amusing tiffs is the story of the "baked beans."

One of their co-pilots on mess duty took pride in always having food served on time and plenty of it. The other co-pilot late for dinner after refueling a plane, saw that there were not enough beans left in the pot for the mechanic who was still outside working. Without ill intent, he went over to the storage rack and opened up another can of beans and emptied it into the cooking pot. This somehow incensed the mess cook, who put up his fists and started swinging. In the ensuing scuffle they almost fell over me on the bench where I was visiting.

The intervention of Lassiter and others brought the battle to a close temporarily. But the fight was renewed late in the evening on their way over to their sleeping quarters in the Jamesway huts, and I happened to see them from a distance. The two men were rolling around in the snow with fists and legs flying—just like two roosters. Once again their associates dragged them apart.

I gave solemn thanks that this was not my affair. These men had been together only a few weeks and were already at each other's throats—what if they had spent the winter with us?

This was the first and only fist-fight I saw at Ellsworth although I knew that several of my boys had rubbed noses at some of the Saturday night parties.

Around Christmas time there was some visiting back and forth with the British at Shackleton and the Argentines at Belgrano. Otherwise, we kept to ourselves, and I kept mostly to myself when not actually working during daylight hours.

Lieutenant Barroli, of the Argentine base, confided in me on one visit that they were having a great deal of trouble with one man who simply would not adjust to conditions as they were. I did not return the confidence, but I was having an equal amount of trouble with one of my civilians, who had become totally defiant.

We were coming to an end of our time now. Perhaps I might expect some change in him, as I had already seen it in many of the others, as the end of our year in the Antarctic drew near.

CHAPTER 16

LEAVING THE HELL-HOLE

On Christmas Eve, my seventh in the Antarctic, I was pleasantly surprised to find a note on the floor of my quarters from Skidmore, discussing our differences, and stating that he was willing to put them aside in the interest of the job at hand. This note was a happy change in his attitude. Perhaps we could have a friendly, co-operative time the few remaining weeks we had to be together on this floating shelf, I thought. When I saw him the next day I expressed this to him and commended him on his stated "willingness to put aside personality differences in the interest of the job at hand."

I felt that settled the problem, and inwardly was only sorry he had not shown so much common sense six months before, when his actions really began to get out of hand. Two weeks before the ships were scheduled to arrive seemed a late date to begin a program of reform. Yet, I was pleased, because Skidmore had become my greatest personal problem, and if he would behave, those last two weeks should be far more comfortable than many I had spent until this point.

But we were not the only Antarctic group with serious problems. The British Trans-Antarctic surface party had left Shackleton base in the middle of November to begin their overland journey to the South Pole. After great difficulty their tractors and dog teams had reached their "South-Ice" station, 250 miles south. It had taken them thirty-seven days to cross the Filchner Ice Shelf and climb the heavily crevassed glaciers to their elevated outpost. In doing so they had consumed more fuel in their tracked vehicles than originally anticipated. As we were in almost daily radio contact, both with the four men who remained behind at Shackleton, as well as Fuchs' own surface party moving southward, we learned of their hopes and disappointments and the many problems that always crop up in such an undertaking. In the first radio talk after reaching South Ice, Fuchs told me that he was in desperate need of fuel for the vehicles and in doubt that he could go on without it. With two additional C-47 planes under my operational control, I told him I would be most happy to give him all aid possible. This was now a matter of international co-operation, so I decided to have Lassiter (who was agreeable) to use one of the C-47 planes and fill her up with aviation gasoline I had earmarked for IGY emergencies.

On Sunday, December 22, with the Air Force crew aboard we flew over to Shackleton to load their fuel cargo. The fourteen remaining drums of their special Sno-Cat fuel had to be dug out of the snow drifts. Then we loaded it along with other material that Fuchs requested and flew south, heavily loaded. In the plane with us now was Fuchs' pilot, John Lewis, who had flown back and forth to "South Ice" many times. He knew every crevasse and rock-outcrop on the way. Lewis, with the other three remaining Britishers, intended to fly non-stop from "South Ice" to Scott Base at McMurdo Sound.

While still ten or twelve miles away, Lewis spotted the "South Ice" station. It was just a speck on the serene white surroundings. Later the tracked vehicles came into view and men on the surface signaled the direction for landing. Immediately, the men in Fuchs' party transferred the much-needed fuel to their tractors while our men made a quick survey of their small base now buried twelve feet below the surface. After a brief visit over a "spot of tea" with "Bunny" Fuchs and his men, we headed back over the crevassed areas through which their surface party had crossed. After viewing the network of crevasses from the air, it is a wonder to me that they had succeeded in getting their loaded sledges and tractors across without any serious casualties.

As a result of our many pleasant associations with Dr. Fuchs and his men throughout the year, we took a very personal interest in their crossing of the Antarctic continent. To their wide acclaim on their victory, I add on behalf of the Ellsworth station personnel a more personal tribute: "It couldn't have happened to a finer group of fellows."

For all practical purposes, Shackleton was almost deserted, although the British had left a great deal of material about, some of which might be used by following expeditions.

The more personal items of the men and expensive instruments they were unable to take along with them on the crossing were also left at Shackleton. I offered to take custody of these items and have them brought to Ellsworth where they would be stored until our ships came in. Then they would be taken to Norfolk, Virginia, for transfer to a British ship and sent to England. The four men at Shackleton made an inventory of it all and crated it.

John Lewis, the British pilot informed me by radio that the cargo was ready for us to pick up including a plane-heater we had lent them some time ago. We were supposed to fly over for it on the morning of December 27. But that same day our planes, or at least one of them, was to make a survey flight for the traverse party. This was in addition to the re-supply flight being made that day by Captain Roderick. We needed to scout for the best and shortest return route toward Gould Bay, so the traverse party could arrive in plenty of time to cache their equipment at the agreed spot, and still not delay the sailing of the ships from Ellsworth's ice barrier.

Again this brought up my unpleasant situation of split command with McCarthy regarding the use of the planes.

I asked McCarthy to send one plane on the traverse route and the other to Shackleton. He replied that he planned to send both planes to Shackleton, and to take all the VX-6 personnel over there, eleven of them. Lewis, without my knowledge, had asked them to visit him before the British left.

I knew why they were anxious to get over to Shackleton. The British had some liquor left over when they departed, and our supply had been diminishing for some time. I was anxious to prevent any renewal of the drinking bouts and subsequent unpleasantness for the few remaining weeks before the ships arrived. In view of my arrangement with Lassiter who could take the entire British cargo in one plane-load, when he had completed his mapping stop at Shackleton, there was really no reason why McCarthy's group should go at all.

It ended up by my asking him if the weather was good enough to travel west—toward the traverse party. He said he did not think so. That ended that particular conversation.

A bit later when I came outside to see what was going on, I saw both OTTER planes ready to fly. I asked McCarthy where he was going.

"To Shackleton," he said.

"The weather man tells me that the weather is good westward," I said. "Winds are only nine miles per hour, and clear sky, and I think we should go for the traverse party today."

McCarthy was terse. He said: "We have an invitation to go to Shackleton. We were invited. And that's where we are going."

I was angry. "I am in charge here," I said with some heat. "Any international relationship I am able to handle, and I do not approve of this trip. If you want to send one plane over there to pick up your heater, that is okay."

McCarthy's dark, penetrating eyes flashed. He said: "You do not have control of the airplanes. If you wish, we will wire Captain Dickey for a decision."

"I will be glad to," I said. "Let us wire and say that you wish to send two plane-loads of VX-6 personnel to Shackleton to say good-bye

233

to a few Britishers, when I want to use the planes to determine a safe route for the traverse party to return to Ellsworth to catch the ships."

McCarthy clammed up. "All right," he said. "I will fly on the reconnaissance flight west, but I have no place for you in the plane."

"I don't particularly want to go," I said. "I will be satisfied as long as you have competent men in the plane to bring me back a chart showing where crevasses are and the distances involved, so I can make a recommendation as to a route for the traverse party to follow."

That was the end of our discussion this time. But now I considered that McCarthy had taken the personal responsibility for guiding the traverse party back to Gould Bay. It was nonsense there being no room for me in the plane. What was it, personal revenge? It did not matter.

That particular reconnaissance flight did not come to anything. The two aviation mechanics, Beiszer and Lewis went along with McCarthy on a three-hour flight on which they had nothing to report on either terrain or crevasses—a complete waste of time and gasoline. But that afternoon, I wrote out a set of direct orders to McCarthy. This brought the matter to a head. He retaliated by inserting a statement about this in his "situation report" to Captain Dickey and to the Lieutenant Commander at McMurdo Sound in charge of the VX-6. I had no recourse then but to send a copy of my directive to McCarthy on to Admiral Dufek and ask that he back me up.

Of course, this conflict immediately became common knowledge among the men whom McCarthy by now had rejoined in their nightly beer-drinking jamborees in the Recreation hall. The other officers and some of the enlisted men came to tell me that McCarthy now was considered a hero for having "guts" to stand up to a Navy Captain.

But with the rumors came some relaxation among the men. Lieutenant Smith, who had been morose and taciturn during most of the winter, now extended his apology and showed more friendliness than he had shown all the year. He really had been turning in a most creditable performance since he had taken over McCarthy's administrative duties.

In addition, he was able to boost the morale among the enlisted men under him by initiating programs for their entertainment at a time when the going was rough. On Sunday evenings he arranged a "music appreciation" course in his room in the administration building, and during leisure time he associated in games with the men in the Recreation hall. With the general step-up in all our activities he also devoted a great deal of time to working the "ham-radio" to arrange phone-patches for the men. During meal hours, I noticed that the atmosphere took on a more congenial air. I was happy to note these changes and even more pleased with the greater bond which had been established between Dr. Smith and myself. He was among the nine men I later recognized for outstanding performance of duties.

Interestingly enough after particularly depressing periods on previous

234

polar expeditions, I have noticed somewhat similar reactions and changes among men. Men can be judged only by their complete performance— some drop by the wayside under the strain, others develop an inner strength which carries them through to a flashing finish, some are steady throughout, while still others never get the message at all. It requires an extraordinarily steady temperament for a man not to turn sour when he does not get what he wants out of an experience. But turning sour in a small Antarctic community can produce much more serious consequences than when similar things occur in civilization.

After the traverse party had received a more powerful transmitter on their second and last big supply consignment flown by Roderick, they resumed their daily radio contacts with us. From their communications it was obvious that they had not given up their idea of remaining in the field beyond their present supply limit in spite of Admiral Dufek's directive to return. They constantly requested more fuel and supplies, even though they already had sufficient, if they intended to follow the order. On one such radio contact Neuburg bluntly stated: "We are disappointed in Lassy's complete failure in supporting us." Lassiter, who was over at Shackleton base preparing to set up one of his control stations, just happened to be working the British radio unit at the time and overheard Neuburg's conversation with Ellsworth. The imprudent remark naturally riled Lassiter. Immediately he cut in on the frequency and let Neuburg have a few choice words on the subject of appreciation—or more appropriately the lack of it.

Of course, we had no intention of honoring Neuburg's request as the traverse party had gone the limit of their available time and were under orders to turn back.

On December 30 we had an unexpected radio call from the British "South Ice" station which by now we thought was unoccupied. John Lewis told us his attempt to fly across to McMurdo had failed. They had taken off the day before and reached 87 degrees and 40 minutes south when heavy overcast fronted them. Their radio contact with the South Pole station and Scott base at McMurdo also indicated foul flying weather, so there was nothing else John Lewis could do—but return to "South Ice."

He told us he was short of gasoline for a second attempt, and he very much needed our assistance in flying to "South Ice" three drums of gas, now at Shackleton. Roderick made the trip and brought me back a letter from Lewis. If his flight failed a second time he hoped I would be able to make arrangements with Naval authorities to take the four of them and their airplane back to a South American port.

But a few days later John Lewis and his crew successfully made the first crossing of the continent, *via the South Pole,** a distance of 2,100

---

*Lincoln Ellsworth was the first to fly across the continent in 1936 from Dundee Island, off Palmer Peninsula to the Bay of Whales.

miles in the same type of plane in which we were restricted to fly only 250 miles.

All our men began working harder. All were anxious to begin the long trip home. And as is often the case, the men began to repent as the expedition drew to a close. For the most part the enlisted men had always taken pride in the cleanliness of their living and working spaces. Our Saturday morning inspection had insured the weekly scrub-down and the results invariably produced a favorable impression. Now, the men turned to for a general house-cleaning before our replacement took over.

All unnecessary gear was removed from the buildings. An inventory was made of the spare parts and they were restored neatly in their proper places. The floors were scrubbed and polished, and all snow and ice accumulation was removed from the roofs of the buildings and tunnels.

How close we were to home became apparent when we began having regular radio contact with the *Wyandot,* to determine what preparations need be made for their arrival. On January 3, 1958, the *Wyandot* was at 63 degrees South latitude, about 1,000 miles away, but had not met ice yet. We hoped they would move into base by the tenth.

After messages back and forth, the aviation unit problem solved itself, just after the first of January. Despite the fact that my orders specifically stated that all military personnel at this station come under my command, including Air Development Squadron Six (VX-6) and that I was responsible for their performance of duty, morale and well being, my superiors did not wish to back me up and instead left the plane situation at Ellsworth in the hands of the VX-6 squadron headed by a lieutenant commander who was stationed at McMurdo Sound. This was another example of the inexplicable interpretation of the chain of command set-up which had caused considerable confusion and lowered morale from the beginning. But by this time it became evident that there was no more need for reconnaissance flights—and I was glad to have no more to do with that muddled situation. However, I did make one more flight.

My relations with McCarthy had suddenly become very formal. I officially requested by memo that he cancel the flight to look for a route for the traverse party.

He responded that a plane would be available to me at any time I wanted to make another flight. He knew that I was still interested in a scouting flight for the traverse party due west from Gould Bay, and at the same time I was also anxious to determine the western extent of the high land which by now I was positive was a huge island.

It was on January 4 with Jaburg as pilot that I made my last survey flight following the high barrier to the penguin rookery about ninety-five miles away. I quote from my notes: "From the rookery we continued southerly and determined the northwest escarpment and cape of the island. There is no doubt in my mind now that there is a huge island to the west and south of Gould Bay."

236

I had now seen the entire outline of the island from the air. All the features revealed on my December 15 flight had been verified and I was certain that the traverse party would have no difficulty getting onto the island by using the crevasse-free entrance at the southwestern cape. Lieutenant Sumrall, my pilot on most flights, agreed with me.

Now, by carefully plotting the ground speed, courses flown and drifts of all my flights, I was able to give the size of the new island as about 180 miles long with three indentations on the eastern coast. The widest point, which is in about latitude 79 degrees, 40 minutes South, I found to be about 165 miles. The highest elevation of about 3,200 feet above sea level is located in the center of the southern half of the island at latitude 79 degrees and 55 minutes, longitude about 48 degrees West. The average height of the northern half of the island is about 2,200 feet above sea level.

And Skidmore . . . I thought all was settled with him until one day when he came bursting into the radio room, while I was sitting there with Lassiter. Skidmore asked if I had taken some pictures off his door while I was in the science building. He was very upset, and he seemed to accuse me of taking them. In fact, I did not even know what pictures he was referring to. Lassiter listened, and stopped Skidmore as he began to walk away. Lassiter then gave him a dressing down for talking to his commanding officer in that fashion. When Skidmore went out, Lassiter told me I ought to have Skidmore moved to the ship, and kept in the brig until it arrived in the United States. Later, I learned that Skidmore had also accused Dr. Smith of taking his pictures.

It was strange, for all the rest of the station was beginning to relax a bit. This was the time when men usually reverse their antagonistic attitudes. As time drew to a close and the replacement personnel would be here very shortly, I was pleased to receive a number of messages of a congratulatory nature. This was a sign that our mission had been accomplished to the full satisfaction of both the military and IGY officials as shown by the following excerpts: "Ellsworth Station under your leadership as both military and scientific leader has successfully completed its assigned mission. My sincere congratulations and hearty well-done to you and your men. Signed, Rear Admiral Dufek."

Similarly, the chairman of the U.S. Antarctic Committee said: "I know that the National Academy of Science will always be in your debt for your fine contribution. Signed, Dr. Joseph Kaplan."

Also, I received a message from the secretary of the British Trans-Antarctic Committee in London, England, thanking me for the assistance we had rendered Dr. Fuchs and his party in their journey. These messages along with others I posted on the bulletin board in the messhall.

After Roderick's final C-47 flight to the traverse party they had moved on westerly toward Mount Hassage. Crevasse areas were encountered and the detours delayed the party many days. Near their turning point, the party crossed a crevasse field about two miles wide and climbed to an elevation of 1,300 feet. This highland probably forms a part of "Orville Escarpment" which I discovered here in 1947 along with a number of unnamed nunataks, one of which the traverse party sighted at their northernmost point. At the turning point they were about 75 miles short of Mount Hassage which they never sighted.

With time running out, the IGY men started on their return journey. Their disappointment at not reaching their objective is understandable; but the reasons, I believe, were entirely of their own making. Their original short-cut to the cape of the island escarpment left them immobilized in crevasses for twelve days. Later, the week that the traverse party had spent at Dufek Massif had produced some worthwhile geological results. But both ventures had proved costly ones to be measured against the additional information which could have been obtained in the IGY glaciology, seismology, gravity and magnetic disciplines had the party spent that time reaching their Mount Hassage objective. They then would have tied in their traverse results with the mountain chain beginning in the western part of Edith Ronne Land.

January 9 was a big day for us. Captain Edwin McDonald who returned once again to take us back home, arrived from the icebreaker *Westwind* by helicopter in the middle of the afternoon. We had heard of their coming when they were off Shackleton, and had flown out to see the two ships as they sped toward our ice cliff—one of the nicest sights I have seen in many years. Then we were back on the ground, and Captain McDonald was with us, for the first time in nearly a year.

I now drove McDonald down to the edge of the ice in my weasel, to examine the new landing place we had selected for the *Wyandot*. He was very pleased with it. Shortly after our inspection, he boarded his helicopter and returned to the ship, still a short distance off. At 8:00 o'clock she was off-shore, and the icebreaker inside shaving off the snow edge of the cliff for landing.

The next morning the ships were tied up at the landing site when I got down to the barrier edge. After a brief visit aboard, Captain Frank M. Smith, the "skipper" of the *Wyandot,* Captain W. J. Conley, the icebreaker "skipper," Captain Mark Hermansen, a task group officer and McDonald came ashore with me—they were all anxious to see the station. These and other officers expressed surprise at the orderliness of Ellsworth Station and went so far as to comment that it was the cleanest station of the five that individually they had visited on the continent. For the moment, at least, I felt our vigilance had paid off.

Sled loads of supplies for the new wintering party were arriving steadily in the camp area and being unloaded in the tunnels by the men from the ships. These men were responsible for unloading the material, but many of them were sleeping around the camp or wandering around, and while it did not disturb us, it was not as well organized a job as it might have been.

When we came here in January a year before, I found it difficult to justify stocking the base with heating fuel for five years, about 300,000 gallons, but only limited supplies of aviation gasoline. Now, I discovered that when the resupply ship *Wyandot* came in this time they were again loaded with an additional five-year supply of fuel. I suggested to McDonald that they take it back again, and they did leave it on the ship. Through an oversight, however, much of the greatly desired and critically needed aviation gasoline was not unloaded.

The IGY supply system was no better. Originally no spare clutches were sent along for our two Sno-Cats, so when the *Wyandot* arrived she brought along and unloaded ten spanking new Sno-Cats—which averaged about one Sno-Cat to every three or four men at the station. They cost about $9,000 apiece—so what!

One of my first moves when the ships came was to have Skidmore transferred to the *Wyandot* immediately. His replacement came out to the station to take over his ionospheric duties, and Skidmore went aboard ship, to stay out of my hair—for a while—the little I have left, that is.

I flew down in a helicopter with Captain Hermansen and Captain Smith for lunch on the *Wyandot*. I had fresh milk and fresh eggs for the first time in more than a year. Then I set about opening the two bags of mail that had accumulated for me—most of it from stamp collectors wanting Antarctic cancellations. I was sorry that I could not accommodate the many philatelists all over the world, but little did they realize that Ellsworth Station was not given the postal facilities accorded most of the American bases under the IGY program. Both the British at Shackleton and Halley Bay and also the Argentines at Belgrano base had mail cancellations. Since the Ellsworth Station was located in an area where two nations (Argentina and Great Britain) claim land, I thought it would have been a logical place to have United States postal facilities, but such was not the case.

The *Wyandot* was scheduled to leave on the twentieth of January (later moved up to January 17 by Captain McDonald), which gave the men only nine more days to complete the resupply of the station. It also gave the engineers of the *Wyandot* time to repair the bent propeller blade their ship had suffered when she struck some unidentified object at sea. The accident made the propeller vibrate the ship so that she could not be speeded above ten knots. Now the men were trying to straighten it out by first heating it.

The Skidmore incident continued to plague me. With Captain McDonald's approval Chief Kent presented me with a $50 check from Skidmore, to cover the deposit for the penguin he wanted. I thought McDonald had made a mistake in accepting Skidmore's story. Without discussing it with me, he overruled my decision in the penguin question, and let the man keep the bird.

In trying to get onto my newly discovered island, the traverse party moved far south of my planned route. By doing so they hit crevasses and they were then forced to detour still farther south where they got themselves so hopelessly entangled in crevassed areas that they never did gain entrance to the island. McCarthy was prepared to pick them up when the time came. But to my surprice, Captain Hermansen sent a message out to the traverse party that four men from the ship would be coming to visit them—completely without my knowledge. At the rate the party was moving, it seemed hard to believe the men would be back in time to sail with the ship.

Day by day, the situation ashore deteriorated—and the discipline of the station collapsed completely, from the old ailment: Too many chiefs. I was no longer the senior officer present and many of the functions were being directed from the ship. It was hard to discern what was going to come up from hour to hour.

The men from the ships wandered almost at will around the camp, lolling and drinking beer instead of working. They were in camp twenty-four hours a day. Finally, I asked to be given a twenty-four–hour shore-patrol to keep the men under control. Nothing happened quickly enough unfortunately, to avoid an unpleasant incident.

I went to the *Wyandot* to the movies on January 12, and was sitting in the movies when Captain Smith called me to tell me there was trouble at the station and they wanted to speak to me on the radio.

Chief Spear was on the other end. He told me men from the ice-breaker *Westwind* had come and had begun drinking. Someone had gone into the enlisted men's head and thrown a flare which started a fire, and almost burned down the house. Spear had caught two of the men and held them. After this incident occurred a twenty-four–hour watch was put on the station.

On the other side of the ledger, the young mechanic who took that wild ride in the weasel early in the year had promised me then he would not take another drink of any kind without my permission. Now he came to get my permission to indulge with an old shipmate who had come down aboard the *Wyandot*. He had been a solid citizen for many months and one who later had performed beyond the call of duty. I gave him the permission along with my blessings.

The men began trickling back to the ship to make room for their replacements. Brown had asked that Skidmore be allowed to come back to the station to teach the new man the ionospheric-record scaling process. He completed his work of instruction and went back aboard, although he managed to leave seventeen days of unscaled records for his replace-

240

ment. Malville went aboard ship. So did Brown and Fierle. Finally, on January 15, there were only five of us of the old wintering crew at the station.

But I had a run-in with Malville that day, when I found him eating in the messhall at the station. The new station messhall crew complained that so many of the old fellows were still having their meals there that they ran short of food for those who were already a part of the permanent crew.

Once they moved aboard ship our men had been told to get their meals there and give the new shore group a chance to get organized. But to the very last, some found it difficult to comply with the very simplest attempt to maintain systematic procedure.

I was grateful, at least, that we had handled our own problems without resorting to court-martial proceedings. A couple of such cases did occur at other stations and were referred to Little America where the authority to take the necessary legal action was vested.

It was the old story of the *New* Antarctic men wanting nothing to do with the old ways of doing things. For some time I had been aware my days of exploring the frozen continent were at an end, unless some drastic changes were made in facing up to our present haphazard, bureaucratic ways of doing things. The entire command set-up was impractical, and unrealistic for efficient maneuverability. It wasn't just a question of being part of a team, but rather part of an octupus whose arms had no idea of what all the other appendages were up to. But even more disheartening I saw—no chance for any major revision in our policy in the foreseeable future. It was really no one person's fault. But the fact remains that such an enormous government undertaking tends to become unwieldly and lacks unified central direction. That, perhaps.was the trouble, for the IGY-Navy command set-up was a decentralized muddle from the very beginning. The true miracle was that the end-results far over-shadowed the confusion.

The new way certainly left something to be desired, from my experience. An expedition leader usually can obtain far better results when he operates as a free agent—unhampered by bureaucratic control. In this case, I was given the responsibility of command at Ellsworth Station, but I was deprived of the necessary authority to discharge the responsibilities.

Lieutenant Paul Tidd, a naval reserve officer, the new military officer of Ellsworth, and Dr. Mathew Brennan, the new scientific leader, came to me several times with questions about running the station. Tidd told me just a few days after their arrival that trouble had broken out between the new group of civilians and the military—even before the old group was out of camp. It came first over bunking spaces.

The new unit had two mechanics, a civilian, Hoffman, and a sailor. The civilian, of course, had officer status, and the sailor was an enlisted man. They had begun to fight already over the bunking space that my mechanic, Walter Davis, had made for himself in the garage. The sailor, Tidd said, was telling the civilian that he would throw him out of the garage bodily if he tried to get in without permission. That sounded like the beginning of a good winter in isolation!

But that was not all. Even the new civilian scientists were already quarreling among themselves. Dr. Brennan told me that the new ionospheric man (21 years old) did not like his room or his roommate.

Our own traverse party was the subject of much confusion in orders. Since they could not possibly make the trip to the cache at Gould Bay in time, there was some talk of leaving them, and having other ships pick them up at Halley Bay a few weeks later by flight from Ellsworth. But Admiral Dufek ordered the men out, and rightly so. In effect, he ordered them to leave the equipment where it stood and come out by air.

At McDonald's suggestion in the early afternoon of January 16 we held a brief ceremony to turn the station over to the new complement. Officers and men that could be spared from the two ships gathered around the permanent flag pole along with the incoming and departing groups. After a brief introduction by Captain McDonald, I had the pleasant task of passing out commendations for nine military men lined up in front of me. In the final analysis these were officers and men who had served at times beyond call of duty during the year at this remote station, and in doing so had maintained the highest tradition of the Navy. Those receiving commendations were: Lieutenant Smith; Lieutenant Sumrall; Chiefs Spear, May; Walter Davis, the mechanic; Edward Davis, the commissary stewart; and second-class aerologist Gary Camp. Included were also the two enlisted men, Clyde McCauley and Ronald Brown, who had shown such bravery in putting out the fire in the Air Force's C-47 plane. The group was congratulated by the ship's officers and others passing in line before them.

Then the station was formally turned over to my two replacements, Dr. Mathew Brennan who would be station scientific leader for the International Geophysical Year Program, and Lieutenant Paul Tidd, USNR, who would head the Navy's support group. Hand-shakes and good wishes were given the new crew taking over duties for the year ahead.

As a climax to the ceremonies, we arranged for refreshments for all hands in the messhall, after which some withdrew to the cozy surroundings of my own quarters until early evening when I moved aboard ship. I felt as though a great load had been removed from my back. For the first time in a year I was free of any responsibility for the non-congealing group of extreme individualists. Aboard the *Wyandot,* I was comfortable, too, for Captain McDonald had transferred to the icebreaker *Westwind* of the Coast Guard, and I got his quarters on the ship.

Early in the morning of January 17, Captain McDonald flew with McCarthy and Tidd to be certain of getting the traverse party out. Everyone knew by then that the traverse party men had tried to make arrangements with the Air Force unit to have them evacuate the party much later. The civilians were enjoying their carefree life on the trail and didn't want to go home. For days they had been holed up in a crevassed area south of my newly delineated island. After some delay, McDonald was forced to get stern with them and finally got them into the two planes with their personal gear and records.

When they came out they were bedraggled, dirty and tired. Three of the five men had spent eighty-one days on the trail. Thiel and Behrendt had been out seventy-two days. During this period they had traveled with the Sno-Cats a total distance of 816 miles, or an average of about ten miles per day. (The results of the traverse party as well as all of our other scientific work is fully detailed in the Appendix.)

Within a few hours after our traverse men returned on the afternoon of January 17, the ships departed. Our five men had remained in the field until the last possible moment, so late in fact that they had no opportunity to instruct their replacements in the operation of their respective programs. As a result, the new glaciologist was unable to locate the bench mark for the glacier movement triangulation survey, thus making comparison of records for the two IGY years impossible. Nor were the new personnel checked out on the seismic and gravity equipment they were to use in the field. Nearly a month was lost by the newcomers in getting men and equipment ready to resume the traverse—all because our group had adamantly refused to return from the field at the designated time.

Once the ships reached open water it was the intention of McDonald in the icebreaker to separate from the *Wyandot* and head into the Bellingshausen Sea, on the west side of the Palmer Peninsula. He wanted to make another attempt to land on the elusive coast to the south of that sea. Many previous expedition ships had tried to make a landing there, but all met with defeat because of the tremendous heavy concentration of rafted pack ice. The Belgian expedition ship the *"Belgica"* was caught in the ice there in 1899, and a year of drifting and general misery passed before the first ship and men to spend a year in the Antarctic were freed.

McDonald did not succeed on this occasion, but two years later in the Navy's largest icebreaker *Glacier,* he did reach Thurston Peninsula, the first group to do so by sea.

When I went through my pay-record aboard ship, I was shocked to learn after a year in isolation, I had only a few hundred dollars coming. I had spent some advance money coming to South America by plane instead of ship, but very little else. As a Navy officer, some $800 had been deducted for my meals. At least no one could say I had gone to the Antarctic to make a fortune, for the expedition had brought me practically no remuneration at all. However, in this respect it was no different for me than all the other expeditions I had been on. Money had never been one of my driving incentives as an explorer.

There was much detail to be wrapped up during the first days aboard ship. I had the pleasant duty of preparing the letters which would be inserted in the personnel jacket of the nine military men who had served me so excellently during the year. I had to make out fitness reports on the officers, stating my views on the way they had carried out their jobs. I also had to formulate a written summary I would later prepare for the IGY officials in Washington.

A psychiatrist from the Navy's Bureau of Medicine and Surgery with two assistants came to me for an interview designed to give my views in selection of personnel for future Antarctic wintering missions. I answered his questions in the best way I could, but I could not refrain from telling him that there was really no point in this interview. One has to live through it to appreciate why. Our daily problems as an isolated unit ceased and the variety of views concerning them changed as soon as the ships appeared on the horizon. The fact was that men were not the same at all in isolation of the Antarctic as in the towers of civilization. The raw, bitter winds of the frozen continent strip the veneer of civilization from men, and reduce some of them, as low as one can reduce civilized beings. The man who can control himself in such surroundings is rare. It is my belief that he is not to be discovered by the present system of selection which was used for this particular expedition.

Our mixture of civilian and military personnel did not turn out well. The military and IGY civilians with me barely managed to tolerate each other, as a rule. Some will dispute me on this and there were exceptions, of course, but all too frequently the gap between the two philosophies is too wide to bridge without the understanding co-operation of all parties concerned.

The fact that the IGY personnel were being paid more than eight times the amount of some of the enlisted men did not help. The problem, of course, is that too little time is spent in adapting humans for the region in which they will serve.

These were my thoughts as we threw off the mooring lines of the ship and sailed on the evening of January 17, first worming our way through the pack ice, then speeding as we came to the fringes, where the only danger lay in big bergs that broke off from the ice shelfs and made their way to the open sea.

Ten days after we sailed from the ice barrier we were well on the high seas. I received favorable word from my request to provide my own transportation back to the States from Argentina. The voyage was drawing to an end for me.

On the evening of January 29, two days before we were to dock in Buenos Aires, the captain of the ship and I were invited to dinner in the wardroom below. We enjoyed a steak, and the Executive Officer, Commander Herbert Waddell, in his formal speech said the company was bringing together all the officers and civilians who had wintered with us as well as the ships' officers, who were also aboard the previous year.

I was called upon to say a few words. I told the group I was happy to be with them that evening. Even though we had some tough times together on the ice, I noted, as I have always believed that time heals everything. That the ill feeling some men might have toward others as a result of the intimate living conditions which had prevailed during the year would be placed in proper perspective with the passage of time. I then thanked the enlisted men, the officers and the IGY civilians for the sacrifices they had made in the furtherance of science for which the nation should be grateful. I then wished them all the best of luck in the future, and said good-bye. My year in the "Hell-hole of the Antarctic" was over.

EPILOGUE

As our ship eased up to the dock in Buenos Aires, my wife and a few close friends were waiting on shore. Together with her traveling companion, Kay Sweeney, we spent a leisurely three weeks traveling through South America on our way back to Washington.

By the time we arrived home all the former occupants of Ellsworth Station had scattered. Members of the military contingent had been granted a much-deserved home leave before reporting to their future assignments on which they had been informed before we left the frozen continent.

The nine civilians of the IGY flew with the group of military wintering personnel from Sao Paulo, Brazil, directly to Washington where the IGY officials staged a briefing with each individual.

Of the nine IGY men in our party four have returned to the Antarctic for further work. The first summer I received a post card from Thiel reminding me of my previous prediction that he would return. The strongly motivated ones always do.

For two successive summers Thiel joined an air-reconnaissance unit of the Navy to make additional seismic soundings in the area between the Weddell and Ross Seas, to ascertain whether a deep and narrow frozen strait connected the two enormous seas.

The first summer Neuburg worked on glaciers out of McMurdo Sound, and returned the following year to go on a summer traverse. The 1960-61 season he wintered for the second time with the military personnel at McMurdo. Augenbaugh went to Little America the first summer after our return to do glaciological survey work.

Chief Walter Davis, my very capable Navy mechanic returned also. He wintered at Byrd Station during the 1960-61 season, and was one in a group of Americans first to reach the South Pole station by tractors.

In January, 1959, a year following my return from the IGY, I made my fifth trip to the Antarctic continent. Upon the invitation of the Secretary of the Argentine Navy, I accompanied the Argentine Task Force aboard their icebreaker *General San Martin* on a return voyage into the Weddell Sea. On this occasion I enjoyed one of the most pleasant and companionable Antarctic trips I ever had. Without the resources which

246

are at our disposal, the Argentine Navy ran a taught, efficient ship. Under the most difficult conditions their seamanship was beyond reproach.

After first visiting their Belgrano base, we moved on to Ellsworth. When the International Geophysical Year ended on December 31, 1958, the United States decided to decrease its Antarctic operations by closing one of its stations (Little America) and by turning two other stations over to foreign governments. Wilkes Station was to be lent to Australia, while Ellsworth would be turned over to Argentina. McMurdo Sound, the Naval operating base, the South Pole, Hallet, and Byrd Stations would remain, as they could be resupplied by one U.S. Navy task force. Officials aboard the *General San Martin* were prepared to receive Ellsworth Station in a semi-formal transfer ceremony from officers aboard the *USS Edisto*. But the icebreaker *Edisto*, caught in the ice, did not arrive in time for the ceremony. We unloaded supplies and deposited the overwintering group composed entirely of Argentines with one American observer, Floyd Johnson. He was one of the meteorologists who spent the first winter at the South Pole station in 1957.

Another American, representing the U.S. Weather Bureau was also scheduled to winter with the Argentines. He was returned to the ship, however, just before we cast the mooring lines off. His infringement of normal camp rules had already compelled the Argentine Naval officer in charge to take stern action in order to prevent an early breakdown in camp discipline. I could not have agreed with the officer more wholeheartedly; it was one way to show his authority as a warning to the rest of the men that law and order would prevail. Unfortunately, I was void of such power during my reign there.

On our passage out of the Weddell Sea we had almost open sailing with only light pack ice and passed within fifty miles of the trapped American icebreaker. The Argentines offer of going to their aid was rejected. Eventually they got loose and reached the Ellsworth Station in time to relieve the eleven Americans we had left behind. The other thirty Americans, we had taken to Ushuaia aboard the Argentine icebreaker and later they were flown home.

The visit had given me an opportunity to view the condition of the Ellsworth Station and the accomplishments of the American crew that had taken over its operations when I left the year before. That experience was quite an eye-opener.

Interiors of the buildings and tunnels were in a sad state of deterioration because of maintenance neglect. According to the senior civilian, morale among the men was no better than when our group held forth. Insubordination, drinking, and problems in the split-command set-up, between the senior civilian and the senior naval man, a naval reserve lieutenant, had been the major factors in lowering the morale. This in turn had been allowed to affect the general cleanliness of the station. The dispensary and the galley-messhall were the only areas which met the standards I had insisted upon. The dispensary specifically, was in a most spotless condition.

Despite any personal feelings I might have had concerning our policy of relinquishing our base in this remote area of the Antarctic continent and its historical interest to Americans, I was embarrassed by the lack of personal and national pride which permitted the inhabitants to turn over Ellsworth Station to a foreign government in such shameful condition. I indicated as much to the Argentines, who were to receive the station. They were polite and understanding, but their wonderment at our all-too-obvious weaknesses away from home were not completely concealed. Is it not understandable why other countries are often tried by our attitude of superiority and self-righteousness?

While actively engaged in this strongly competitive and highly emotional field of Antarctic exploration, I refrained from making public any of my privately held views of our previous Antarctic operations, but now I feel I can speak out: The way our endeavors in the Antarctic are run today there is no place for the strongly motivated explorer of yester-year to plan, organize, command, and execute future field operations. This fact, coupled with my seniority, and the knowledge that I have already weathered most of life's storms, including four winterings in the Antarctic, leaves me in a position to speak frankly about the conduct of our operations there.

As we race headlong into an era of scientific clean-up in the Antarctic the success of new methods will depend on a critical review of the old ones. In order for one to be progressive he must also have a respect for the past. More men participated in the IGY program than the total complement of all previous expeditions combined, and public funds were used exclusively to finance the entire IGY project. The public is entitled therefore to know how and why these funds were used.

In the IGY program, time for preparation was not a limiting factor. Organizing and planning commenced several years before any Antarctic unit left the U.S. Money was no particular problem. Once Congress was convinced of the long-range importance of the program, it willingly voted financial appropriations. Department of Defense budgets also were utilized freely. The U.S. Government has perhaps spent more money on the IGY and the subsequent SCAR (Special Committee for Antarctic Research) organization which replaced it, than the combined cost of all previous expeditions of all nations recorded in Antarctic history.

Nor was there lack of material resources. This was the best-equipped project ever to enter Antarctic waters. And personnel could have been selected from the entire country. Therefore, the casual observer might well assume that some of the organizational problems I have dealt with could have been resolved efficiently and adequately beforehand.

It is difficult to understand why previously trained Antarctic men were not consulted. With a single exception, no member of any previous over-wintering expedition was in a position where his advice and knowledge was other than superficially sought. With but few exceptions the advice or constructive criticism of the Antarctic veterans was neither wanted nor accepted.

It would be extremely difficult, if not impossible, to estimate with a reasonable degree of accuracy the exact cost of the Antarctic activities of the IGY. More than $200,000,000 was spent, with by far the largest cost absorbed by the Department of Defense budget. It has been estimated that for every dollar appropriated to the IGY for science, the Department of Defense spends eight dollars for logistic support. I estimated that during the IGY it cost us $1,000,000 to put each individual scientist or technician on the Antarctic continent for a year. That is a very high figure, but on the other hand I am sure we then had and still have the finest scientific program of any nation in the Antarctic.

Both from scientific and public relations accomplishment in terms of world-wide co-operation the results of our IGY efforts are considered excellent. In comparison with previous Antarctic expeditions these results were remarkable. It is reasoned, therefore, that the expense in obtaining them was justified. This may well be, but there are those of us who believe we paid excessively for those results by our lack of efficiency in planning, organization, and execution.

With a nearly inexhaustible supply of men and equipment in relation to the nature of the mission, a goodly amount of creditable accomplishment would seem inevitable. And it was largely unlimited resources at many well-equipped bases, aided by numerous ships and airplanes provided by the military, that let us make a substantial net showing. In the past the military often has justified its overwhelming contribution in the polar regions as providing good training for its personnel under polar conditions, which is certainly true. But after one or two brief summer cruises the men invariably are shifted to other assignments. The training therefore is spread lightly over a great number of men and it produces exceptionally few seasoned authorities to carry on.

We wasted money because of lack of experience, knowhow, and efficiency. It was unnecessary, in my opinion. We bought our results above the going market price. Less affluent countries, such as England, Norway, France, and Australia, showed greater results per dollar invested. I recognized that this problem is not unique with our Antarctic operations. And, while I can understand how it can happen in our growing bureaucratic society, I do not agree that this cannot and should not be rectified. It is far too easy to spend money which is not your own—the account of which can be charged off as expendable.

We must and should go on. We have much to be proud of. It would behoove us, however, to make a very thorough review of the U.S. future objectives vis-a-vis the Antarctic and make a clear appraisal of how to reach these objectives most efficiently. This study should be undertaken by those who are most experienced in the field, in conjunction with those who have a broad conception of all our national objectives, rather than by those with limited knowledge of conditions and possibilities. Nor should the scope of our future objectives be limited entirely to the purely scientific approach. We have many other legitimate national interests in the Antarctic.

Accounts of problems in human relations on Antarctic expeditions have been circulated and analyzed among explorers since the continent was first sighted. All expeditions suffer from the same malady, although few such stories and their causes have ever been widely publicized.

In order to appear more successful and heroic, expedition leaders (as well as their followers), have consistently minimized their difficulties in human relationship. Even on occasions when human relationship has become the balancing point between success or tragic failure, we have attempted invariably to cover or gloss over these frailities. Perhaps this has been a mistake and a distinct disservice to those who follow. It has certainly considerably delayed bringing any national focus on a very serious problem.

In my opinion, this area of human relationship under abnormal conditions should be a fundamental area for immediate intensified study. On the ability of humans to adapt themselves hangs the future success of undertakings under similar conditions. This application goes further than to the polar regions. The problems are the same as sending men into outer space. An analogy of the two fields will find many similarities between the necessary mental preparation required to deal with abnormal physical conditions. The Antarctic probably offers the best example of isolated stress and strain to be found on the face of this planet.

Never has sufficient interest been taken in this human problem, nor has much serious attempt been made to find the answer. Several summer transients have professed some understanding and have even had the courage to set forth their views. But the real answers will only come from those who have and will live through an Antarctic winter night, not only once but several times. The psychiatrists should stay a year or two in the Antarctic, not merely visit and ask questions. The true answers to those questions change with the first sight of the relief ship.

Exploration of the Antarctic demands youth for aggressiveness, age for mature judgment, skilled technicians for specialized practical jobs, and well-rounded scientists to pursue the scientific objectives sought. In such diversified groups there will be divergent opinions regardless of where they are located.

250

In civilization long-established conventions have a controlling effect, whereas in the remote, cold, cramped, isolated, womanless, abnormal society of the polar regions views that would be mildly divergent elsewhere often become nearly irreconcilable.

Money has no place here, for there is nothing to buy.

First-timers are often unprepared and bitterly surprised by the lack of established tradition which has governed their life heretofore. The complete isolation from civilization makes a man lose interest in the outside world. Technically there is no set of laws to govern the actions of such a community. A new set of norms is needed. The world becomes a narrow daily life with limited associates. Man's basic animal instinct of survival is laid bare. Either he faces up to the challenge and gets along or he makes himself miserable and endangers the lives of his fellowmen.

Those who have gone through the ordeal of an Antarctic winter tend to mellow. They are considerably more adaptable and stable the second winter. But regardless of all the flowery words that have been written to the contrary, I do not believe that the conditions experienced on Antarctic wintering expeditions bring out the best in most men. The personnel of American expeditions in particular no longer seem to show the rugged resourcefulness, moral fiber, and mental discipline so often associated with the pioneers of this country less than 200 years ago. I have known only a dozen or so men who possessed the qualifications of the ideal expeditioner.

There are few life-long friendships among Antarctic explorers—competition and jealousy become overwhelming somewhere along the way. It is possible that having been brought up in a hero-worshipping society, a man subconsciously identifies himself with the great-name explorers of the past when he ventures into the Antarctic himself. I have watched men suffer such delusions. Have they always been this way; or are life's frustrations so magnified in the isolation that man's common sense no longer governs his reasoning? Perhaps some day the answer will be found.

I hope that my frank revelations will not be assessed as an attempt to distract from the world-wide acclaim of the objectives and accomplishments of the International Geophysical Year. This is not the first time in the history of the Antarctic, or of the world for that matter, that human nature has been found to be imperfect. Human reactions of expeditions have changed very little since the time of Columbus. We cannot eliminate human weakness, but through infinitely more careful selection, training and preparation, we can reduce it. At best, life is a series of major adjustments. The most successful men face this reality with an open mind and receptive attitude.

The problems of any leader of a group of men in polar isolation are many and varied, and I found the Ellsworth Station to be no exception.

251

Fortunately, the results proved to over-shadow the vicissitudes and for this reason I am happy to have had a small part in the successful undertaking of the International Geophysical Year.

By telling my story in considerable detail, it is my hope that some constructive thought may be given to the realities of operating in the isolated areas on this earth as well as in outer space. If this book should stir a few men to action, it will have accomplished its purpose.

APPENDIX

At THE CONCLUSION OF THE INTERNATIONAL GEOPHYSICAL YEAR, three world data centers were established to receive the IGY scientific findings. One of these centers is located in the United States (with sub-centers at eleven institutions). Another is in Russia, with four sub-centers. The third center is sub-divided into twenty-two sub-centers in eight western European nations, Australia, and Japan. That material is divided according to specific scientific disciplines.

Much of the material collected in the various scientific studies undertaken at Ellsworth Station, as elsewhere, was of such basic nature that it may require years of digestion before the material is meaningful. In some cases the research was so basic there may never be any tangible results apparent to the layman.

In most cases the recordings at Ellsworth require correlation with findings of similar groups working at other Antarctic bases and/or other IGY stations throughout the world. A considerable amount of analysis may be necessary before the information can be translated into results, theories, or principles.

There were, however, certain areas in which the results of the studies were more easily explainable. I deal briefly with these below.

HEAT AND WATER AREA

Oceanography.

Oceanographic programs of the IGY in the Antarctic were limited to shipboard operations on Navy and Coast Guard icebreakers en route to and from the continent. These investigations in widely scattered sections of Antarctic waters played a small but important part in this world-wide undertaking. Information was gathered for correlation with data obtained from results conducted on a larger scale elsewhere.

The over-all quest concerned the movement of currents to understand the circulation of the ocean waters and sea level changes and their relationship to other oceanic, glaciologic and atmospheric phenomena. Water temperature, baththermy readings, marine geology, and biology as well as cores taken from bottom sediments all provide some clue to circulation patterns.

Studies made in the Weddell Sea showed very little change in density with depth of water. Between a depth of about 400 to 2,200 feet along the ice-shelf at the head of the sea, the temperature remained uniformly about 28.4° Fahrenheit (-2 C.), while air temperatures were between 20.8° (-6.2 C.) to 26.9° Fahrenheit (-2.8 C.). In late summer, winter cooling had begun and the sea was already losing heat to the atmosphere.

The theory was verified that the Weddell Sea's bottom water is formed by cold, heavy surface water, originally coming from the continental shelf, mixing with warmed circumpolar sub-surface water.

Striking differences were noted in the bottom composition of the sea. Samples taken in the deep water off Cape Norvegia, at the entrance to the sea, show typical deep-sea ooze, whereas, off Gould Bay, at the head of the sea, almost pure sand was brought up from 900 feet. Stones are often found in bottom sediments. Glaciers pick up the stones from the continent. After glaciers break up into icebergs, these float until they disintegrate and the rocks and stones drop to the bottom.

It is hoped that such studies, giving some information on the climatic changes which have taken place in the past, can be correlated with other material for more accurate predictions in the future.

Meteorology.

As a result of gathering weather information from fifty bases during the IGY many new things were and still are being learned about the compositions of Antarctic weather—one of the major gaps of knowledge in our world-wide understanding of the weather network. The Weather Central at Melbourne, Australia, still staffed by meteorologists from several nations, still receives daily reports from all bases. The day-to-day synoptic weather analysis are broadcast to all Antarctica and the southern hemisphere twice daily as background for local forecasting.

On September 17, 1957, the Antarctic took the record from northeast Siberia ($-90°$ Fahrenheit) as the coldest spot on earth. That date the United States South Pole station recorded $-102.1°$ Fahrenheit (with a subsequent average for the year of $-56°$ Fahrenheit). But the following year (on August 17, 1958), the Russians registered a new world record low of $-124.5°$ Fahrenheit, in an area several thousand feet higher, about 400 miles from the South Pole station. Again this temperature was lowered when, on 24 August, 1960, they registered $-126.9°$ Fahrenheit.

The weather at Ellsworth was similar to that at the South Pole station but notably warmer. On May 10, 1957, we recorded our lowest temperature of $-67°$ Fahrenheit. Our yearly mean temperature was $-8.5°$ Fahrenheit. During the year we experienced an unusual number of cloudy days, even for the Antarctic. However, the Ellsworth area was not as windy as some others.

High altitude balloons and sounding equipment gave us much information about the structure of Antarctica's stratosphere. The high level, deep cyclonic weather is not stationary as suspected but changeable in location and intensity. This activity continues throughout the year, but is more pronounced in summer than in winter. A temporary average rise in temperature precedes the big drop that accompanies the setting of the sun for the winter. During the winter the temperatures drop steadily, with the lowest point usually before the reappearance of the sun in the spring. In the spring an extremely rapid warming is denoted by sudden swift temperature changes, which start at the northern fringes and encircle the stratosphere over most of the continent. Beginning at Ellsworth Station on October 22, 1958, a twenty-four–hour period of warming of nearly equal intensity swept over the South Pole and a large part of the continent before diminishing somewhat and centering over the polar plateau. There is considerable evidence that both maximum temperature and its change occur last over the high plateau of east Antarctica.

Irregularities in the ionosphere and the earth's magnetic field occurred simultaneously with one spring's swift rise in temperature, but at present it is not known whether this has some physical connection or is merely a coincidence. Dr. Harry Wexler of the U.S. Weather Bureau (Senior Scientist for the IGY) has suggested a possible meteorological relationship between disturbances in the lower atmosphere and in the ozonosphere, that layer of ozone lying between heights of about twelve to twenty-one miles, depending upon the season and latitude.

Three members of the international team of meteorologists at Little America's weather central in 1958 stated in a report that a belt of low pressure appears to surround the whole Antarctic continent. In four areas of this belt strong depressions are most common: The Ross Sea, the Weddell Sea, the Mawson-Mirny area, and the eastern coast of Queen Maud Land. The general circulation of air over the Antarctic appears to be an integral part of the circulation throughout the whole southern hemisphere. The three main areas of outflow: Western Victoria Land, Palmer Peninsula, and western Enderby Land, while the three main areas of inflow of warm air are: Marie Byrd Land, the eastern Weddell Sea-Queen Maud Land sector, and Adelie Land. The shifting of cold and warm air masses takes place mostly in the lower half of the troposphere, that portion of air which is below the stratosphere.

As all of this data is continuously accumulated and analyzed it will ultimately help to clarify the influence of the frozen continent upon global, as well as southern hemisphere weather patterns. The IGY program has made possible the preparation of daily weather maps of the entire world.

Glaciology.

Glaciers are among nature's most sensitive indicators of past and present climatic trends. About thirty-five feet beneath the surface of a glacier there is a constancy in the annual temperature of the ice and usually is very close to the average annual air temperature above the surface (often varying no more than a fraction of one degree Fahrenheit). Such a reading from a deep pit provides a relatively simple way of estimating the mean temperature or general climate of an area where long-term meteorological observations are not available and without the need for a permanent station.

By counting the stratified snow and ice layers beneath the surface (something like counting the rings of a tree), a fairly accurate estimate can be made of the accumulation over a period of years. The layers also reveal past annual meteorological events such as warm spells during a particular winter which caused melting, or a cold summer when no melting occurred. The variation in accumulation of the yearly deposits provides important evidence on shrinkage, advance, or retreat of the ice fronts.

At Ellsworth, a snow pit was dug during the two darkest months of the year (June-July) by the five men of the traverse party. The pit was located less than a quarter of a mile due east of the station—in a trough or shallow depression in the Filchner Ice Shelf. The pit reached a depth of 102 feet, and in the floor of the pit a fifty-foot–deep borehole was drilled with a four-inch auger. This allowed seismic and glacier studies to be made to a total depth of approximately 155 feet.

Dr. Harry Wexler points out that this decrease in temperature with depth at Ellsworth Station differs from Little America and Maudheim where temperatures increase slowly with depth in the top 185 feet. A significantly different thermal history for the ice shelf around Ellsworth is therefore suggested.

According to Dr. Thiel the density of the ice measured in the deep pit was twice as dense as that on the surface and higher than any previously recorded at similar depths of deep pits in either Antarctica or Greenland.

From the surface to a depth of 102 feet it had required seventy-six years for that much ice and snow to accumulate.

The stake system which the glaciologists set up around Ellsworth Station was used to measure the amount of snow accumulation from week to week. Drifting winds may increase the height of the snow, or extremely strong winds may cause deterioration or ablation; i.e., lowering of the snow level. From studies of deep pits, core samples and stake measurements the average annual accumulation at Ellsworth is estimated at eighteen cm. (seven inches) water equivalent, which in seventy-five years would amount to about 13.5 meter (approximately forty-four feet). In comparison Little America's average annual net accumulation in terms of water equivalent is twenty-four cm., Byrd Station sixteen cm., and South Pole Station seven cm.

Through the application of certain heating, melting and accumulation formulas Dr. Wexler suggests that the upper layer of the Ellsworth ice represents snow which accumulated for about 75 years as the ice moved rapidly at about two km. a year (about five times faster than the ice at

256

Little America) toward the northwest from Coats Land. Further IGY data analysis indicates that the strain rates obtained on the Ross and Filchner Ice Shelves show that the creep of the ice, or the slow, continuous horizontal strain, is about one meter per kilometer per year, and is at a maximum in the direction perpendicular to that of absolute ice flow.

At each seismic station site on the traverse the glaciologists dug a shallow pit about four by six feet in area to a seven-foot depth. Surface temperatures were taken and penetration values were established by the rommsonde method of letting a controlled weight fall a certain distance on a rod. The weight would force the rod down into the snow and the distance it penetrated was measured. Snow blocks were taken from the smooth wall of the shallow pit and were returned to the station for further studies of crystal forms, radio-activity, and isotope analysis. Strata of the snow crystals were measured as to angle and composition. A thirty-foot borehole was made to measure the temepratures at various depths for an estimate of the average annual air temperatures and to ascertain the variation of this average with latitude and elevation.

General glaciological investigations indicate there has been relatively little change over the years. This finding supports the assumption that Antarctic glacier movement is sluggish. The British reported that the movement of the Filchner Ice Shelf appears to be slight but definite. The Argentines reported their astronomical fixes indicated that the portion of the Filchner Ice Shelf from General Belgrano Station eastward nearly to the Moltke Nunataks is moving northward at approximately 1,300 meters a year.

On the basis of air observations made by the Australians over wide areas of the MacRobertson Coast, their report states that ice shelves lose very large volumes of ice by calving each year and offer the most important source of icebergs. Only repeated astronomical fixes over a period of years can determine accurately the movement of the inland ice sheet. The faster-moving ice streams or glaciers are directed toward short lengths of coast composing only about ten per cent of the total length of Antarctic coastline. However, their velocity, which at times is twenty to fifty times greater than the general ice sheet, indicates that they remove at least as much and probably considerably more ice than the sheet flow over the remaining length of coast.

The important question as to whether the Antarctic ice cap is increasing or decreasing has not as yet been established. Russian and some Australian scientists believe that there is a definite build-up of ice taking place on the South Polar continent of about 293 cubic miles per year, while scientists of other nationalities are inclined to refute this hypothesis.

Within the past year preliminary results of University of Kansas scientific studies on the thermoluminescence of Antarctic limestones give 170,000 years as an approximate minimum age for Antarctic glaciation.

As the important instrument of seismic soundings plays such an integral part in studying Antarctic glaciology other results of this program are related under the next scientific heading.

EARTH'S SCIENCES

Seismology.

Prior to the IGY there was very little knowledge of the thickness of Antarctica's ice cap. On the second Byrd Expedition 1933-35 I assisted Dr. Thomas T. Poulter, senior scientist and second-in-command in making the first seismic soundings on the Ross Ice Shelf in the area of the Bay of Whales. Later, the Norwegian, British, Swedish expedition of 1949-52 under Captain John Giaever made a 300-mile–trip from the sea ice over the ice plateau in Queen Maud Land, demonstrating the feasibility of seismic and other scientific surface traverse operations.

Information on the thickness of the ice cap reveals facts of the Antarctic's glacial history, world climate, and the earth's crustal strength. Many sciences are used to gain this information (such as glaciology, gravity, magnetism, and geology), but for measuring the ice thickness the techniques of seismology are primary. Seismological investigations are based on the precise measurement of the time required for a sound wave from a small explosive charge to penetrate the surface and be reflected back from the rock or water underlying the ice. The speed is not always the same but changes with the change in the physical properties and depth of the underlying snow and ice.

At Ellsworth Station on the floating Filchner Ice Shelf, where the nearest land was eighty miles away and thus prevented the use of seismographs to record any earthquake disturbances, seismological studies were confined to soundings for measuring the thickness of the ice shelf and the water depth to the ocean floor. The thickness beneath our station was found to be 760 feet, whereas at Shackleton base, just fifty-five miles to the east of us, an IGY report gives the measurement there as 1,300 feet. The depth of the water beneath Ellsworth Station's floating shelf is 2,600 feet to the bottom of the ocean floor. This same measurement was also obtained by the traverse party nearly 250 miles farther inland at a point just before the upland grounded ice eventually raised the actual land to above sea level. The contact between the floating ice shelf and grounded inland ice was mostly a disturbed zone. This contact was crossed ten times during the traverse and caused the party many detours and delays.

In addition to seismological soundings the Ellsworth traverse party also used the sciences of glaciology, geology, magnetism and gravity measurements to learn more about the ice shelf, land, and mountains as they traveled inland.

The traverse party departed from Ellsworth Station on 28 October, 1957, and was evacuated by aircraft from a point about 220 miles south of the station on January 16, 1958. In the eighty-one days they traveled about 816 miles in their Sno-Cats. During this period they set up twenty-seven seismic stations at intervals varying from five to fifty miles apart, with an average distance of about thirty miles. Between seismic stations stops for gravity, magnetism, and rommsonde (hardness) measurements were made. All of the information they gathered enables an intelligent guess to be made on sub-surface formations. A deep trough averaging about 3,500 feet below sea level was found starting near Belgrano Base, about thirty-five miles southeast of Ellsworth. The trough cuts through an otherwise even depth of ground beneath the bed rock sea bottom and runs for a distance due south before turning to the southwest and going between the newly discovered island and the Pensacola Mountain Range on the mainland of the continent to the south. The detection of this deep, narrow trough, which was still evident when crossed by the traverse party for the last time at 82 degrees South, some 300 miles inland from the ice shelf edge, reopened a fifty-year–old hypothetical question. Is the Antarctic divided into east and west segments by a down-warped, ice-filled depression stretching between its two greatest indentations, the Ross and Weddell Seas—off which the world's two largest ice shelfs are located.

Griffith Taylor, geologist on Scott's second expedition (1910-13) subsequently suggested that an ice-filled strait or trans-Antarctic trough might join the deeply indented Ross and Weddell Seas because of the distinctly different geographical and geological characteristics of their surrounding mountain areas. Albert P. Crary's traverse party from Little America also increased the speculation of such a possibility by locating a record depth of 4,400 feet to the bottom of the sea beneath the Ross Ice Shelf. It was therefore hoped that a traverse party from Ellsworth to Byrd Station the following year would detect the missing links to the hypothetical continental divide. Instead, a shallower distance of bedrock was recorded which extended above sea level to a mountainous region (part below sea level), in the general area where the trough must lie. A simultaneous airborne seismic traverse under Dr. Thiel in 1959 found the ice grounded at the seven locations where he landed, thus eliminating the possibility of any interchange of water, or any broad connection between the two seas.

Unless this hypothetical trough cuts sharply east to the south of the Ellsworth-Byrd traverse route, it is now felt that a mountainous land connection probably exists between the South Pole land mass and the Palmer Peninsula. Whereas, the evidence now points strongly to a broad ice-trough-like connection between the Ross and the Bellingshausen Seas, to date the likelihood of a connection between the Ross and Weddell Seas has diminishd.

A combination of magnetic, geologic, and seismic evidence indicates that the major sub-ice channel located between the Ross and Bellingshausen Seas represents a fundamental division between three major geologic provinces separating the Palmer Peninsula from the volcanic structures of Marie Byrd Land and sedimentary formations of the Horlick Mountains farther south. Gravity studies show West Antarctica to be in approximate isostatic equilibrium, i.e., that the rocks have subsided to compensate for the added load of ice. They also show that the crust is continental in character, with the base of the crust at a relatively high average elevation.

In this connection, the deep basin found in Marie Byrd Land, the land at Byrd Station far beneath sea level, and the new huge island discovered in Edith Ronne Land, all strongly suggest that the continent is not one continuous land mass, but rather that West Antarctica contains several large islands covered by an enormous sheet of ice grounded on them and exerting considerable pressure upon the land beneath. An extensive program of analysis of seismic, gravity, and magnetic traverse data is being conducted at the University of Wisconsin.

Our Ellsworth traverse ascertained that the ice shelf extends much farther inland (about 300 miles from the edge of the shelf) than previously thought and estimated its size at about 160,000 square miles.

As a result of the various studies of ice-thickness conducted on the three major traverses from Little America, Byrd and Ellsworth Stations (covering a total of 4,000 miles) the indications are that Antarctica contains as much as forty per cent more ice than was originally estimated. And according to George P. Woollard, Department of Geology of the University of Wisconsin, this ice sheet can be estimated as about 8,000 feet in average thickness.

It is interesting to note the results of the seismic soundings taken by Dr. Fuchs' party on the crossing from Shackleton to our South Pole station. The British found that the ice thickness increased steadily the farther south they went. Over much of the route the ice was about 6,000 feet thick. At a point less than 100 miles from the South Pole the base of the bedrock appeared to rise to within 2,000 feet of the ice surface. Earlier seismic soundings taken at the South Pole station by Father Urban Joseph Lineham gave an ice thickness of about 8,300 feet overlying a rock surface about 900 feet above sea level. Interpretation of seismic records obtained by New Zealand scientific teams at Scott Base and Hallett Station all contributed to knowledge of the crustal thickness of the land beneath the ice cap in East Antarctica where the existence of a true continent has now been confirmed.

An analysis of all the seismic and related data obtained throughout the Antarctic has allowed G. P. Woollard of the University of Wisconsin to state: "After even a crude calculation . . . it appears that the eastern half of Antarctica is a continent and the western half is an archipelago of islands bridged over by ice."

Gravity Measurements.

The exact location of Ellsworth Station was established at 77 degrees

42.9' South latitude—41 degrees 07.6' West longitude by William Chapman, Cadastrial Engineer with the U.S. Geological Survey. Latitude, elevation, and some information of the underlying crustal structure must be known for the effective use of gravity data. Gravity readings or values signify the distribution of mass beneath the surface; a high reading would mean a great mass and a low reading would indicate some deficiency in the mass. For measuring ice thickness gravity measurements alone could be misleading and inaccurate, but coupled with seismic soundings they become an important supplement to the undertaking.

Thiel and Behrendt's gravity measurements of the Weddell Sea's tide off the Filchner Ice Shelf were compared with the readings obtained at Little America off the Ross Ice Shelf, with interesting results. At both places, the observations were influenced and complicated not only by the rise and fall of the shelf in relation to the movement of the tide, but by a high-frequency movement, previously noted by Crary on the Arctic pack ice, and believed to be oceanographic in origin and influenced by the ice cover. These high-frequency oscillations decrease so rapidly inland from the ice front of the shelf that six to nine miles from the edge the gravity meter can be read with the same accuracy as at a land station.

While the Weddell Sea revealed mixed tidal action, both daily and twice daily, the Ross Sea has only daily tides with the unusual influence of the sun exceeding that of the moon. The range of the tide is greater in the Weddell Sea than in the Ross Sea which might relate to the different configurations of the ocean bottoms south of the two stations. Since the Filchner Ice Shelf is 760 feet thick and the Weddell Sea 2,600 feet deep at the Ellsworth Station, while the Ross Ice Shelf is 610 feet thick and the Ross Sea 2,100 feet deep at Little America, gravity measurements are by far the most practical method of making tidal observations at both places.

The northward drift of the Ellsworth Station is so small that no correction in the readings had to be made to account for it.

The Ellsworth, Byrd, Little America, and Fuchs' trans-Antarctic traverse parties' gravity measurements were made as part of a world-wide program to provide standards for calibration of gravimeters, for international datum control, and to strengthen the international network of auxiliary gravity coverage in areas not likely to be visited in the foreseeable future. In the field, these gravity studies were conducted in conjunction with, but more frequently than, the seismic observations. The results are still being analyzed.

According to G. P. Woollard, the small irregularities in the preliminary gravity values for the various Antarctic bases suggest general equilibrium or stability in the earth's crust but at the same time the minor fluctuations suggest a considerable variation in the thickness of ice, the underlying rock types, or both. Future gravity and seismic measurements in the areas off shore will give an indication of the pressure exerted on the earth's crust in the Antarctic by its heavy ice sheet covering.

All the data obtained in the earth sciences during the IGY and its succeeding program gives the first real glimpse as to the isolated continent's possible influence upon world sea levels and geography.

Geology.

Geology was not one of the disciplines included in the IGY because this branch of science does not require simultaneous observations on an international scale. However, limited geological work was performed in the Antarctic.

From Ellsworth Station the only rock outcrops visited by geologist Augenbaugh were at Dufek Massif (Santa Teresila Range)* in Edith Ronne Land, about 300 miles south of our station. In order to study these mountains, the traverse party made a detour from the predetermined traverse route. From several miles away the various rock layers appeared to be sedimentary in origin, but closer observations revealed them to be igneous instead. The Dufek Massif extends in a northeast-southwest direction for about thirty-five to forty miles, with its highest peak about 9,000 feet above sea level.

During the five days Augenbaugh studied the rock formations on the north side of the Massif he found no fossils but reported that abundant green malachite stains gave evidence of mineralization. He also stated that the range as a whole has been tilted, but not folded or faulted and that the appearance of layering was caused by varying mafic content. Some old sedimentary formations were noted, indicating there had been a later igneous conversion. In contrast to the pinacles in the western part, the eastern outcrops were rounded, undoubtedly the result of previous heavy glaciation. The 400 pounds of rocks collected were brought back and tested aboard ship for radio activity. None was found.

Large ice-free lakes, fairly level valleys, several miles in width, lie along the northern front of the range. The party visited a melt-water lake about 100 yards in diameter in one of these barren ground valleys and collected specimens of low forms of plant life growing in the lake for subsequent biological laboratory analysis. The obvious melting and large areas of exposed ground indicates that a receding ice edge surrounds the northern part of this range.

PHYSICS OF THE UPPER ATMOSPHERE

Aurora and Airglow.

More complete auroral and such related phenomena as ionospheric and geomagnetic effects have been gathered than ever was possible previously despite the fact that results from these fields have been slow in

---

*Discovered and named by the Argentines in November, 1955.

their arrival at the data collection centers. Early in the IGY, British scientists at Manchester, England, definitely ascertained through radar observations that auroras occur simultaneously in the Northern and Southern Hemispheres. Additional evidence of this was obtained by the United States through statistics submitted by radio from the polar regions.

Ellsworth Station is situated close to the aurora zone. Malville operated the spectrograph over a seven-month period. Of the 778 spectrograms taken, 508 of them contained auroral lines. Auroral spectrograms were recorded on eighty-six per cent of the 116 nights. On seventy per cent of the auroral nights, the emission of hydrogen was detected, indicating that its presence is not the rare occurrence previously assumed.

By correlating results obtained at Ellsworth with those taken at the South Pole there is evidence that the width of the zone rather than its radius expands as magnetic disturbances increase. Data analysis from both stations makes it possible to determine the most probable time overhead aurorae will occur in high geomagnetic latitudes.

The displays at Ellsworth occurred most frequently near local midnight, which is typical of stations lying outside the aurora zone, but apparently not so for those well within the zone. However, at the South Pole, on the opposite side of the aurora belt, the greatest maximum is nine hours before midnight, indicating that the time of largest display is earlier the closer the observations are to the geomagnetic pole.

Malville also reported that the direction of auroral drift in the Southern Hemisphere, undetermined previous to the IGY, is shown to be in the same direction as that in the Northern Hemisphere. The close similarity of geomagnetic phenomena in the Northern and Southern Hemisphere is demonstrated through correlation.

In connection with his aurora work, Malville also measured the intensity of the patchy night airglow or luminosity which results from oxygen emissions.

A report by two British scientists, S. Evans and G. M. Thomas, summarized the displays from other Weddell Sea stations at Halley Bay, Shackleton, and South Ice (250 miles south of Shackleton):

"Quiet arcs tend to lie almost stationary for long periods in a narrow range of latitudes. Any increase in activity is likely to show itself first by an equatorward drift of the arc, which may later break into rays or bands. A short period of rapidly moving forms, with bright coloration, gives way to diffuse surfaces and pulsation. Amorphus patches of luminosity may litter the sky for many hours without any noticeable change after a display of this kind. Classification of forms has been reduced to arcs, rays, bands, and surfaces. Although borderline forms will occur from time to time, these four are so distinct that they surely result from four different physical processes of action."

As of this date the National Academy of Sciences reports in their IGY Bulletin that the location of the southern auroral zone has now been fairly well defined, and "magnetic bays" and ionosphere variations shown in the records of various stations has been documented. In general, a surprising degree of agreement between auroral, magnetic, ionospheric, and other upper-atmosphere phenomena has been found, but only a few of the features have as yet been studied in detail.

Ionospheric Physics.

Ability to understand and predict the future condition of the ionosphere has a direct influence on the dependability of long-range, short-wave radio transmission. Nature's electric blanket can reflect radio waves to distant parts of the earth like a mirror or absorb them like an ink blotter. The ionosphere is made up of several layers of electrically charged gases lying between forty and 400 miles above the earth but well below the great heights reached by the "whistlers."

During the IGY the various layers of the ionosphere were studied by forty-one nations at 253 observation stations. Direct probings were made by sending radio signals of various frequencies into the ionosphere for two minutes every hour and measuring how the signals were reflected or absorbed.

When a flare-up on the sun occurs there will be a period of maximum solar activity which often causes fade-outs or complete black-outs in radio communication. During this period the radio signals transmitted by ionospheric sounders are absorbed and not reflected back to earth. On June 28, 1957, such a solar flare of major proportions occurred. A storm in the earth's magnetic field was observed two days later. The ionosphere was charged with electrical disturbances and long-range radio communications were blacked out. On each such date of probable solar disturbances the IGY declared an alert so that all stations would intensify their ionospheric soundings on the same basis outlined for the previously scheduled World Days.

During this year of maximum solar activity several other solar events occurred and for the first time a global picture was obtained of the growth and decay, station by station, of such fade-outs. Also early rocket experiments showed that the first layer of the ionosphere could be lower than previously believed.

With such techniques the United States Bureau of Standards has considerable success in foretelling broadcasters the best possible frequencies for the most successful overseas connections on a specific day, and often far enough in advance to aid communications programming. But the intangibles for greater accuracy are constantly being sought.

Since ionization density increases during the day when the sun is present and decreases at night there was much speculation as to what would happen to the ionosphere during long absences of solar radiation. The polar areas held the clue, with the South Pole station being the best possible observatory. Dr. Hugh Odishaw, Executive Secretary of the IGY, has summarized the results of the investigations: "In spite of the absence of the sun, the electron concentration seems to remain very high throughout the polar night; moreover, there is a diurnal variation that can only, it appears, be associated with geomagnetic activity. The evidence so far obtained suggests that ionospheric behavior in the two polar regions is essentially the same. Analysis of these observations may appreciably alter our concepts of the ionization and recombination processes in the atmosphere."

The statistical ionospheric information continues to be correlated and evaluated for making better radio frequency predictions which, among other things, has a direct application to safer ship and airplane travel.

"Whistlers."

"Whistlers" are naturally occurring radio waves with the frequency of sound. Anyone with a simple antenna and amplifier can easily pick up the long descending noises. They originate from lightning bolts near the surface of the earth and travel back and forth from their point of origin from one hemisphere to another along the earth's magnetic lines of force, arching high over the ionosphere to provide potentially useful information about the high atmosphere and the thin electrified gases there which affect them.

Roger Gallet's traveling wave tube principle has led to a hypothesis regarding these previously unexplained low-frequency radio noises. Solar particles arriving in the very high atmosphere transfer energy to very low-frequency radio waves there and the very low-frequency sounds heard at ground level are an amplification of these waves. They can also occur at times in trains of successive waves.

IGY investigations showed that the ion density and concentration of molecules along whistler paths at altitudes of twice the earth's radius must be much greater than formerly anticipated. British physicist L. R. O. Storey, who first linked "whistlers" to lightning, pointed out that the surprising thing is what they told us about the height of the atmosphere. Previously thought to end at about 1,500 miles, "whistler" investigations first suggested that the atmosphere must extend out several times farther, to at least 7,000 miles. We now know it extends much farther as Pioneer I reached 70,000 miles.

A group at Stanford University under R. A. Helliwell has discovered that above a certain frequency, "whistlers" occur, with both falling and rising components. The shape of the "nose-whistler" is related to the intensity of the earth's field along the "whistler" path and gives information on the distribution of ionization as well. It is therefore theoretically possible to place limits on the path and obtain the distribution of ionization along it. Storey has found indications of the presence of hydrogen ions along the path, and Maeda of Japan has shown that the "whistler" path may depart markedly from the magnetic fieldline path.

In addition to the "Whistlers," there are vlf sounds heard on "whistler" apparatus and a correlation between these sounds and the aurora is being sought since the vlf emissions are evident in every notable display of flaming aurora rays.

Because the science of "whistlers" was so new then the IGY began a very limited program confined solely to Ellsworth Station, was carried on in the Antarctic in 1957. After some initial difficulty caused by interference noise from the generators, later eliminated by moving the "whistler" equipment to another building, the "whistlers" were picked up at Ellsworth and routinely amplified 1,000,000 times onto a tape recorder. But as in many of the other sciences our function was limited merely to collection of this data for future study and analysis by more experienced scientists throughout the world.

GEOGRAPHY

The final phase of the research work accomplished during our year at Ellsworth relates to geography of the area of our station. This branch of science was not one of the disciplines included in the IGY Antarctic program. It always seemed unfortunate to me that this was so because detailed knowledge of the physical surroundings in relation to observations is of considerable benefit to practically all scientific studies.

The report from a government-wide survey conducted in 1949, stated that a reasonably accurate map of the Antarctic was a prerequisite to any further large-scale scientific work being conducted there. In spite of this conclusion, and the fact that more than 100,000 aerial trimetrogon photographs lay unused, the IGY has come, gone, and been replaced by a succeeding organization, but still the all-important detailed map of Antarctica has not been made. As a result of the IGY we find some solace in the increase of public and official interest in Antarctic problems. I am also hopeful that eventually a long-sought, large-scale official map of the Antarctic will be produced, which will utilize details of geographical material gathered during the last twenty-five years.

The responsibilities I assumed as commander of Ellsworth Station, its IGY program, and the safety of its personnel came before any ambitions I harbored for what lay beyond our limited horizon. However, with a background of exploration that dated back more years than the age of most of our personnel, I did not close my eyes to the geography of the area when opportunity arose in line with the performance of my duties.

The final outcome of the restricted flights conducted from Ellsworth resulted in three major geographical discoveries:

1. The determination that the high land sighted in 1947 to the south and west of Gould Bay proved to be a large island.
2. The findings that the Filchner Ice Shelf terminated in a high escarpment running westward from mountains in Coats Land to the new island.

3. The sighting and photographing of new mountains southwest of Dufek Massif in Edith Ronne Land.

These geographical discoveries were mostly made prior to the departure of our traverse party and additional geographical details acquired subsequently were supplied them to aid their trek.

The delineation and elevations of the new island were established in no less than seventeen flights. Courses flown were accurately noted along with ground speeds, and drifts. A number of celestial sunlines were obtained while in flight by Lieutenant Sumrall. Radio altimeter readings were taken on all flights. By this method we established the contours of the snow-covered island with the three marked embayments on its eastern escarpment.

While the elevation of the ice shelf varied between 250 feet and 700 feet above sea level, the height of the escarpment at the edge of the island was generally about 800 feet higher. The eastern side has a steeper escarpment which breaks off sharply to the 700-foot elevation of the ice shelf and ends in a belt of crevasses. In the western and southern areas the elevations of the island increase by more gradual slopes. Between the two southern inlets an ice-fall rises to about 1,000 feet from the otherwise even elevation of 700 feet. The height of the island increases in a gentle rise as you go inland. The radio altimeter gave 3,200 feet above sea level at the highest elevation at the center of the southern half, while on the northern half of the island the highest elevation is 2,200 feet.

When the traverse party crossed the southeastern tip of the island, Thiel told me his seismic soundings, taken at 1,700 feet above sea level, located the land below at sea level or slightly above. This recording substantiated my findings. Providing there is a relatively even snow cover over the entire island, the height of the bedrock above sea level could be expected to rise in comparison to· the increase in levation.

The western side of the island has much gentler slopes. On my December 15 flight with Lieutenant Sumrall we flew westward many miles over the island before getting much change in the decrease of the altimeter readings.

The second major geographical discovery is the prominent escarpment which bounds the southeastern flank of the Filchner Ice Shelf. Now it is known to extend for many hundreds of miles from Cape Norvegia in Queen Maud Land, past Moltke Nunataks in Coats Land to west of Dufek Massif in Edith Ronne Land, tying in all the mountain ranges along the way. From there it probably heads toward the Queen Maud Mountains in the Ross Sea sector.

The existence of the various mountain groups and escarpment tie-in from Cape Norvegia to Moltke Nunataks had been known for many years. I first saw the escarpment from Britain's Halley Bay base and followed it from the ship as we proceeded deeper into the Weddell Sea. But it was a surprise to come upon it again on my first flight to the Dufek Massif. From an elevation of about 1,800 feet, the escarpment rises steeply to 5,200 feet. On later flights I followed it to Moltke Nunataks in the east and to beyond Dufek Massif in the west. The escarpment, therefore, is continuous from Cape Norvegia area in Queen Maud Land to the mountains south of the Ross Sea.

The third major geographical discovery was the new group of mountains southwest of Dufek Massif. These mountains consist of rugged peaks, some bare of snow, reaching to a maximum height of about 10,000 feet. I photographed them from a distance. Later, the Air Force Testing unit photographed them at closer range.

Shortness of time and poor weather prevented the Air Force unit from making more than one photographic mission. Their flight started at the northeast end of Dufek Massif and headed in a southwest direction for about ninety-five miles. The mountains that I had discovered on my October 28 flight received excellent coverage, although no new mountains or other geographical features were seen by the group. Had this test group been blessed with better weather. An additional 150-mile flight in the same direction with photographic coverage might have been extremely beneficial and revealed much additional geographical information.

These and many other findings show the main reasons why men are being sent to the Antarctic today; and that despite the tensions and frustrations of isolation they do manage to collect the important data for which they are sent.

Bay ice — ice of recent formation, so called because forming most readily in bays and sheltered spots.

Beset — so enclosed by floating ice to be unable to navigate a ship.

Bight — an indentation.

Brash ice — ice broken up into small fragments.

Calf — detached masses from 'berg or glacier.

Dock — an opening in the ice, artificial or natural, offering protection.

Field ice — an extensive surface of floating ice.

Glacier — a mass of ice derived from the atmosphere, sometimes abutting upon the sea.

Hummocks — ridges of broken ice formed by collision of fields.

Ice anchor — a hook or grapnel adapted to take hold upon ice.

Ice belt — a continued margin of ice which adheres to the coast above the ordinary level of the sea.

Ice-blink — a peculiar appearance of the atmosphere over distant ice.

Land ice — floes or fields adhering to the coast or included between headlands.

Lane or lead — a navigable opening in the ice.

Pack — a large area of floating ice driven together more or less closely.

Polynia — a Russian term for an open-water space.

Water-sky — a peculiar appearance of the sky over open water.

ABLATION OF SNOW-LEVEL—Wearing away, as of a glacier melting.

ANTARCTANDES—The mountain range comprising the Palmer Peninsula that is structurally a continuation of the Andes of South America by way of the Scotia Arc.

AURORA—The aurora borealis or aurora australis (northern or southern lights).

BARRIER—The steep or vertical seaward edge of an ice shelf along the margin of the Antarctic Continent.

BLACKOUT, POLAR—An ionospheric condition on which density of ionospheric layers increase so that all radio waves entering these layers are absorbed resulting in temporary loss of communication.

CONTINENTAL GLACIER—A glacier originating inland, flowing seaward.

CONTINENTAL PLATEAU—A wide platform that projects, with some abruptness, from bordering lowlands or from the sea.

CONTINENTAL SHELF—The zone around the continents extending from the low-water mark seaward to where there is a marked increase in slope to greater depths.

COSMIC RAYS—Strongly penetrating rays, discovered by Milliken in 1925, coming from beyond the earth's atmosphere and containing particles that move at extremely high speed.

DRY VALLEY—An ice-free area of the Antarctic, especially a series of such areas on the west side of McMurdo Sound, around the USSR base of Oasis and in the northern slopes of Dufek Massif in Edith Ronne Land.

ELECTRON—A minute negative electrified particle with the smallest known quantity of electricity.

FOSSIL—Traces of an organism, embedded and preserved in the earth's surface or crust.

GEOPHYSICS—That part of physics related to the earth, such as the tidal phenomena, magnetism, temperature, meteorology, etc.

ICE SHELF—A thick mass of glacial ice that has flowed from the continent into the sea or an arm of a sea; or a mass of ice that started in shallow water and over years gradually increased in thickness, usually floating but sometimes grounded in part.

IGNEOUS ROCK—Pertaining to, or having the nature of fire, as rock which has crystallized from the molten state.

ISOTOPE ANALYSIS—One of two or more closely allied elements having identical chemical properties but differing slightly in atomic weights.

JAMESWAY HUT—A prefabricated and portable shelter made of fabric and wood units. It has a flat wood floor and hemicylindric roof with no separate walls.

MAFIC CONTENT—Relating to the ferromagnesian minerals in a rock.

MAGNETOGRAPH—An instrument for recording the magnetic force.

MALACHITE STAINS—A brilliant green mineral—copper carbonate.

METAMORPHIC—Involving physical transformation, as rocks derived from pre-existing rocks by changes caused by heat and pressure in the earth's crust.

MORAINE—Stones, boulders, clay, etc., deposited by melting glaciers.

NUNATAK—A small mountain or a rock outcrop surrounded by glacial ice.

OSCILLOGRAPH—An instrument which records or indicates changes of an electric current used to study the wave form of an alternating current or voltage.

OUTCROP—An exposed part of a bedrock.

PENGUIN—Any of several species of short-legged flightless aquatic birds (family Spheniscidae) of the Southern Hemisphere.

PRE-CAMBRIAN—A geologic time previous to the Cambrian era of about 500,000,000 years ago.

PROTON—The nucleus of the hydrogen atom, exceedingly minute and carrying a unit positive charge.

RADIOSONDE—Instrument normally attached to balloon which measures humidity and temperature in the atmosphere.

270

RAMMSONDE—Instrument for determination of snow-layer density.

RAWINSONDE—Combined observation of data obtained from a radiosonde plus radar tracking of the balloon drift for wind speed and direction.

ROOKERY—An area birds establish nests and raise their young.

SCOTIA ARC—Part of the South Atlantic Ocean southeast of the Falkland Islands and South America.

SEDIMENTARY—Having an origin involving settling from or being deposited by water.

SEISMOLOGY—The scientific study of earthquakes and their causes and results.

SOLAR FLARES—Sudden outburst of lights or flashes.

SOUTHERN CROSS—A constellation, Crux, in the Southern Hemisphere, with four bright stars forming the general shape of a cross.

SPECTROGRAPH—An apparatus for photographing or mapping a spectrum.

STRATIFIED SNOW—Snow formed or arranged in strata; to become formed in layers.

STRATOSPHERE—The upper portion of the atmosphere, about eleven kilometers, more or less (depending on latitude, season, and weather), in which temperature changes but little with altitude and clouds of water never form, and in which there is practically no convection; originally, and still often called the "isothermal region".

SUN SPOTS—One of the dark patches or spots visible on the sun's disk, supposed to be of the nature of a syclonis storm in the sun's atmosphere.

SURFACE ALBEDO—The reflecting power of a surface, as of the moon.

THERMO LUMINESCENCE—Light resulting from the release of energy in a mineral by heating to less than red heat.

TRIMETROGON PHOTOGRAPHY—Overlapping aerial photographs for making maps.

TROPOSPHERE—All that portion of the atmosphere below the stratosphere. It is that portion in which temperature generally rapidly decreases with altitude, clouds form, and convection is active.

WHISTLER—An audio-frequency electromagnetic signal generated by some lightning discharges. This signal apparently propagates along a geomagnetic line of force, and often "bounces" several times between the Northern and Southern Hemispheres. Its name derives from the sound heard on radio receivers.

WHITE-OUT—An atmospheric optical phenomenon of the polar regions in which the observer appears to be engulfed in a uniformly white glow. Neither shadows, horizon, nor clouds are discernible, sense of depth and orientation is lost; only very dark, nearby objects can be seen. This phenomenon is experienced in the air as well as on the ground.

ACKNOWLEDGMENTS

I wish to express my appreciation to Rear Admiral Robert A. J. English, US Navy (Ret.), and Ralph E. Becker, Washington attorney, for their review of the manuscript. To Lieutenant William H. Sumrall, USN, and Chief Walter H. May, US Navy (Ret.), I owe a great deal of gratitude for their verification of authenticity that the events did indeed happen as described in this volume. Lieutenant Sumrall and Chief May wintered at the Ellsworth Station with me and experienced the emotional strain on the scene.

Dr. Harry Wexler, Director of Research, U.S. Weather Bureau, and Captain Elliott B. Roberts, Coast and Geodetic Survey graciously checked the accuracy of the scientific results interpreted herein. I also wish to extend credit to the many scientists whose published reports in the IGY Bulletins and other scientific journals were used as source materiel for the conclusions made in the Appendix.

Grateful acknowledgment is made to the U.S. Navy for use of photographs reproduced here and to Mr. Herman Friis, Geographer, National Archives, for drafting the map of the Ellsworth Station area.

The inspiration and unfailing support of my wife, Jackie, was of inestimable value to me in relating this story. The experience she gained as a member of the Ronne Antarctic Research Expedition 1946-48 when she wintered in Antarctica, gave her first-hand knowledge of the reactions of men living under stress in an isolated polar camp, and where she shared the leader's problems and responsibilities. In her I have always had a sturdy brace to leeward.

FINN RONNE,
Captain, United States Naval Reserve

Washington, D. C.
August 16, 1961